THE POSTER ART OF DAVID LANCE GOINES

A 40-YEAR RETROSPECTIVE

Foreword by Alice Waters

Preface by the Author

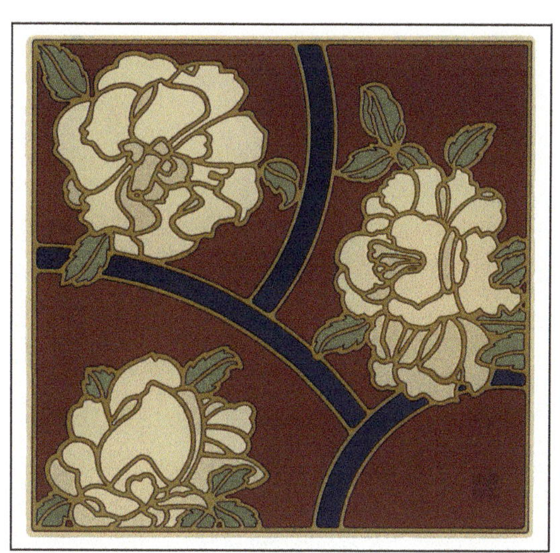

DOVER PUBLICATIONS
GARDEN CITY, NEW YORK

Copyright

Bibliographical Note

The Poster Art of David Lance Goines: A 40-Year Retrospective is a new work, first published by Dover Publications in 2010.

Library of Congress Cataloging-in-Publication Data

Goines, David Lance, 1945–
The poster art of David Lance Goines : a 40-year retrospective / foreword by Alice Waters.
p. cm.
ISBN-13: 978-0-486-47875-3
ISBN-10: 0-486-47875-0
1. Goines, David Lance, 1945– —Themes, motives. I. Title.

NC1850.G58A4 2010
741.6'74092—dc22

2010030020

Printed in Canada
47875006 2025
www.doverpublications.com

FOREWORD

WHEN I FIRST SAW David, I was struck by how beautifully and methodically he worked. I was working on Robert Scheer's campaign for Congress at the time, and I had brought some campaign literature to Berkeley Graphic Arts to be printed, and there he was: small, particular, and so attentive to what he was doing.

He invited me for coffee and Cognac. I had just returned from studying in France and was ready for something new. I was taken by his way of making coffee, which was as careful and precise as his printmaking. He had a big, old-fashioned coffee grinder mounted on a table, where you turned the wheel to grind the beans. As I came to know him, I would realize it was not only the way he worked that attracted me, but also the very way he led his life. It struck me as an artful, simple way of living, of taking time, of doing things right.

In those days I was working as a waitress at a small restaurant in Berkeley called The Quest, as well as teaching at the Montessori school. David was printing and studying calligraphy. We realized we worked well together and decided to collaborate. We started a weekly column for the *San Francisco Express Times* with recipes I wrote and gathered from friends, and David created linoleum cuts to illustrate them. For us, our column brought together a key set of precious elements: taste, aesthetics, beauty, community, and a real way of life. We loved sharing that with people. When David published a selection of the prints in a portfolio, called *Thirty Recipes Suitable for Framing*, it was the first book-like thing either of us had made.

David and I lived together at one end of the block and Charles and Lindsey Shere lived at the other. They would come to our apartment for crêpes and a glass of wine, and then we would go back to their apartment for dessert and coffee. As we talked and laughed around the table, inextinguishable feelings of family and friendship were born.

These were the feelings we wanted to share with our community when we opened Chez Panisse in August 1971. David made the poster for the opening—the Red-Haired Lady—and it set a tone that would continue to characterize the restaurant for decades: not quite Art Nouveau, not quite Art Deco. It was very expressive, like Kip Mesirow's interior carpentry and Carrie Glenn's flowers, and it became a fundamental part of the restaurant's style. From then on, David made a new poster for every Chez Panisse birthday. Art was always a vital, breathing facet of the restaurant for me, and David was integral in shaping a beautiful Chez Panisse aesthetic. We paid for the posters he made in trade. For nearly a decade he ate at the restaurant almost every day.

Everything I have learned from David is special to me. Thanks to him, whenever I look at a sign, I scrutinize the typeface: how it could be different, how it could be better. He taught me italic calligraphy and for years I wrote the menus in that hand. Calligraphy and cooking resemble one another in important ways. In both, something essential and necessary—either food or words—is made beautiful through craft and creativity. David has had a priceless impact on Chez Panisse and on the wider community of Berkeley—and beyond. He has designed posters for the library, for the Cheese Board, for AIDS benefits, and for the birthdays and anniversaries of many of our friends. He has shared so much beauty with all of us.

David represents the ideals that are dearest to me: family, friendship, and living simply in a beautiful, artful way. Many people of the Chez Panisse family were also part of the sixties Berkeley world, and many of them have left an indelible mark on the restaurant. But David was there from the very beginning, and he has stayed with us, both literally and in spirit, for the past four decades. During this time, he has continued to promote the kind of tasteful, imaginative craftsmanship we all believe in. The way he works—with the skill and appreciation for his materials of a true artisan—is exactly the way we will always want to do things here at Chez Panisse.

May 2010

ALICE WATERS

PREFACE

What a Poster Is

A poster is the practical integration of word and image. Each reinforces the other. Without words, the image lacks focus. Without the image, the words lack impact. A poster has one shot at getting its message across, and cannot depend upon a leisurely or sympathetic audience. The text is therefore brief, the image direct.

A poster addresses its viewer on two levels, hoping to attract and focus attention, and suggest action. The picture speaks to the emotions, and the words to the intellect. The picture is taken in all at once, while the words are consumed sequentially.

Posters are the handmaidens of industry, commerce, and opinion, and the poster designer is always looking for a combination of words and images that will do the trick. He has to make his pictures talk: talk fast, talk coherently, and talk persuasively.

Why I Do What I Do

A lot of art is out there competing for your attention, and I create some of it. I make posters and book jackets, wine labels, and announcements. I'm a graphic designer, writer, and printer. My clients want you to eat dinner at their restaurant or drink their wine or attend their event. You might or might not, but you certainly won't if you don't know about it. My job is to get your attention and keep it long enough for the message to get across. This is what I do for a living. I also want people to know about my work and hire me to do more, so every piece of work that I do is also an advertisement for myself. In addition, I want to provide the viewer with something fun to look at. You don't need to be interested in the product or service to enjoy looking at the picture. Not only am I trying to get you to go to Chez Panisse for dinner, and in the process persuade Chez Panisse or somebody else to ask me to do another poster for them later on, but I'm also making an attractive picture for you to put on your wall, even if you live in New Zealand and will never ask me to design a poster for you, or will never go to Chez Panisse in your life.

I set a task for the viewer, which I hope will be performed correctly. The task is to look at my poster and do what it suggests. If the task is too difficult, the viewer will simply turn away. Therefore, I make my designs easy to look at, operating on the theory that what is easier to look at will be preferred to something that is difficult to look at.

Rough lines and soft colors are more pleasing for longer intervals than hard lines and bright colors. If I were trying to get your attention and hold it for a short time, or had something exceedingly important to say, I would do things differently. There is a place in the world for sirens and flashing red lights, but there is a much larger place in the world for things that don't make as much racket.

Graphic work is different from fine art. I expect to be treated a bit roughly. Book jackets get shopworn and tattered; posters get bent, torn, put up on a wall with thumbtacks, and after a while become faded and flyspecked and dirty. My inclination is to work with this reality rather than pretend it isn't there. Things that don't have to be perfect to look good, look good longer. Think of my work as a pair of blue jeans. They're meant for everyday use. If they get dirty it's okay; the dirt probably won't show anyhow. As they fade or get frayed or torn, they might even look better than when they were new. The older they get, the more comfortable they get. Of course, you can't wear blue jeans to the opera, but I'll let somebody else design evening wear.

How I Do It

My posters begin as small black-and-white drawings or linoleum blockprints. After I am satisfied with the basic drawing, I work on color sketches.

The original drawing is called a "key-line," which means that it not only is a rendition of the subject, but also contains information that tells me, as a printer, where every color belongs in the final printed piece. The drawing is then scanned into my Macintosh, and color separations are made in Photoshop. Negatives are then made with a laser film generator that are the same size as the final, printed poster. There is one negative and plate for each color in the finished poster. Generally, there are between five and twelve separate colors. The plates are made by direct contact with the negatives, and are therefore exactly the same size.

I print on a 1954 ATF Solna Chief 18" x 24" single-color photo-offset-lithographic press. This machine has been in my shop since 1966, and was old and beat-up when I got it. My learning to print on it didn't do it much good, either. So, unlike most other graphic designers, I can't design anything I please, and then expect some poor printer to work his magic on my design. I am always the next guy in line: after I design a poster, I have to make the color separations, and then I have to print it, and then I have to trim it. So, I make it easy on the next guy, which is always me wearing a different hat.

When the printing begins, I tack up the color sketch and refer to it throughout. Color is a function not only of the shade and hue and so on, but also of two other exterior factors: the source of light under which it is viewed, and the other colors that surround it. Consequently, I follow the original sketch faithfully, as decisions that were made while looking at the original as a whole will be difficult to copy without this reference in front of my eyes. I compare each new color to the original, and try not to depart from it without careful consideration. Each color is mixed separately to match the original sketch. I mix the color by eye, and when I think I'm getting close, run a few sheets through the press to see how it looks. This "hit and miss" process can go on for quite a while. I need to have enough ink to last for the whole run, which is somewhere between a pound of ink for moderate coverage to four or five pounds for heavy coverage or a long run. I use a few basic ink colors: transparent white, opaque white, yellow, cyan (pure blue), reflex blue, magenta, warm red, rubine red, and black. With these colors I can faithfully create combinations which will satisfy most of the demands made by the eye.

Each plate is mounted on the press in sequence, and the color to which it corresponds is completely printed before another layer of color is put down. Aligning the image on the plate with those that have preceded it is called registration. Another important part of printing is getting the ink balance and density correct for the area to be printed: large areas of coverage call for copious amounts of ink, whereas small areas need only a little ink. Since both large areas and small areas of coverage are often found within the same image, it is important to make them look alike, despite the varying amounts of ink called for. A third part of my task is to make sure that the paper feeds properly and continuously, and is delivered in a neat stack, so that I can run it through the press again. A constant and careful eye must be focused on the printed sheets, as well. Dirt, dust, flaws in the paper, the occasional suicidal insect, the malign influence of evil spirits—all these misfortunes demand unremitting vigilance. Things go wrong all the time.

Barring interruptions, the press runs at 3,600 impressions per hour. Since the press runs vary from a few hundred to a few thousand, this part of the process is relatively fast.

Lithographic ink takes about twelve hours to dry, so I print one color a day. The more that colors build up on top of one another, the longer this drying time can be, so the roughly 24 hours that elapses between colors insures that the sheet will be thoroughly dry on the next pass through the press.

When the poster is finished, it may be that I have discovered a mistake or feel that one or more of the colors is not quite right. When this happens, I make what is called a "touch-plate," which allows me to add another color.

The poster is then trimmed, sorted, wrapped, and delivered to the client. Then on to the next one.

May 2010

David Lance Goines

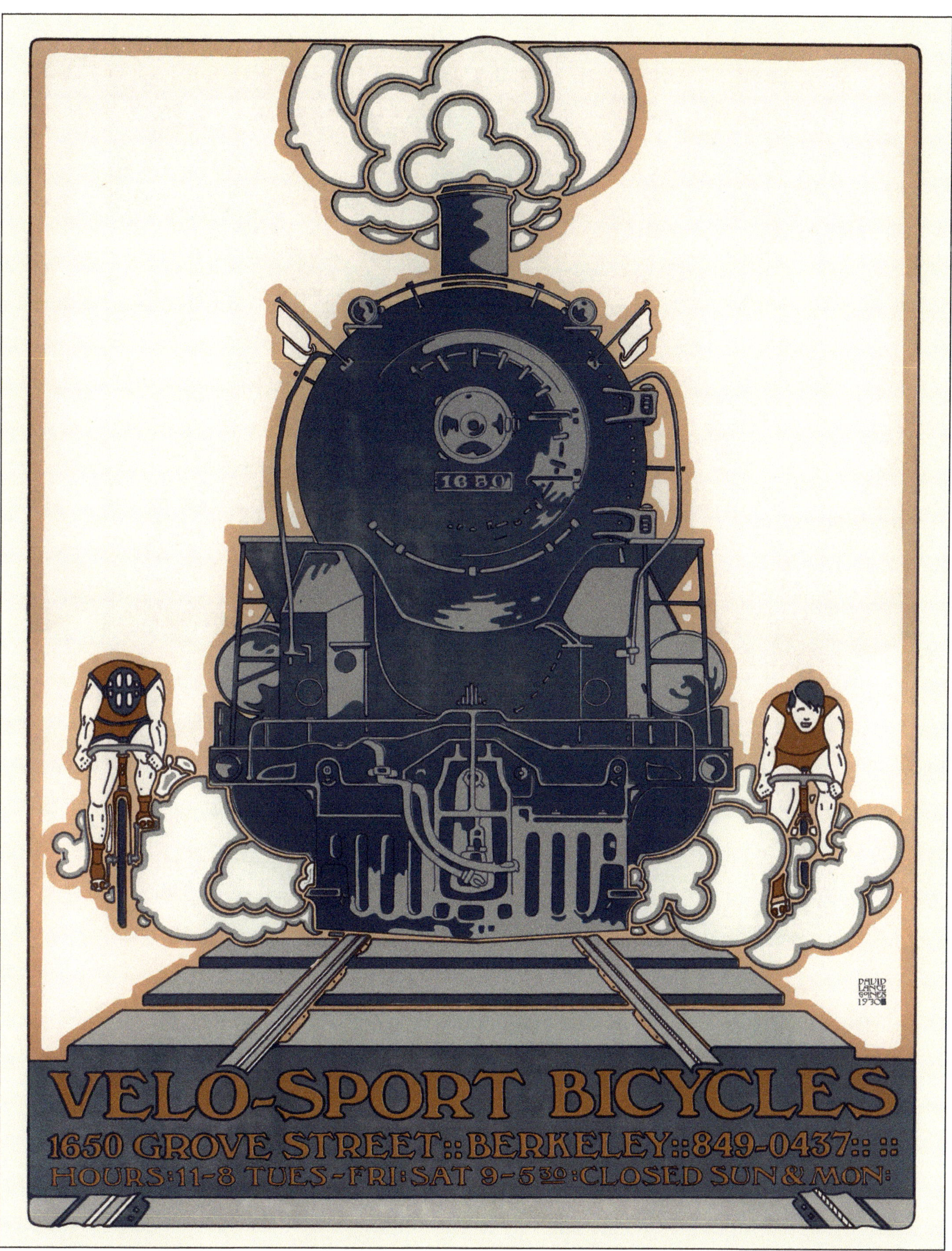

1. Velo-Sport Bicycles, 1970, 18" × 24"

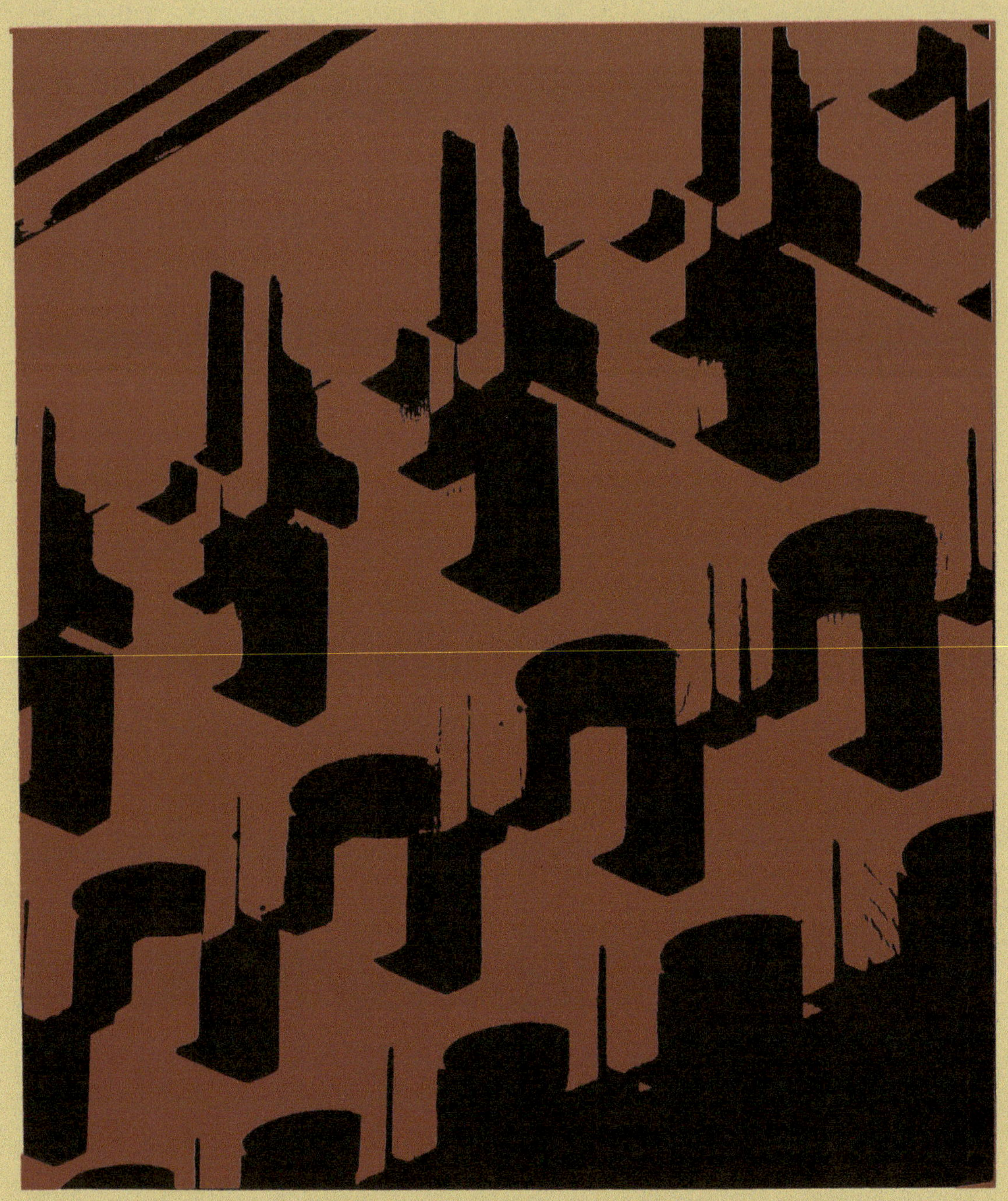

2. Woodwork, 1970, 18" × 24"

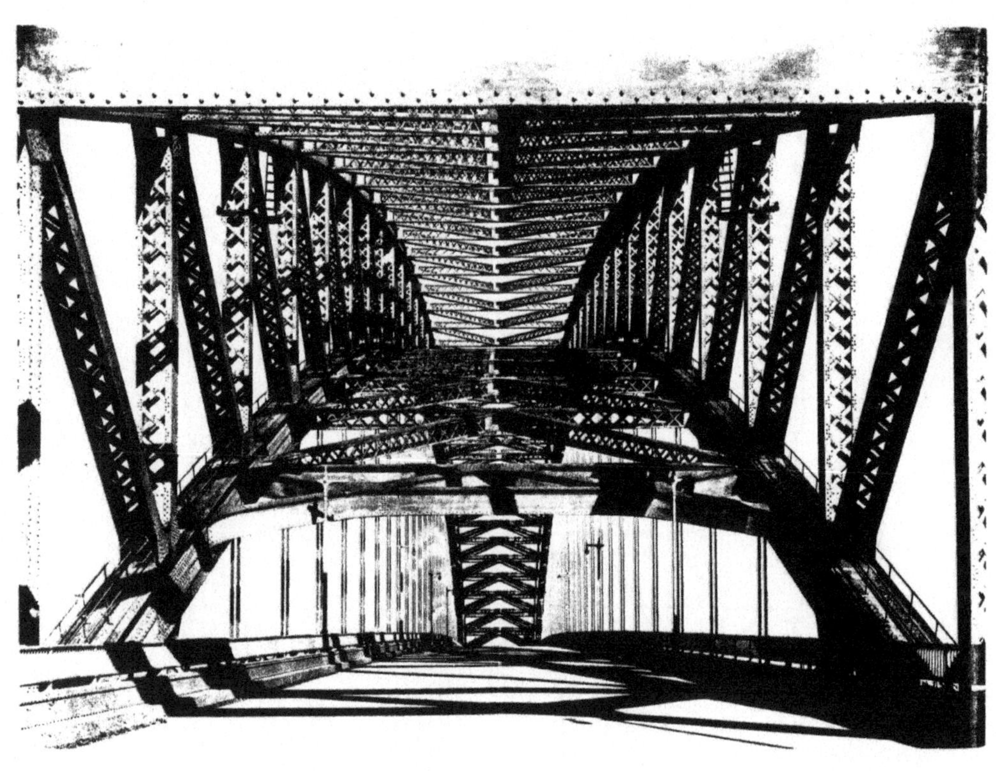

The law,
in its majestic equality,
forbids the rich
as well as the poor
to sleep under bridges,
to beg in the streets,
& to steal bread.

Anatole France

MICHAEL KELLEY IS PLEASED TO ANNOUNCE TO HIS FRIENDS & CLIENTS HIS ASSOCIATION WITH THE FIRM OF FRANCK, HILL, STENDER, ZIEGLER & HENDON, ATTORNIES AT LAW::HIS PRACTICE WILL BE CONDUCTED FROM THEIR OFFICES AT 2905 TELEGRAPH AVENUE, BERKELEY 94705

3. Anatole France Quote, 1970, 15" × 24"

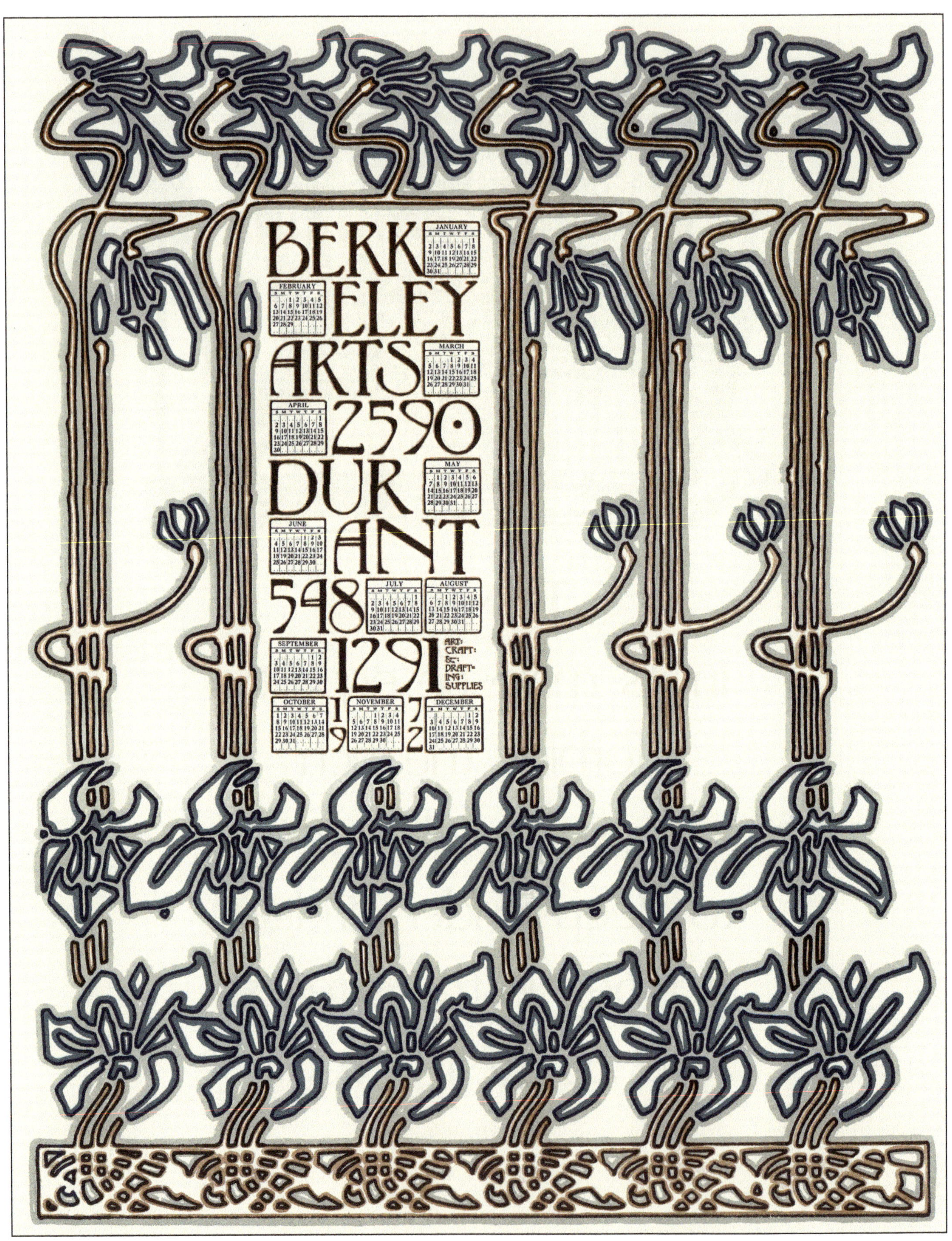

4. Berkeley Arts Calendar, 1971, 18" × 24"

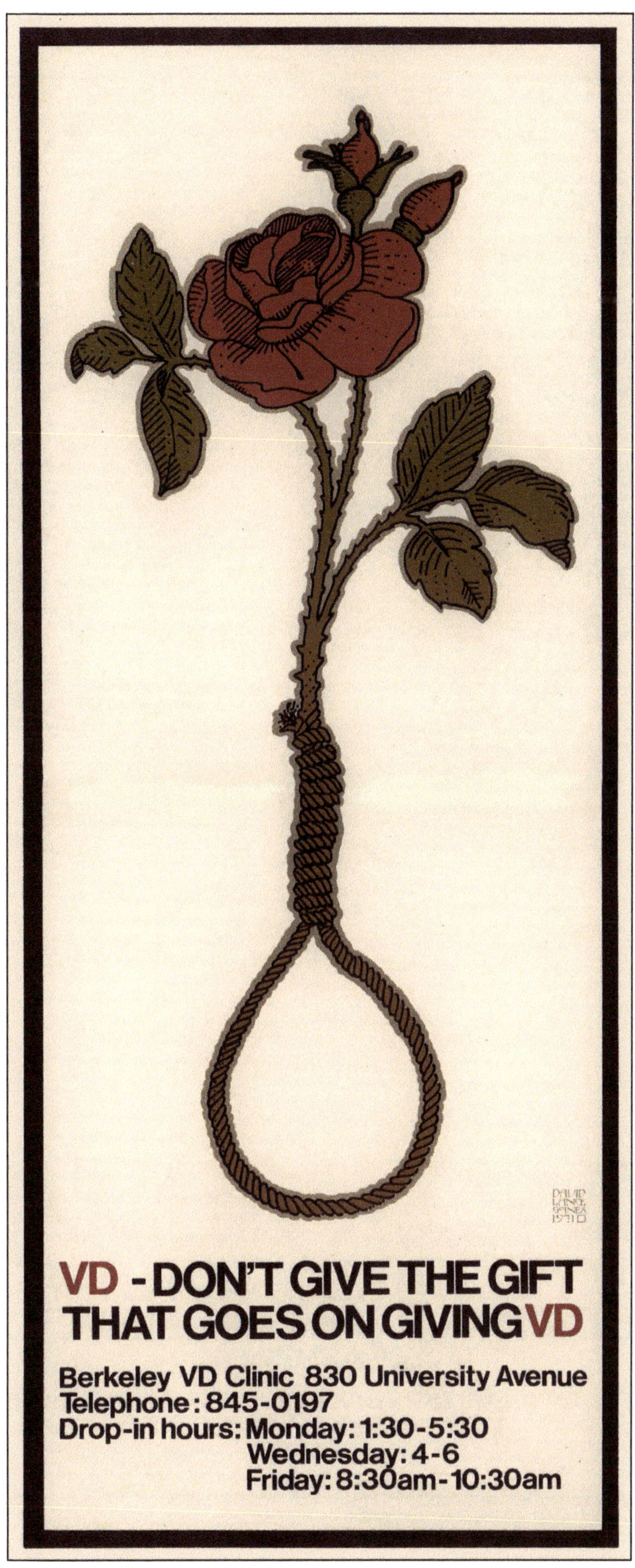

5. Berkeley VD Clinic, 1971, 18" × 24"

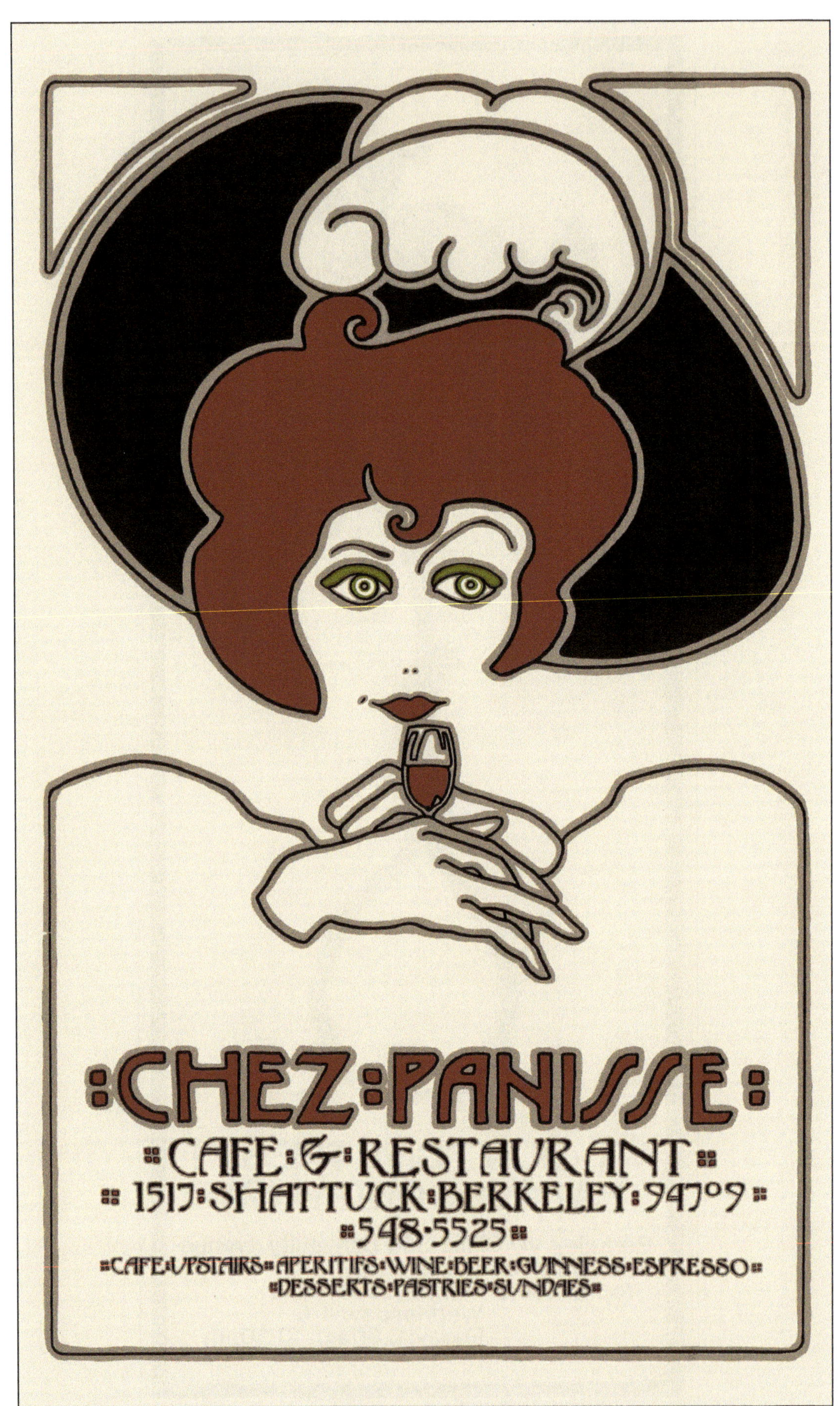

6. Chez Panisse Red-Haired Lady, 1972, 15" × 24"

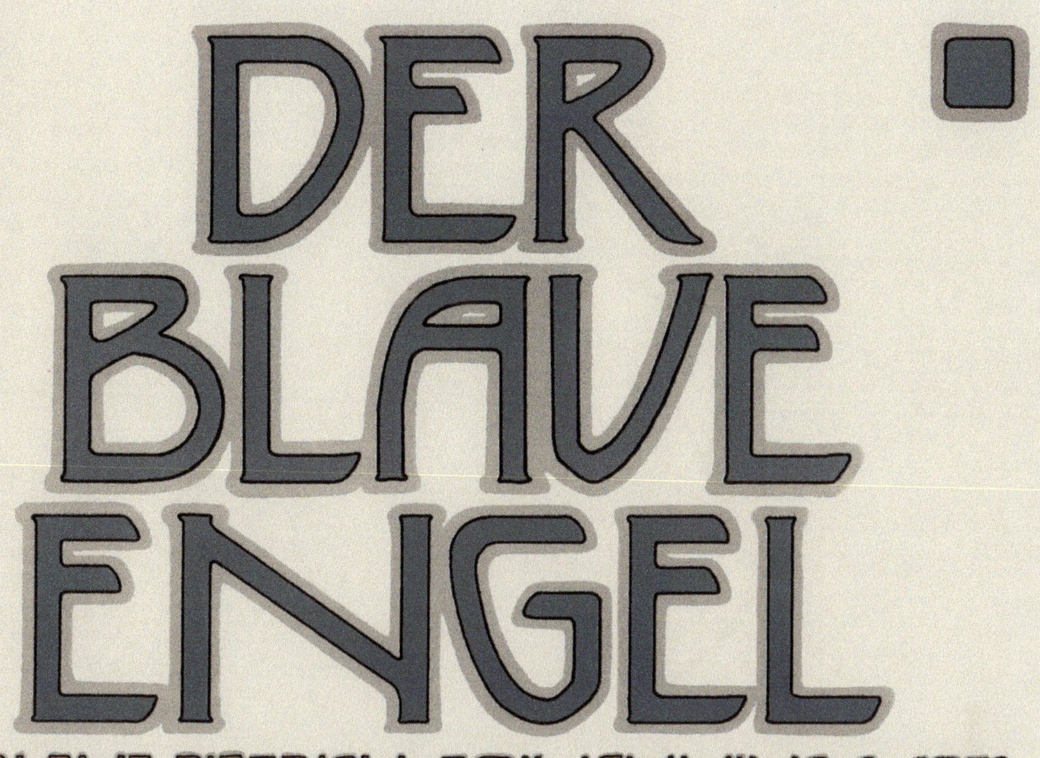

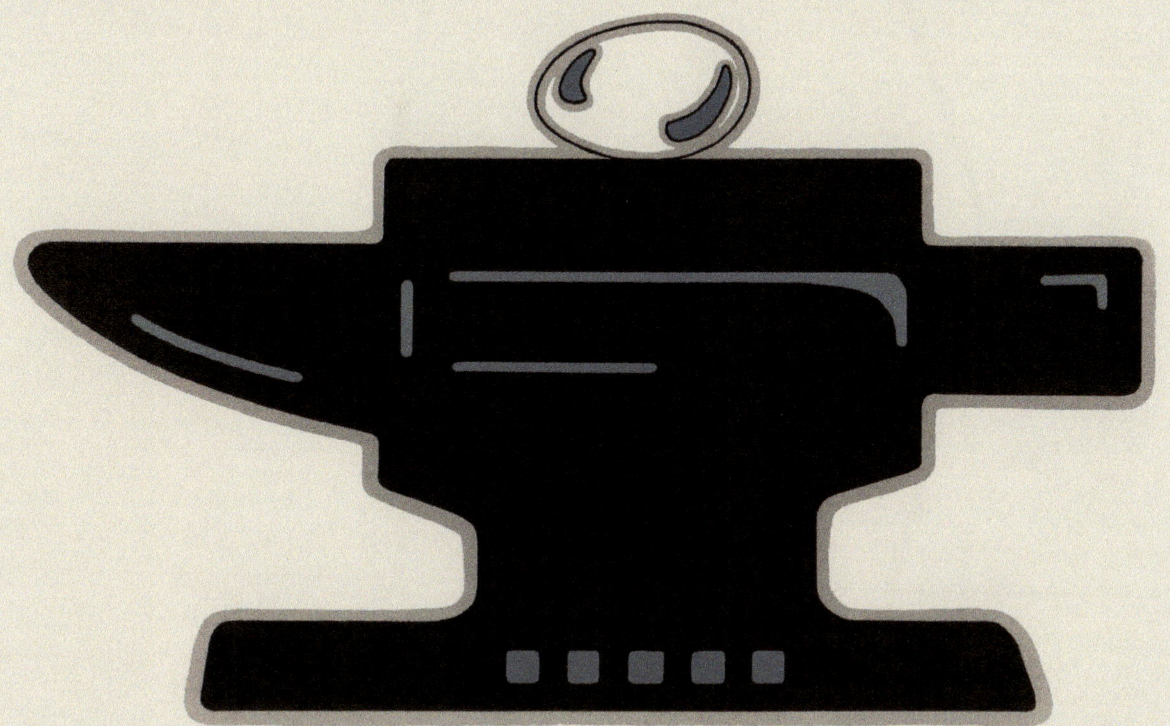

7. Der Blaue Engel, 1972, 16¾" × 24"

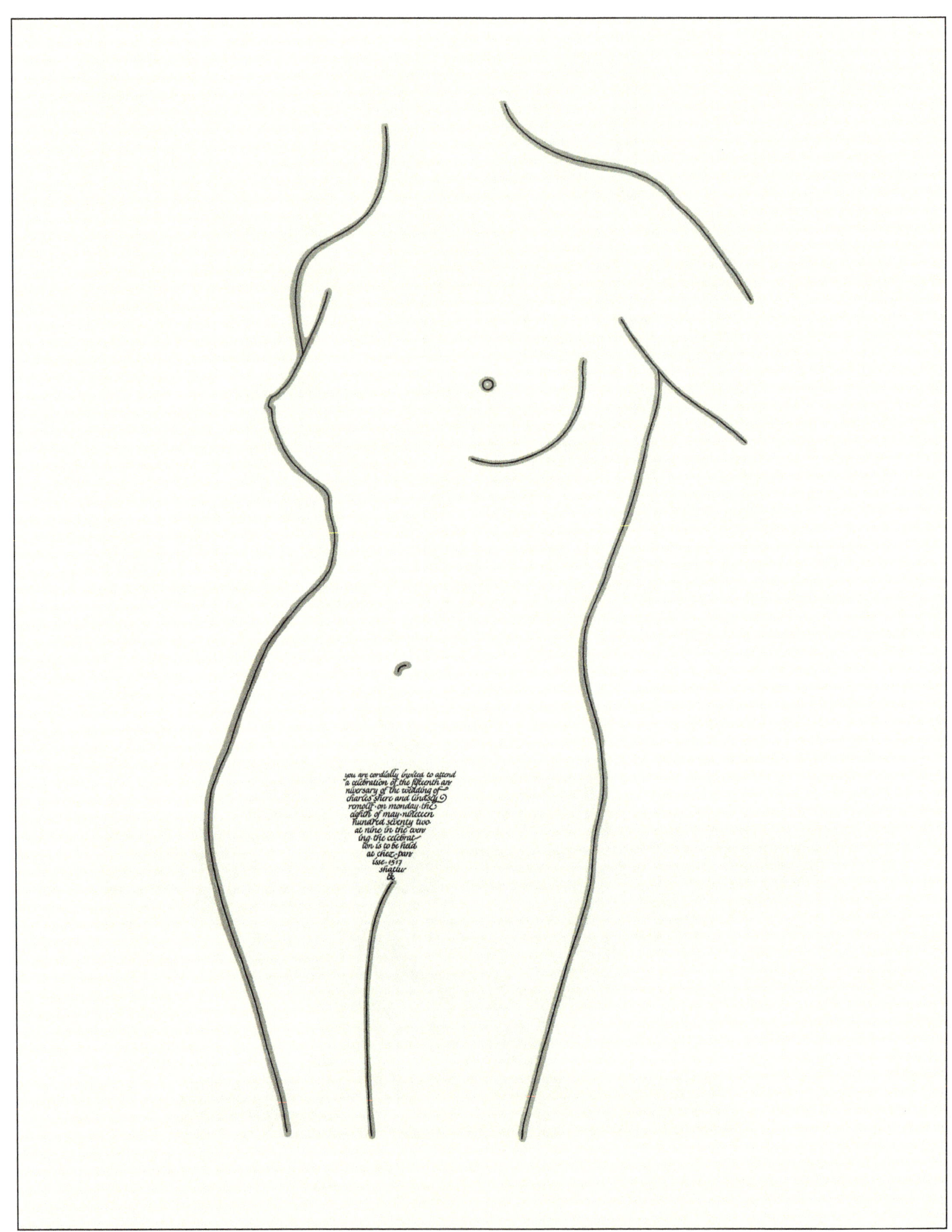

8. Shere Anniversary Invitation, 1972, 16" × 24"

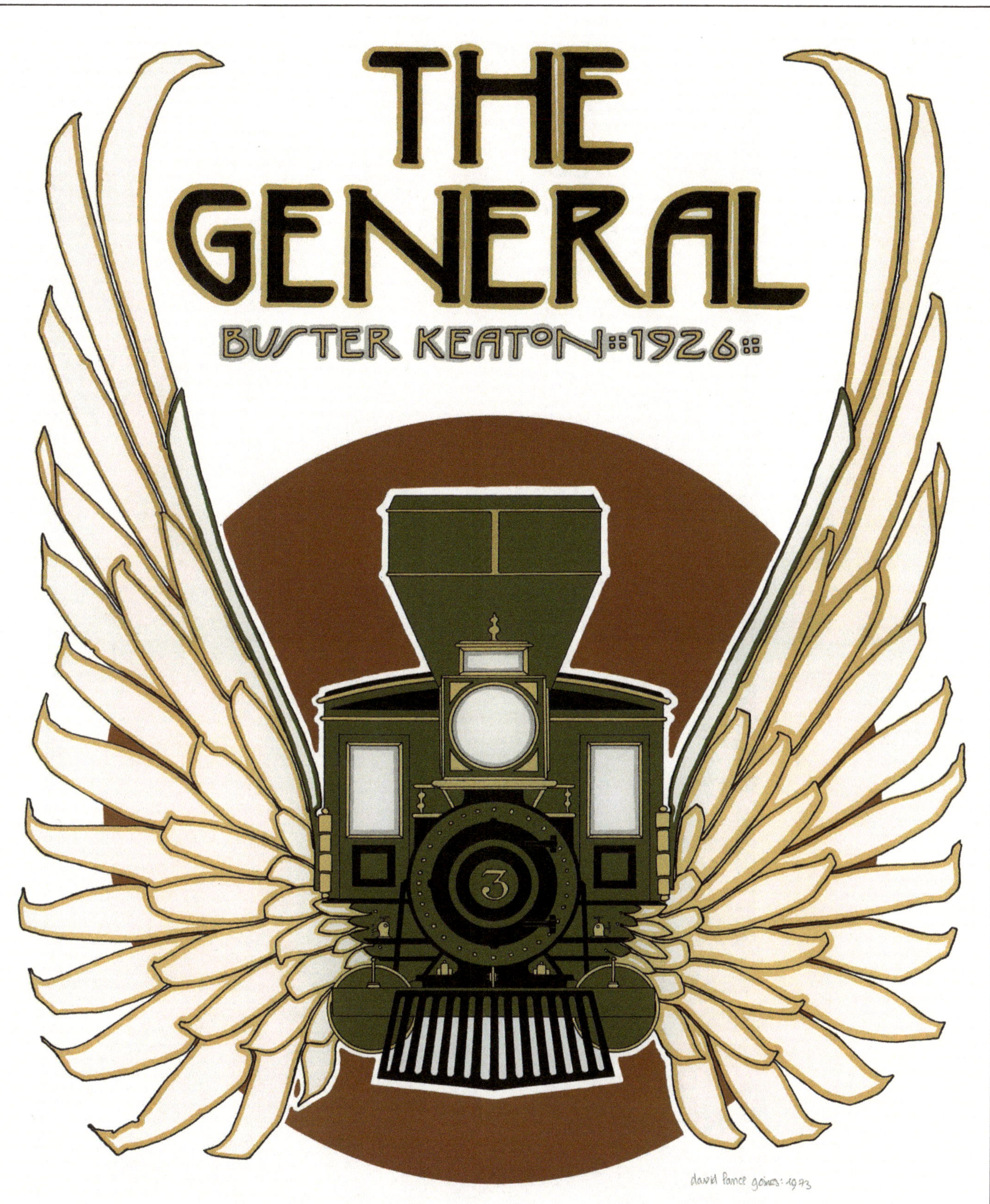

9. The General, 1972, 18" × 24"

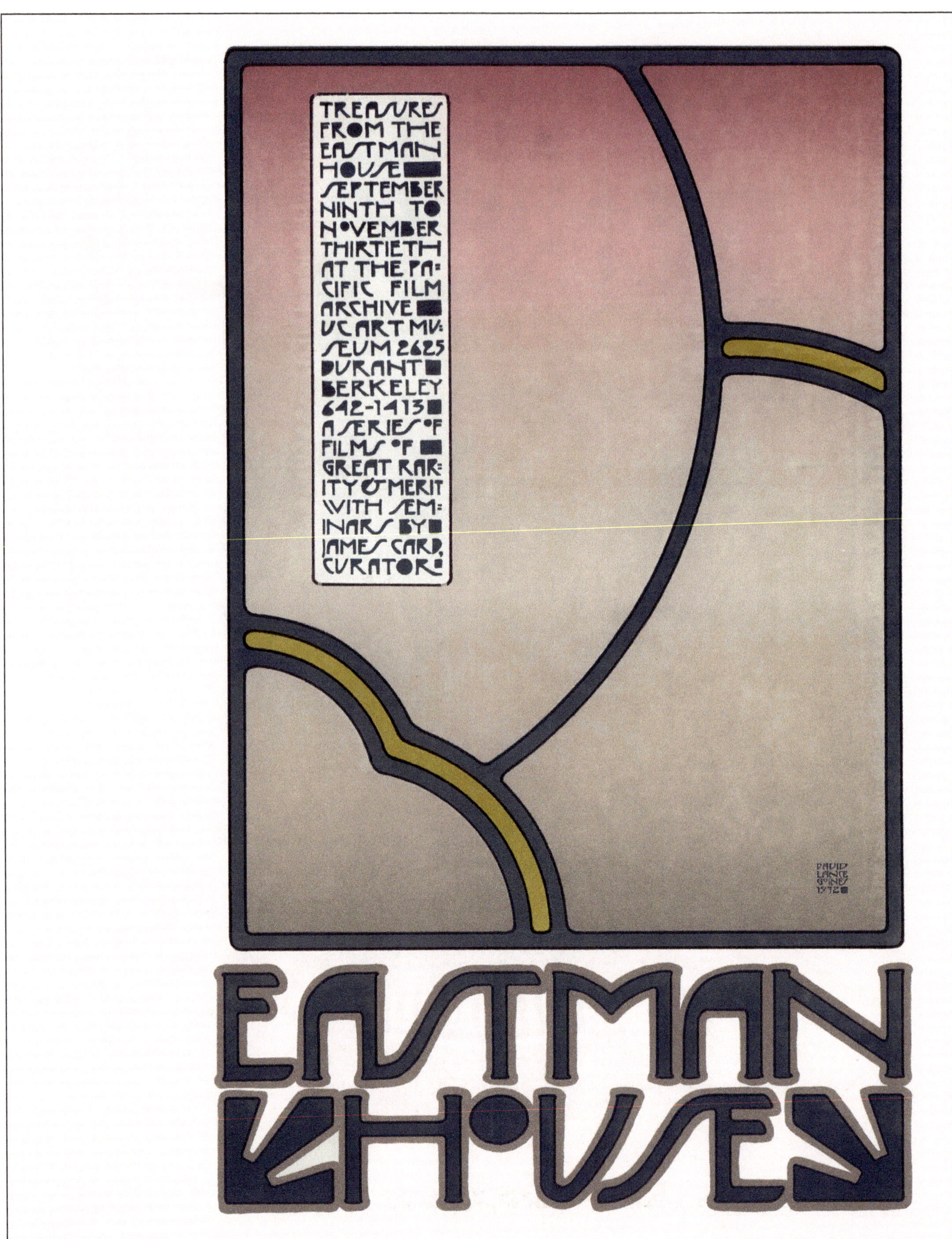

10. Eastman House (Pink), 1972, 15½" × 24"

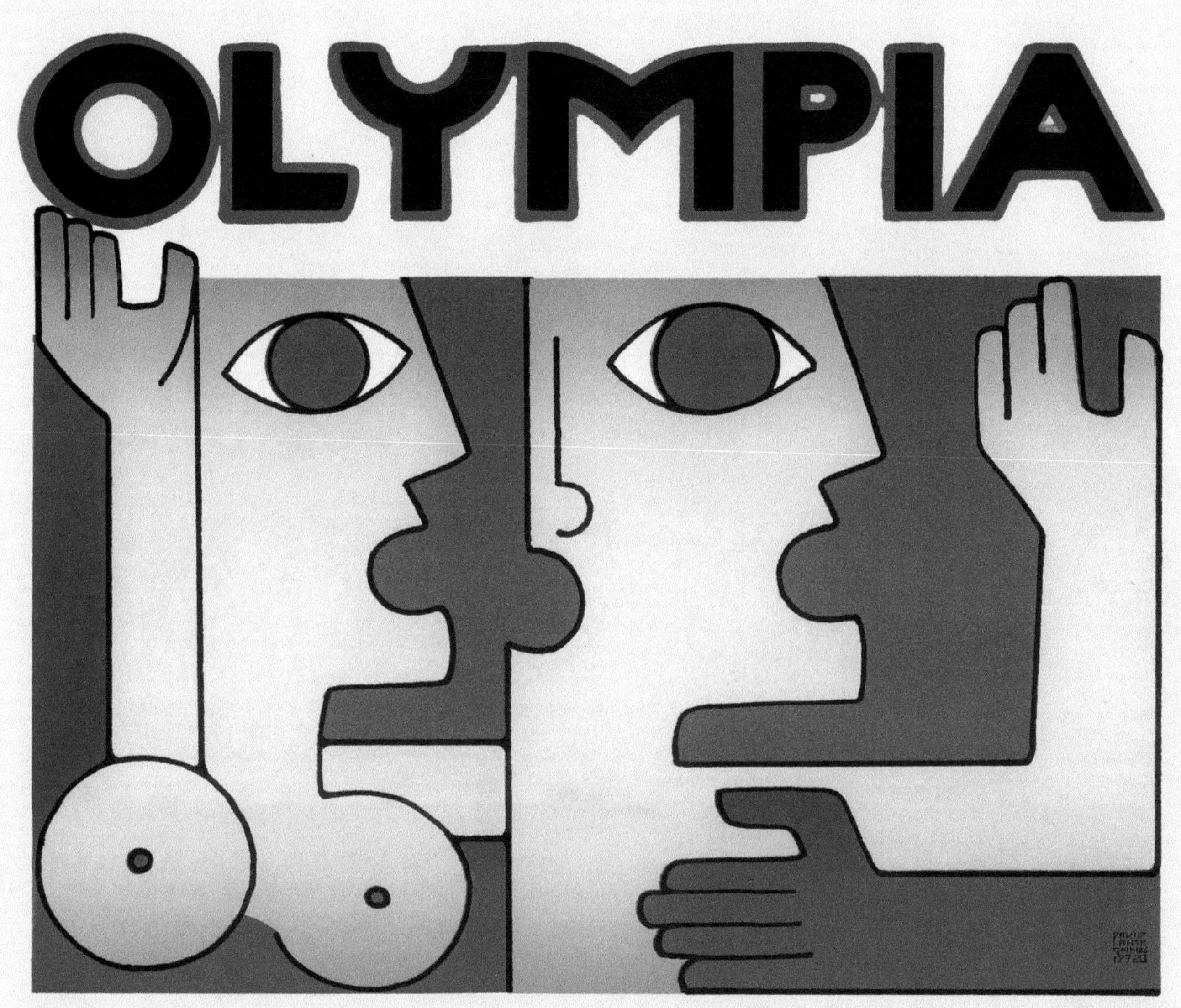

LENI RIEFENSTAHL:1936-1938
PART I:FESTIVAL OF THE NATIONS
FRIDAY:SEPTEMBER 22:AT 9:30
PART II:FESTIVAL OF BEAUTY:
SATURDAY:SEPTEMBER 23:9:30
PARTS I AND II:SATURDAY:3:00
PACIFIC FILM ARCHIVE:UC ART MUSEUM:2625 DURANT::

11. Olympia, 1972, 18" × 24"

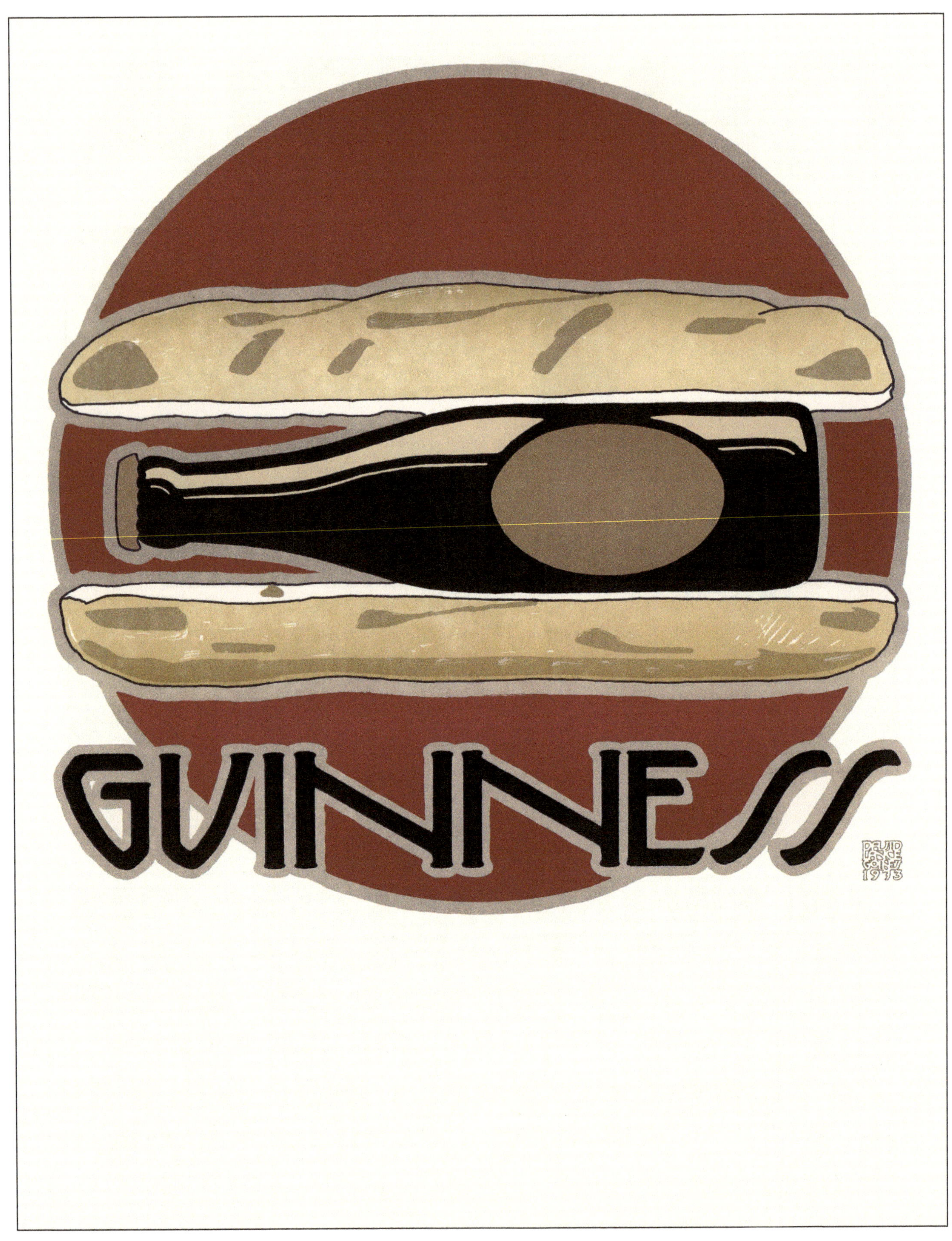

12. Guinness, 1973, 18" × 24"

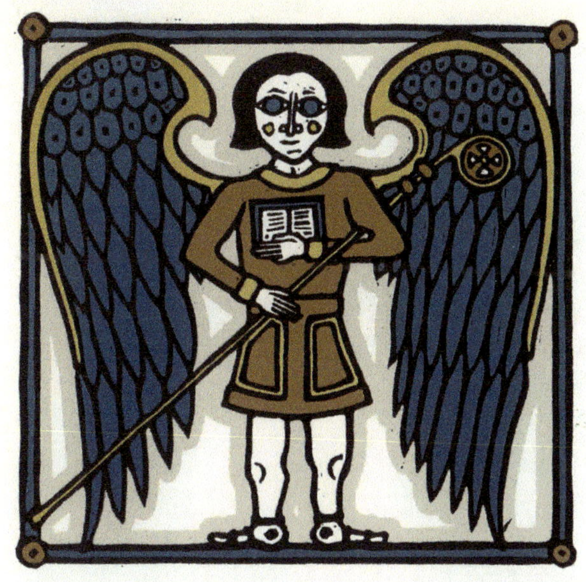

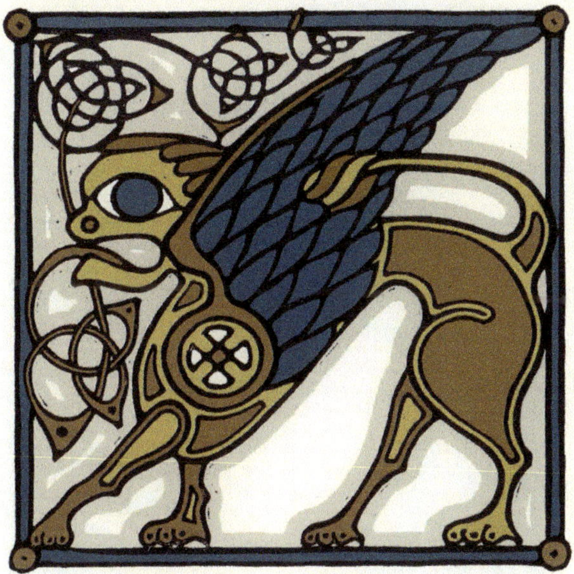

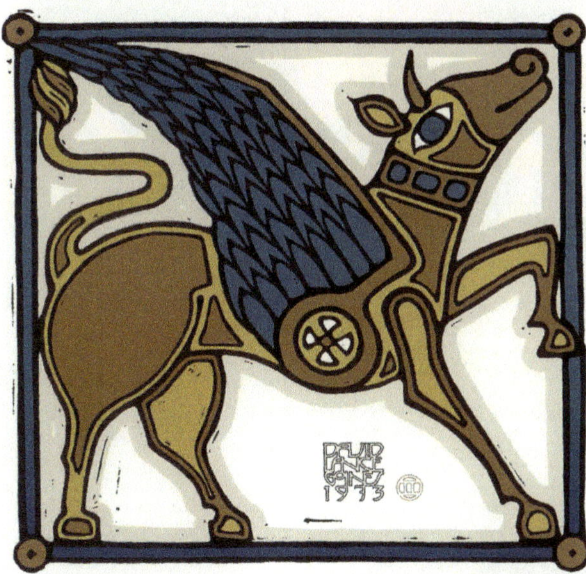

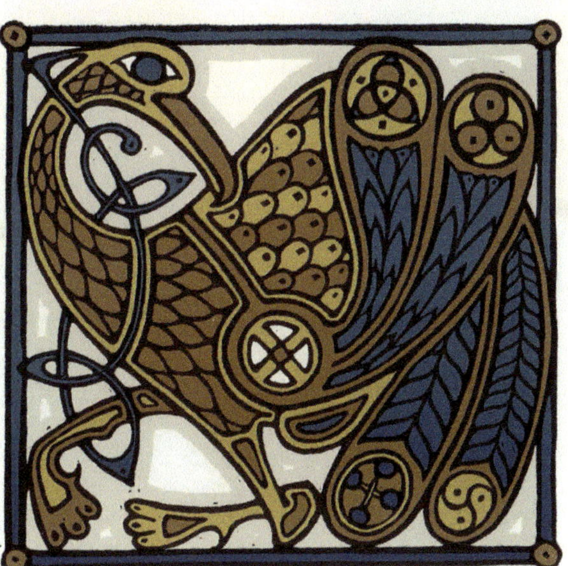

13. Bach, 1973, 18" × 24"

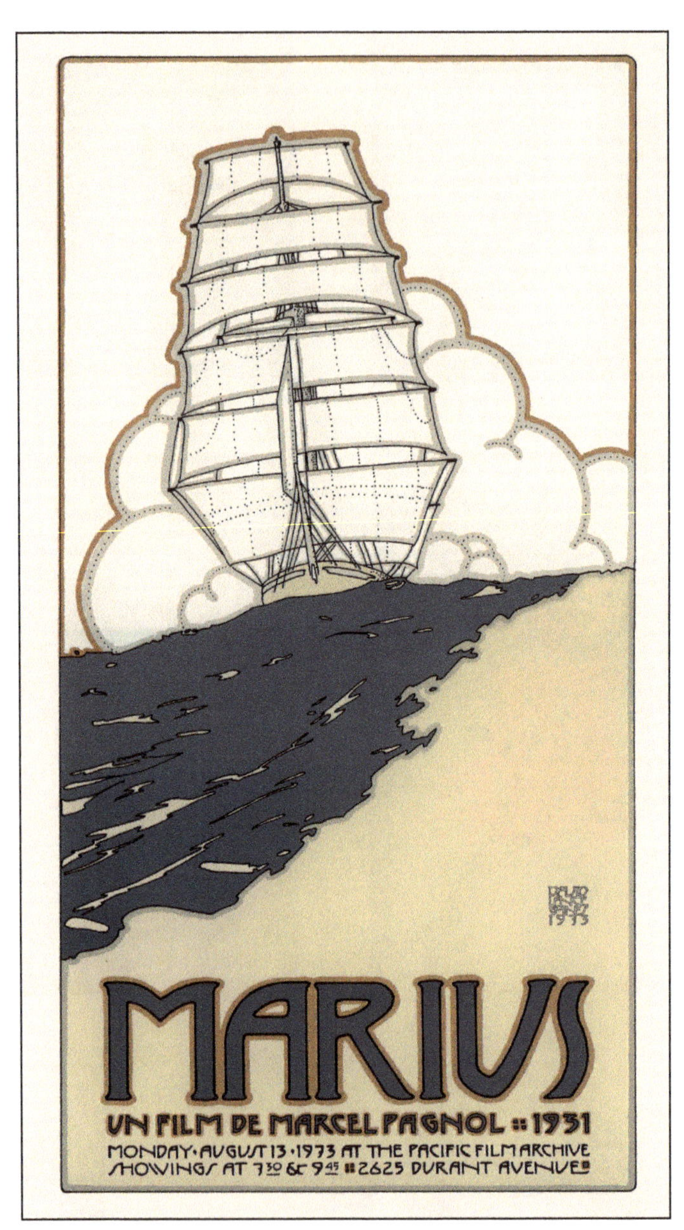

14. Marius, 1973, 13½" × 24"

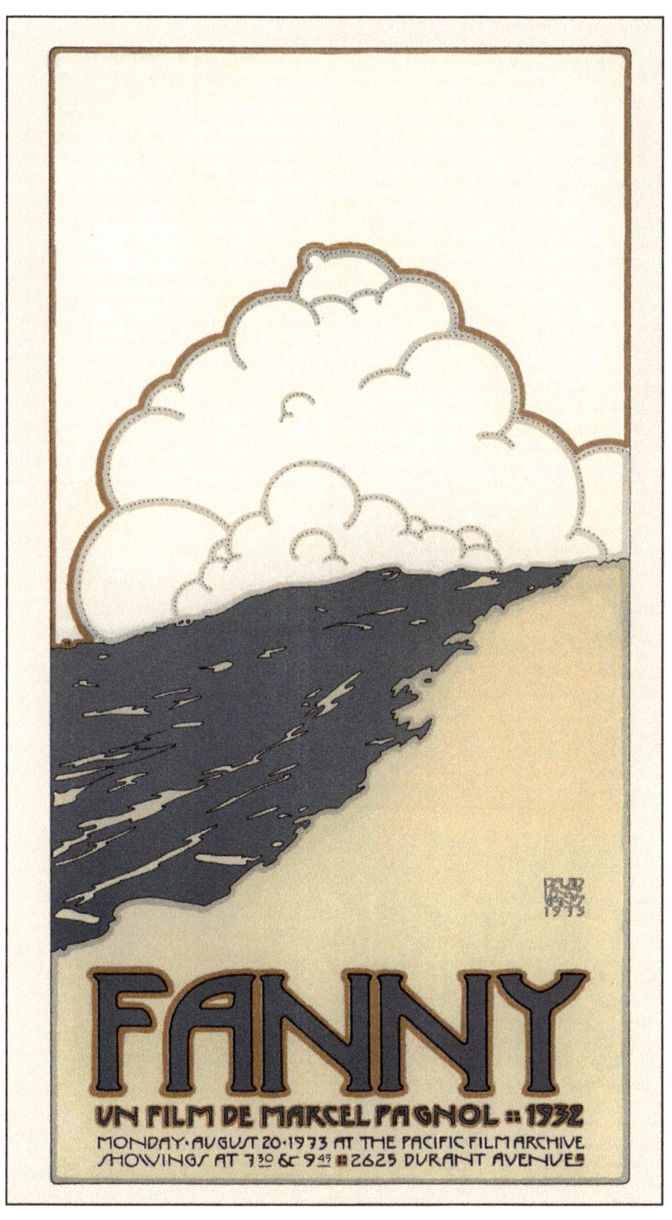

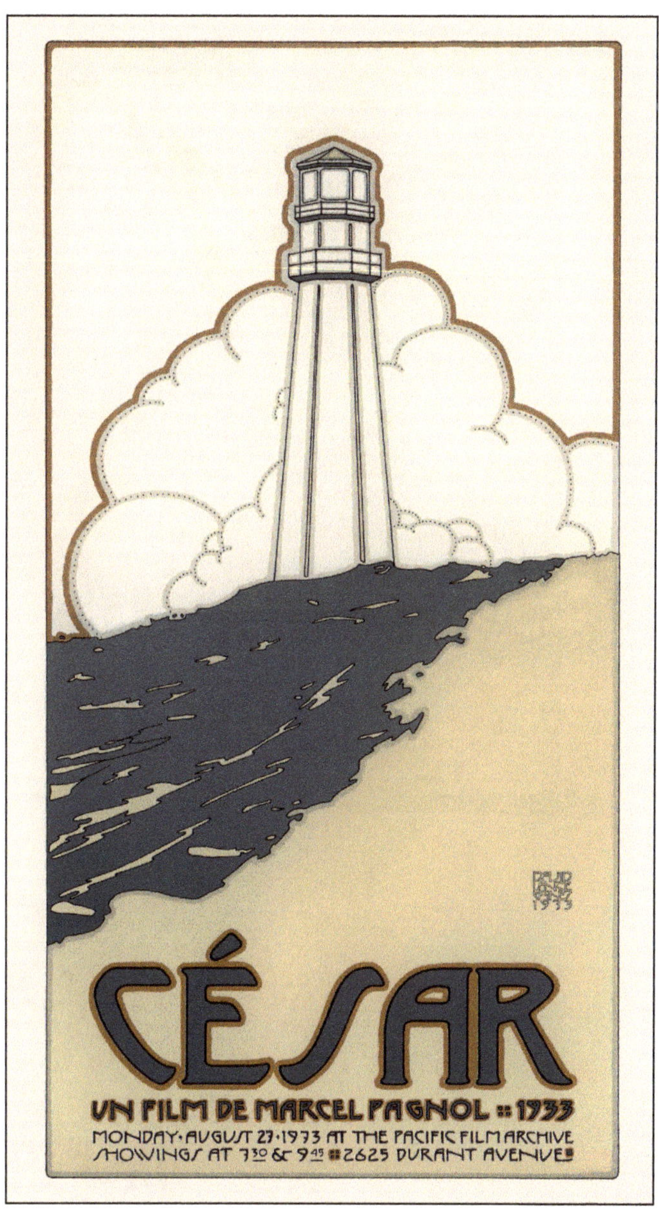

15. FANNY, 1973, 13½" × 24"

16. CÉSAR, 1973, 13½" × 24"

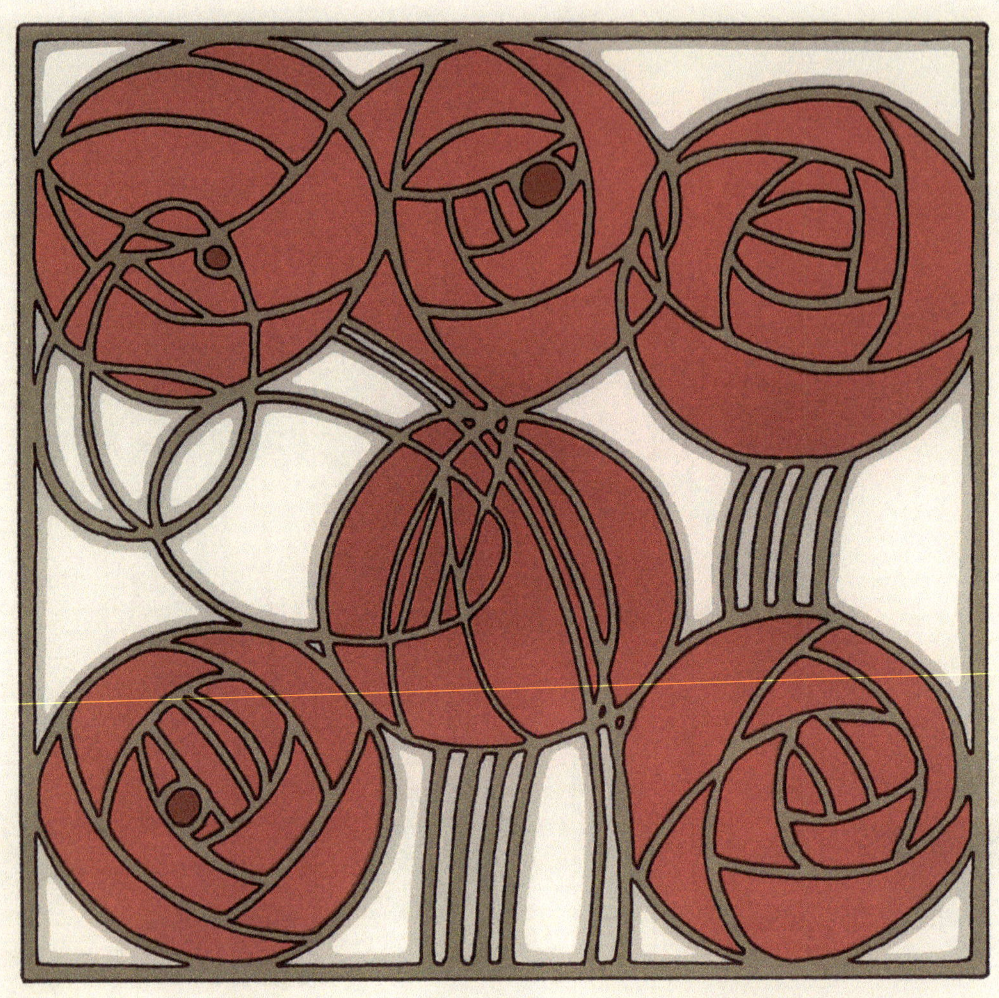

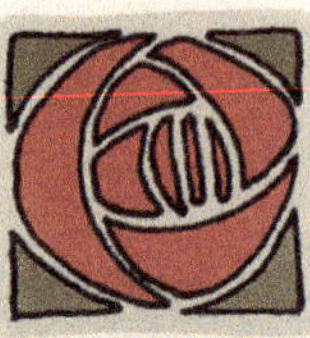

17. Chez Panisse Second Birthday, 1973, 18" × 24"

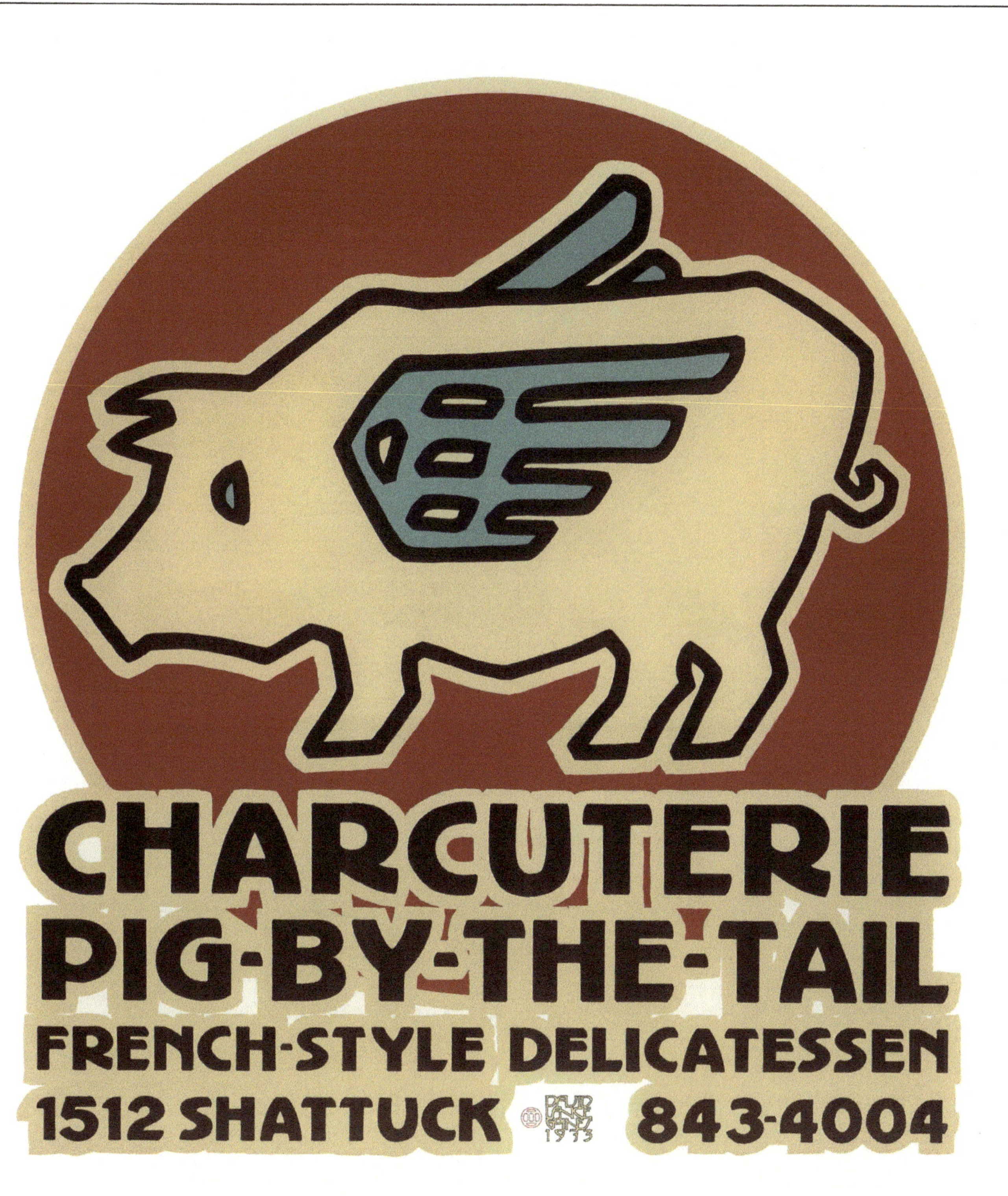

18. Charcuterie Pig-by-the-Tail, 1973, 18" × 24"

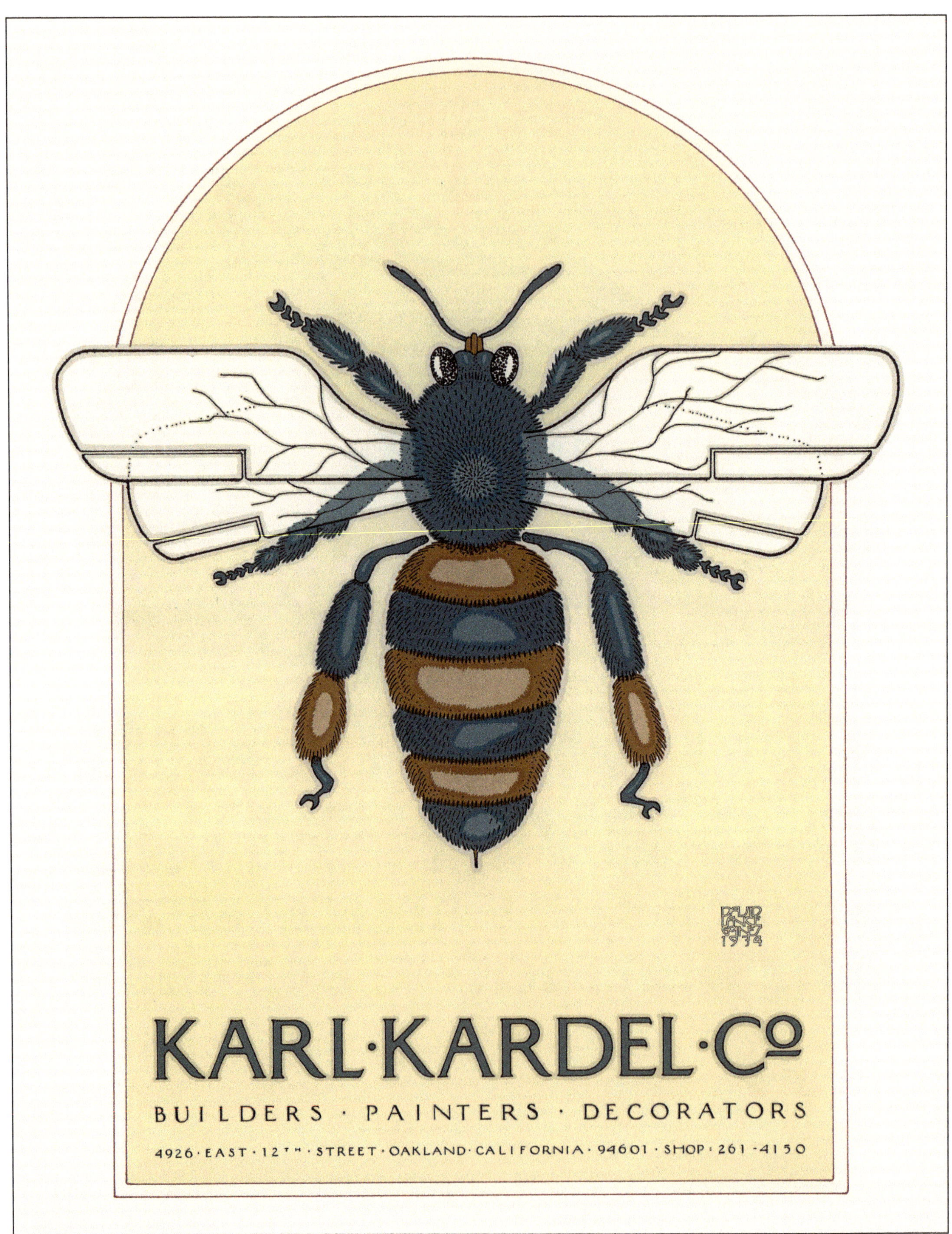

19. Karl Kardel Co., 1974, 18" × 24"

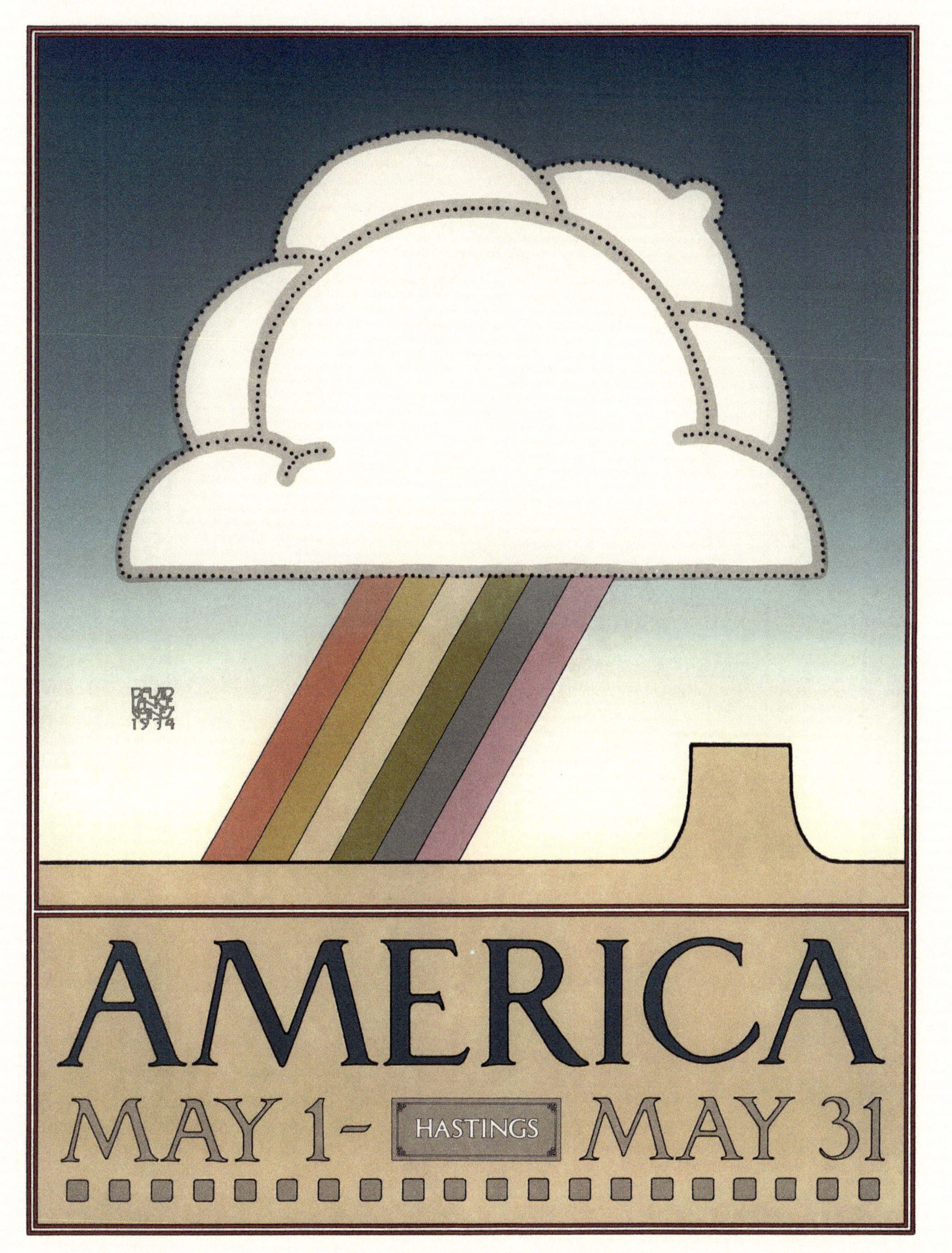

20. America, 1974, 18" × 24"

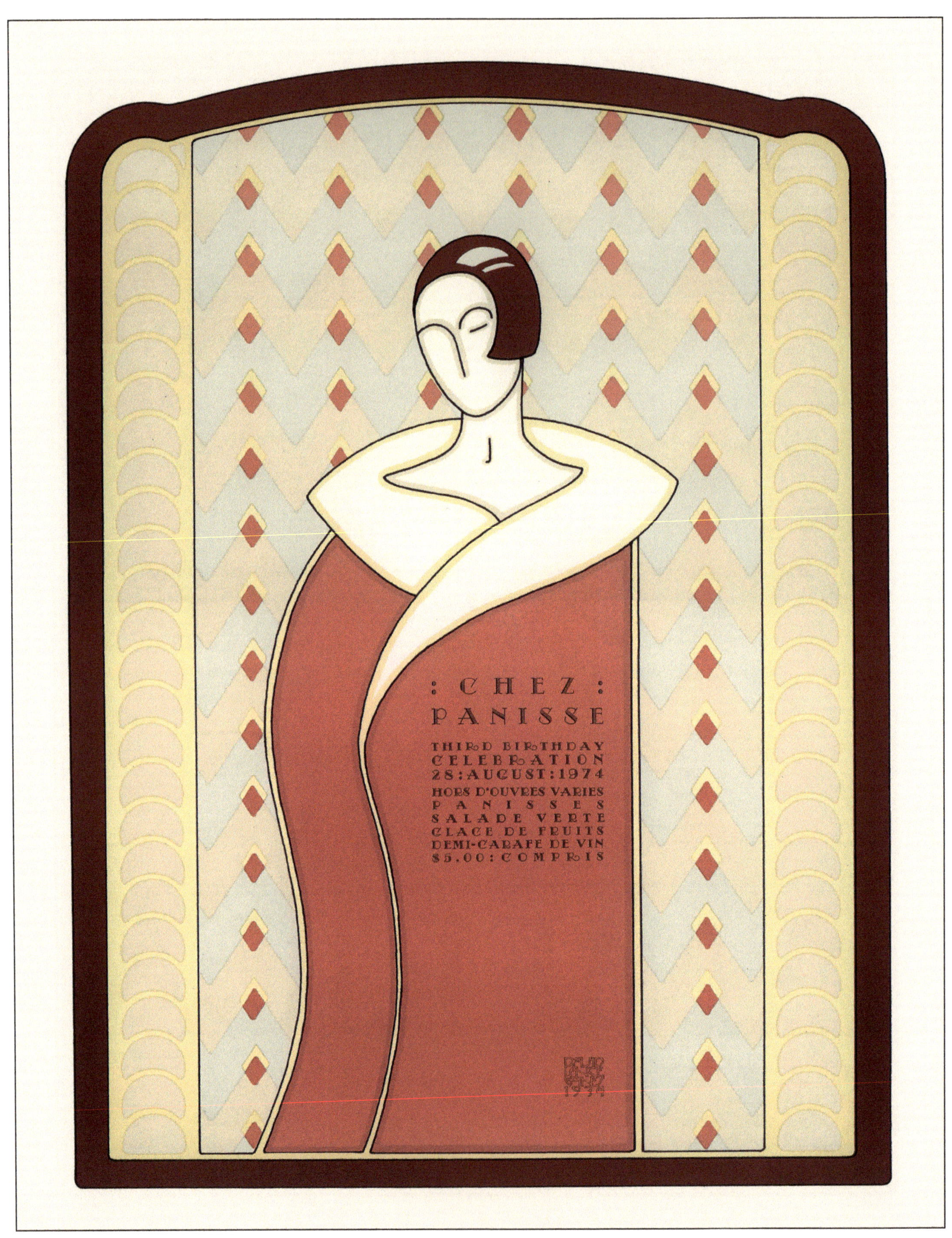

21. Chez Panisse Third Birthday, 1974, 18" × 24"

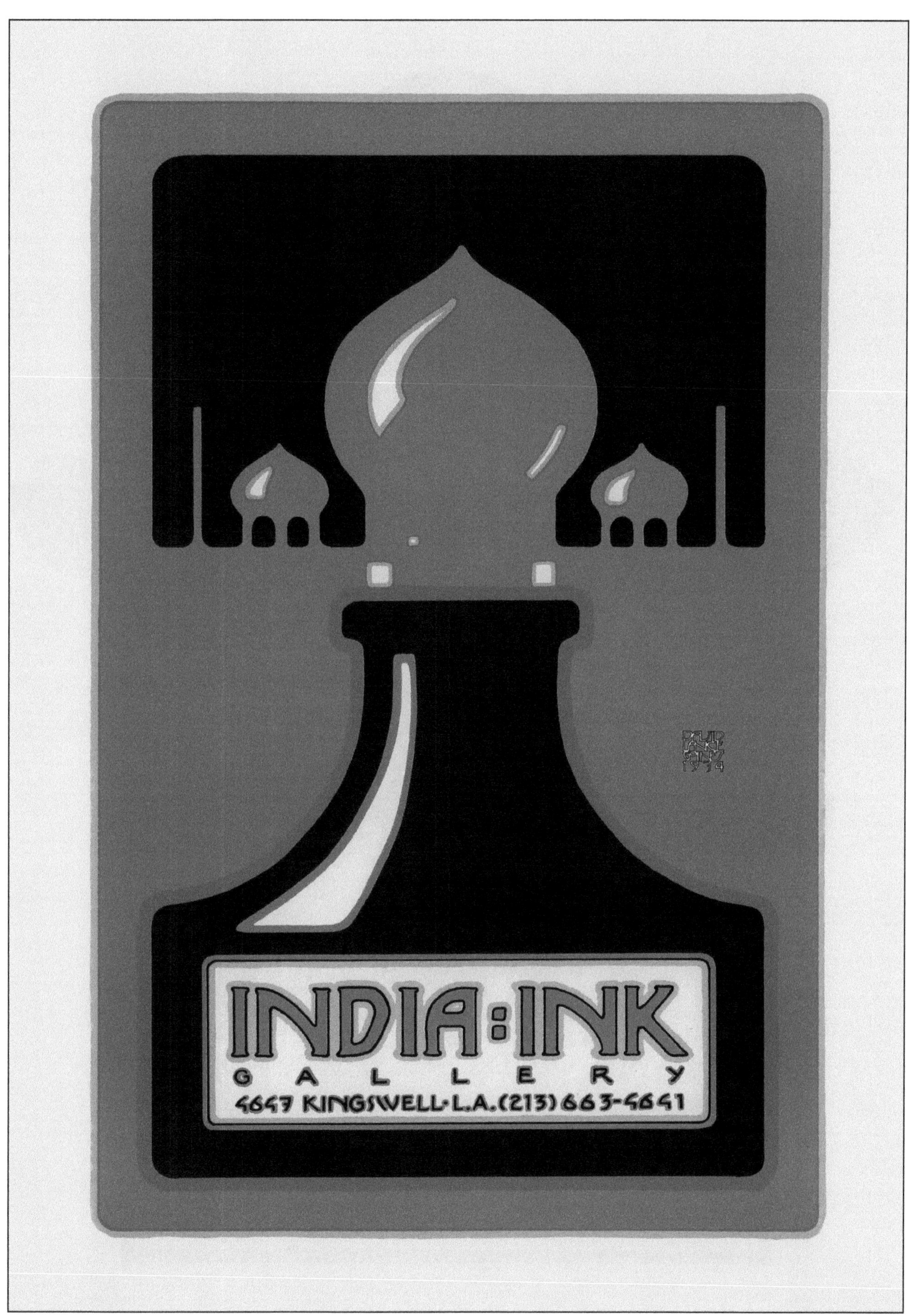

22. India Ink Gallery, 1974, 16¼" × 24"

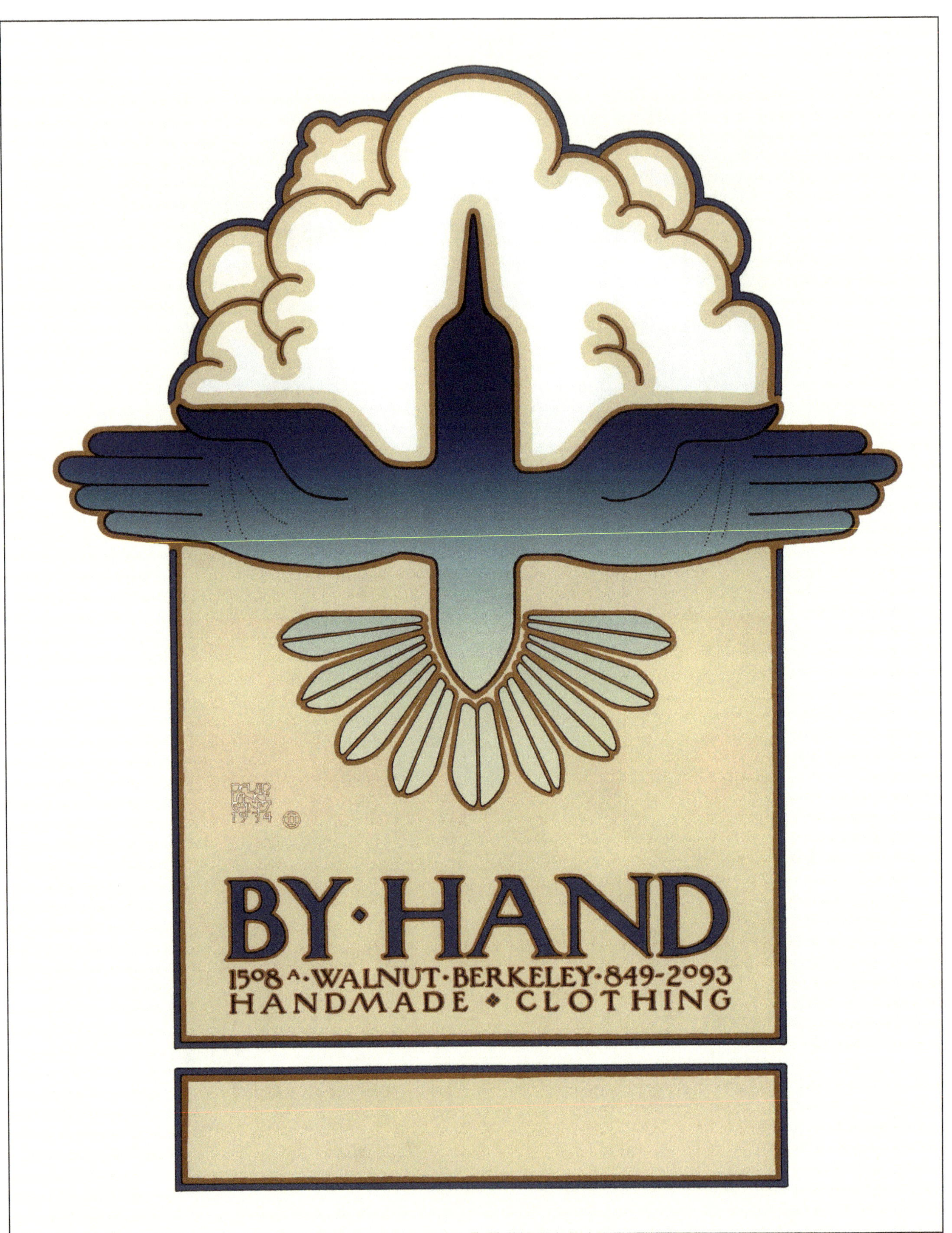

23. By Hand, 1974, 18" × 24"

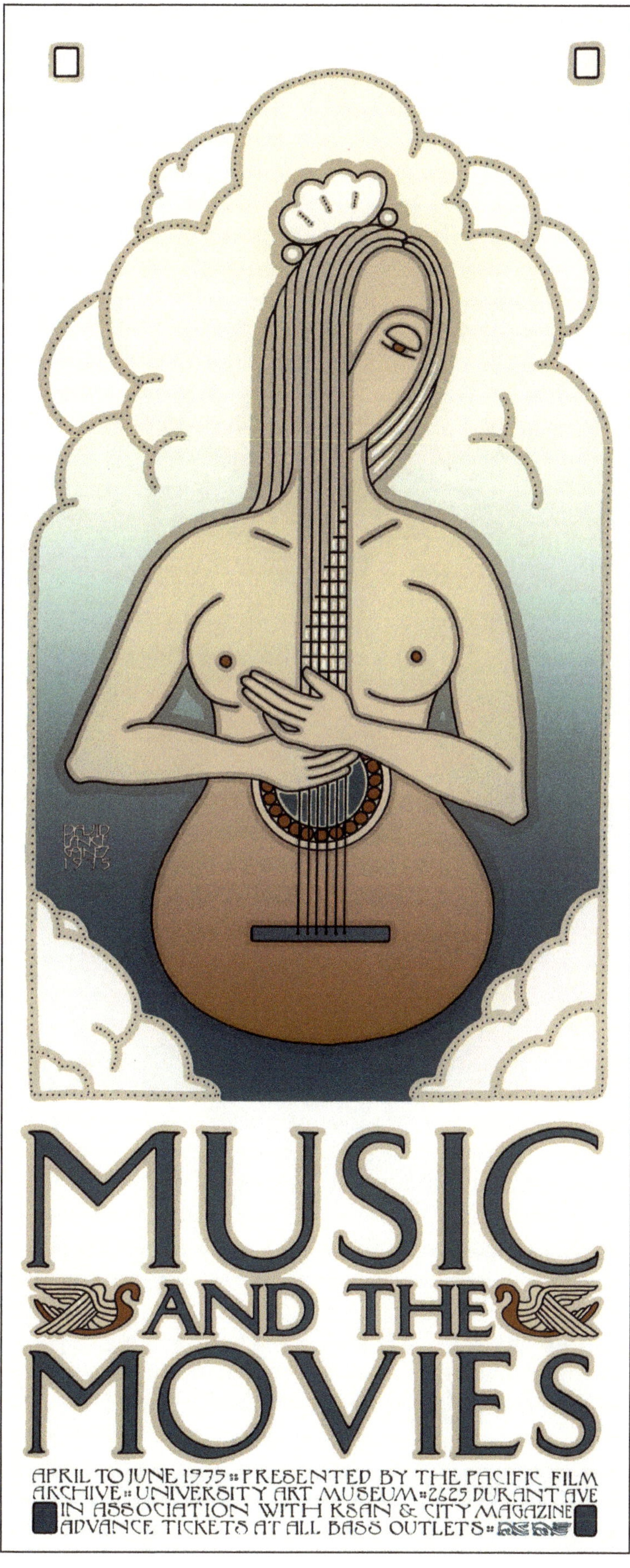

24. Music and the Movies, 1975, 10" × 24"

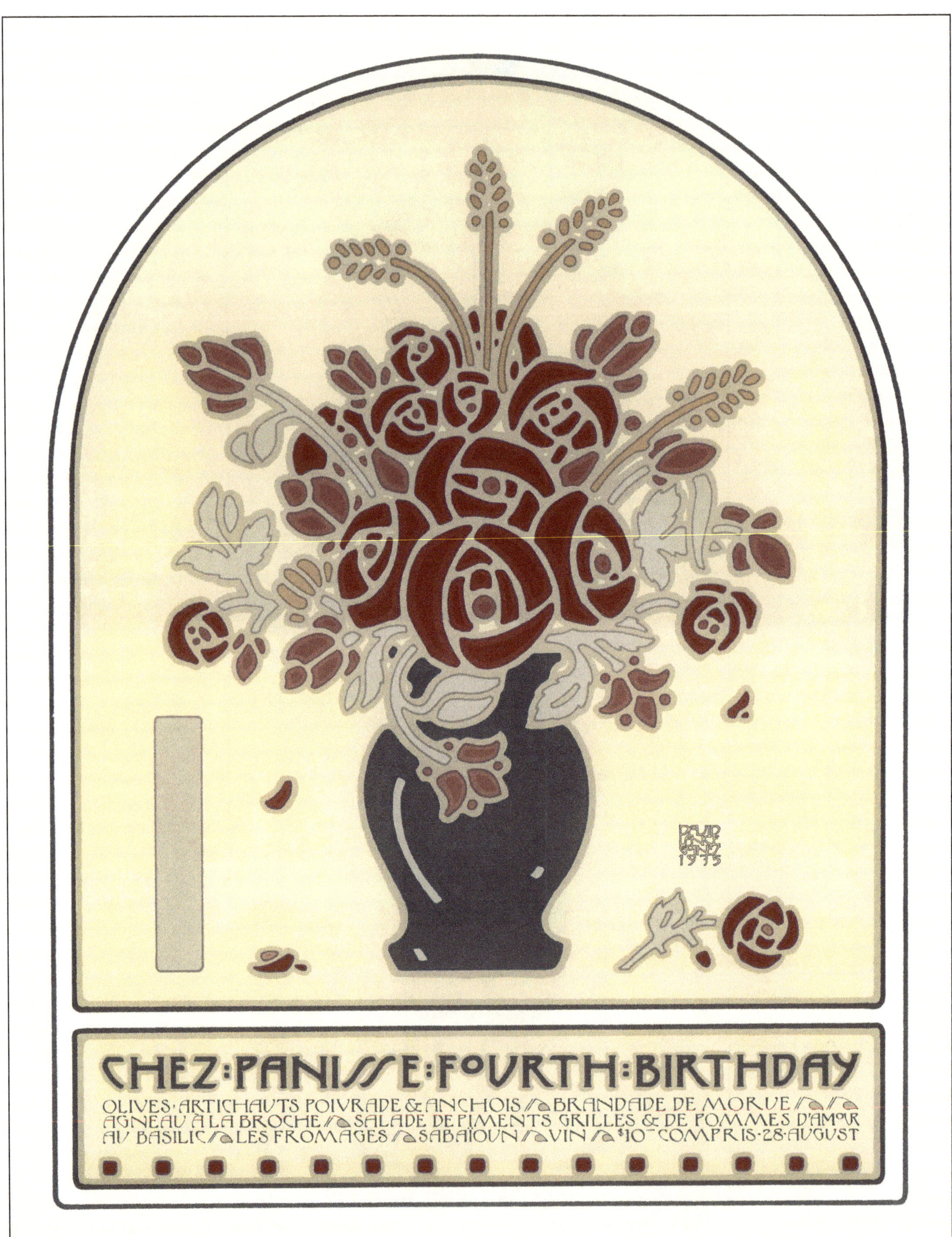

25. Chez Panisse Fourth Birthday, 1975, 18" × 24"

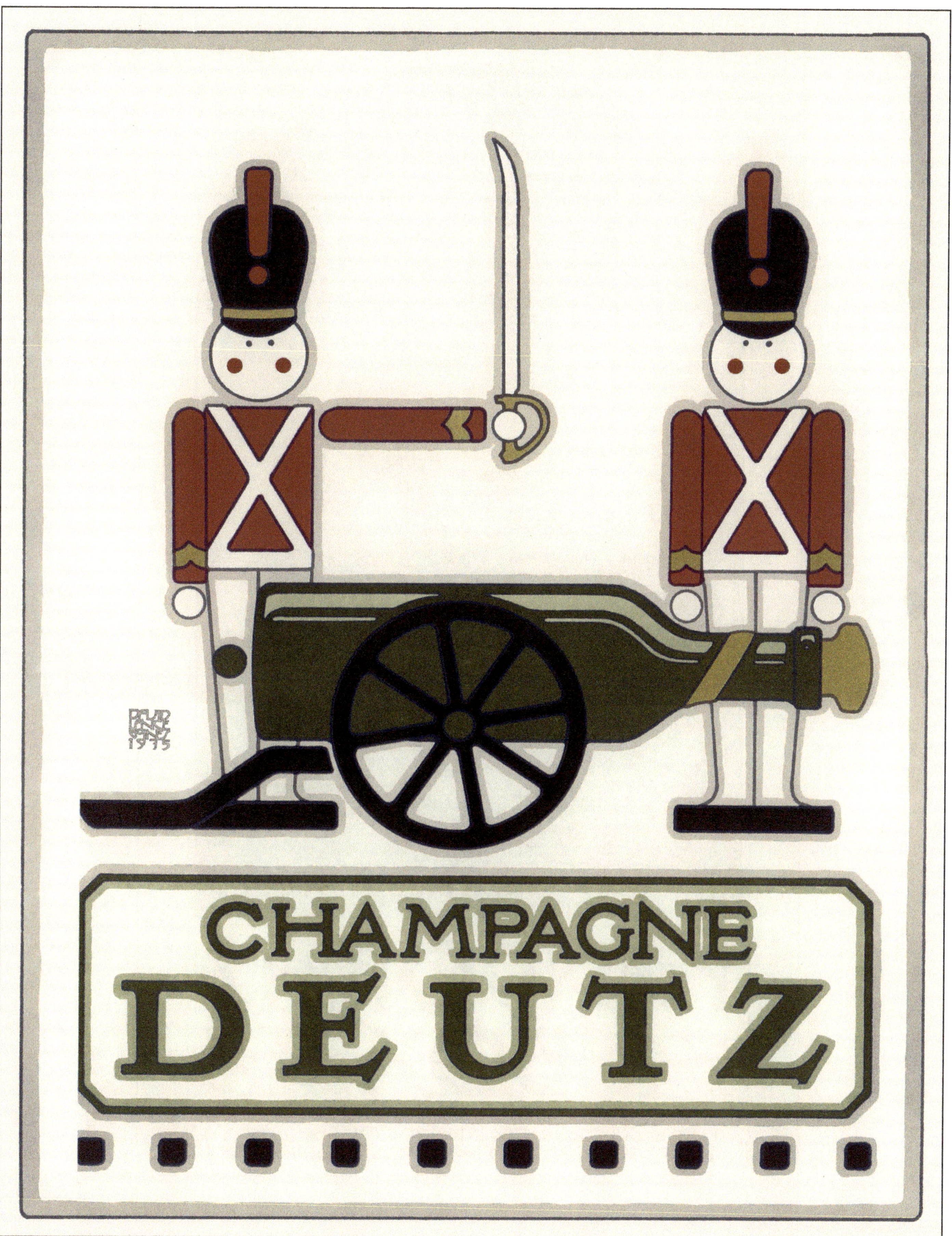

26. Champagne Deutz, 1975, 18" × 24"

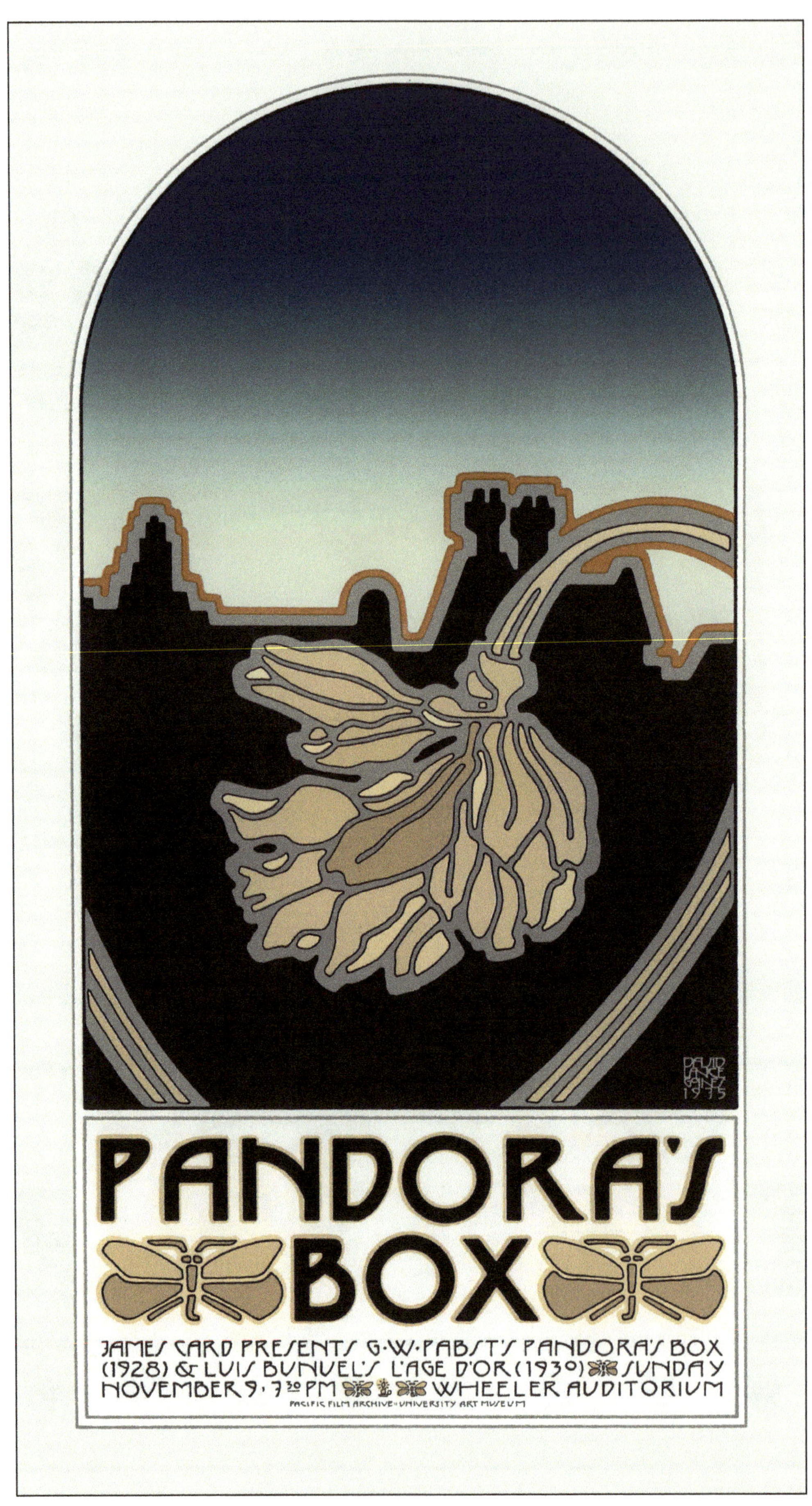

27. PANDORA'S BOX, 1975, 13" × 24"

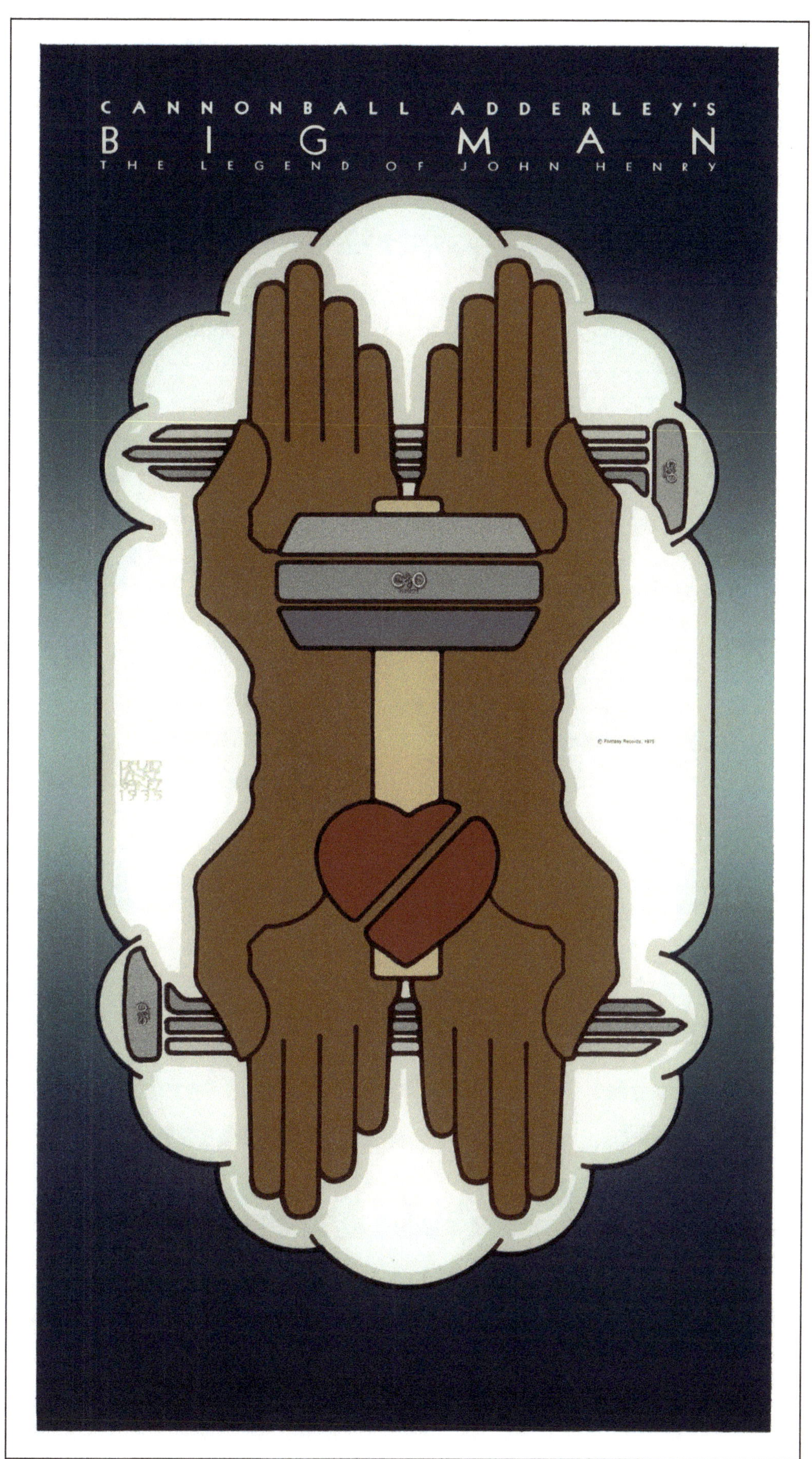

28. Big Man, 1975, 14" × 24"

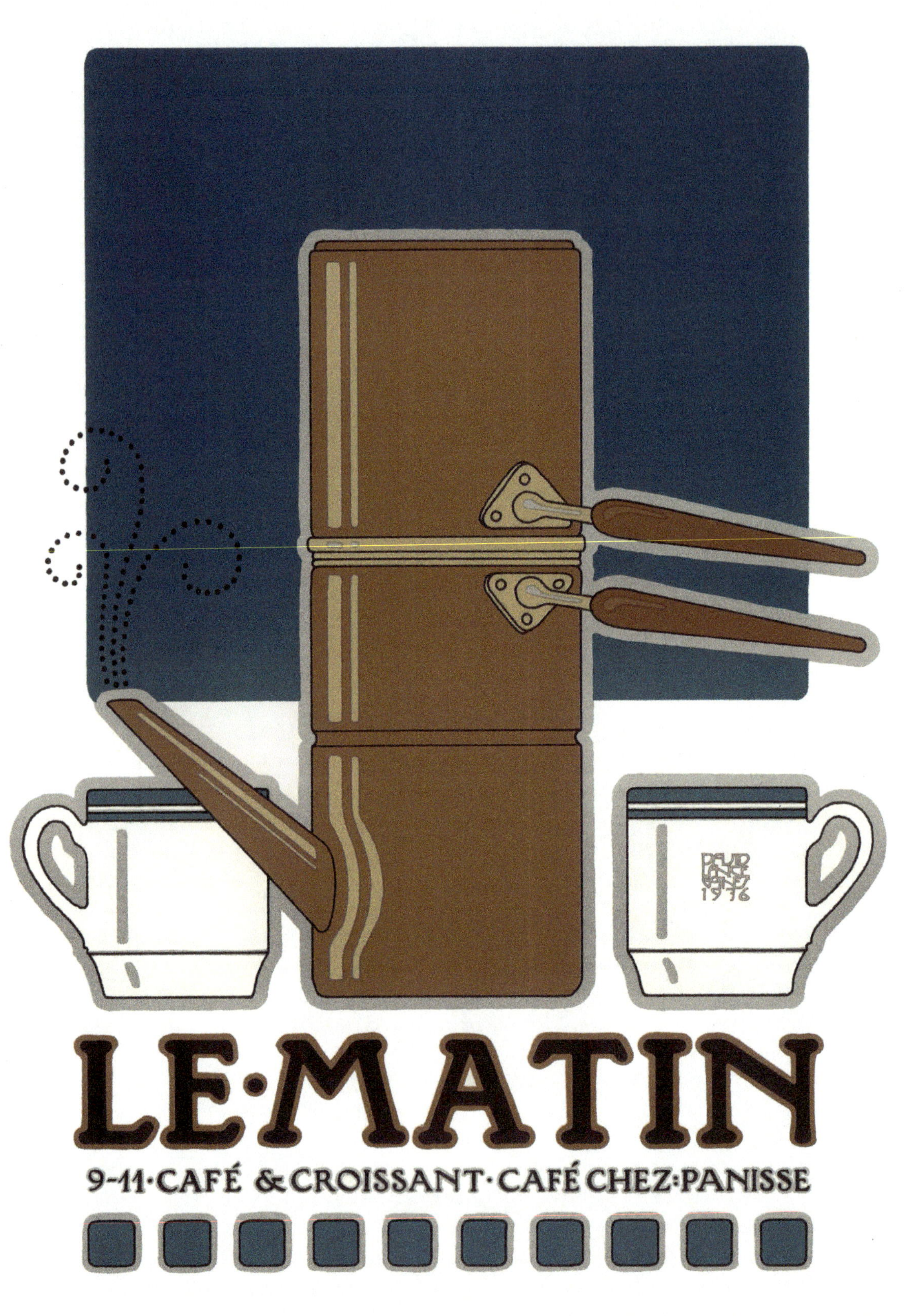

29. Le Matin, 1976, 16¾" × 24"

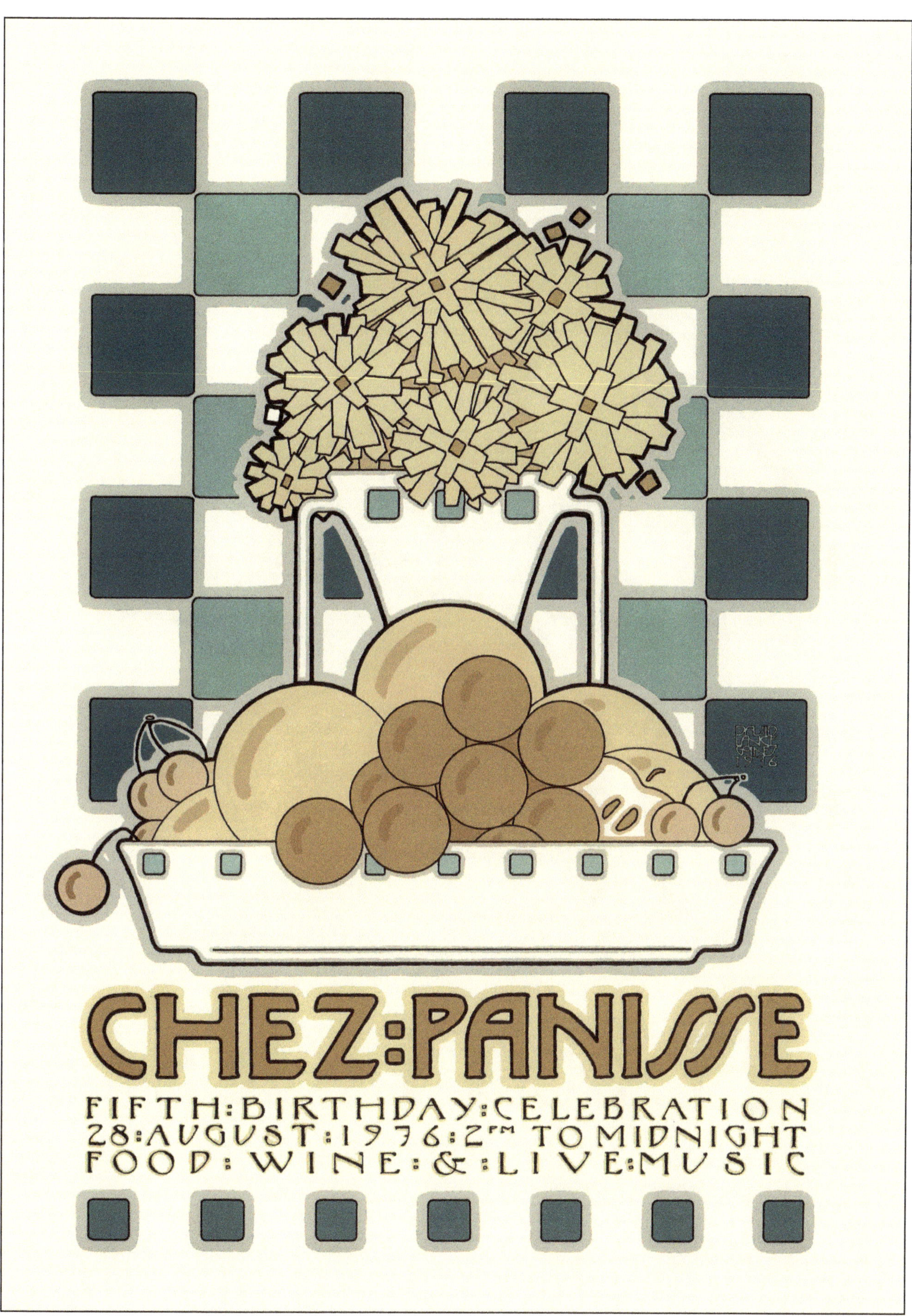

30. Chez Panisse Fifth Birthday, 1976, 18" × 24"

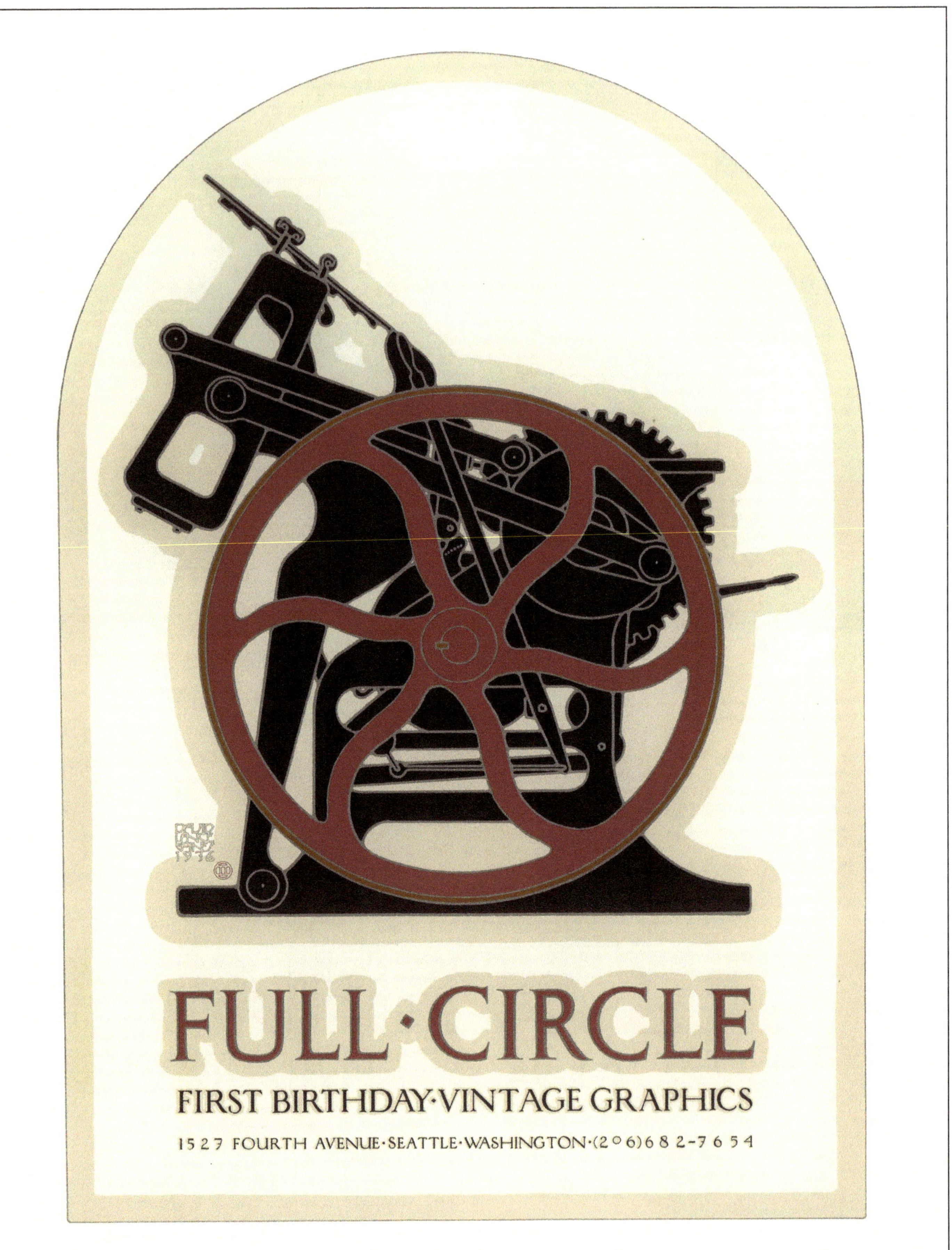

31. Full Circle, 1976, 18" × 24"

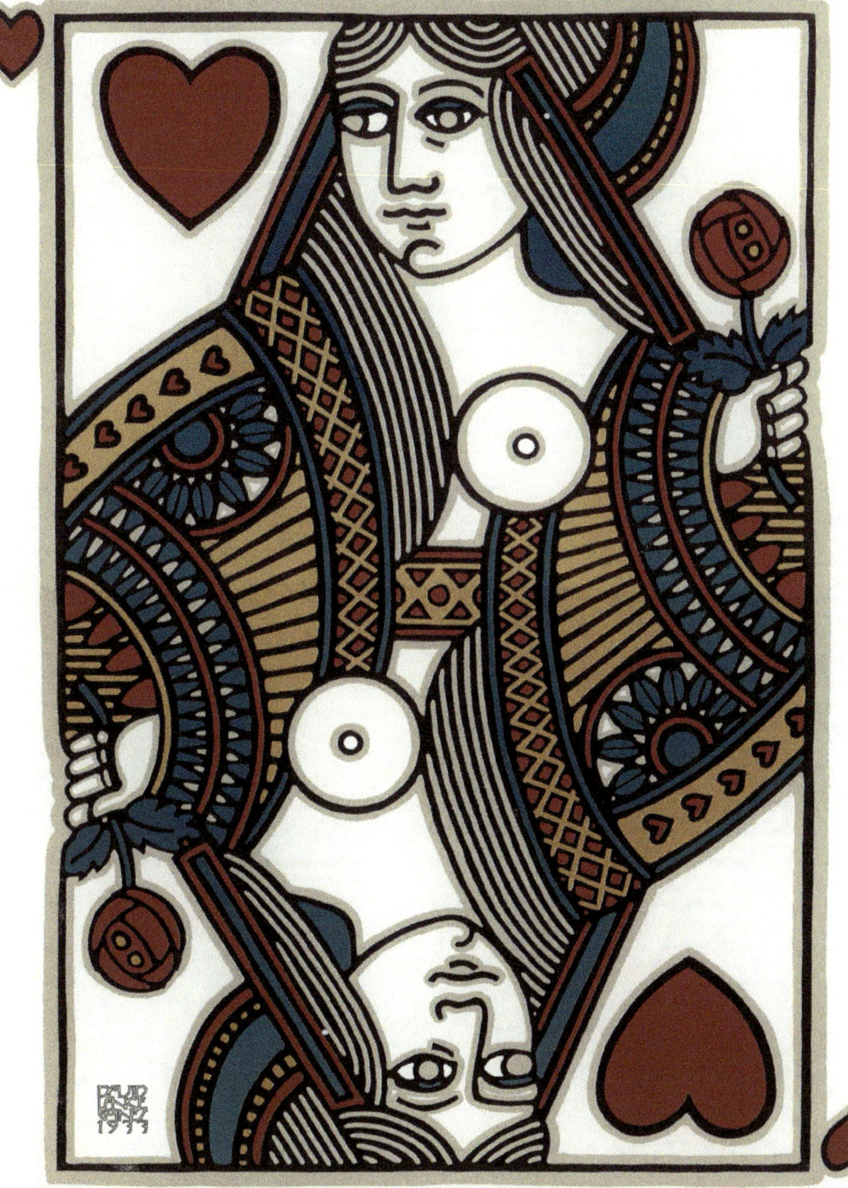

32. Queen of Hearts Ball, 1977, 14¾" × 24"

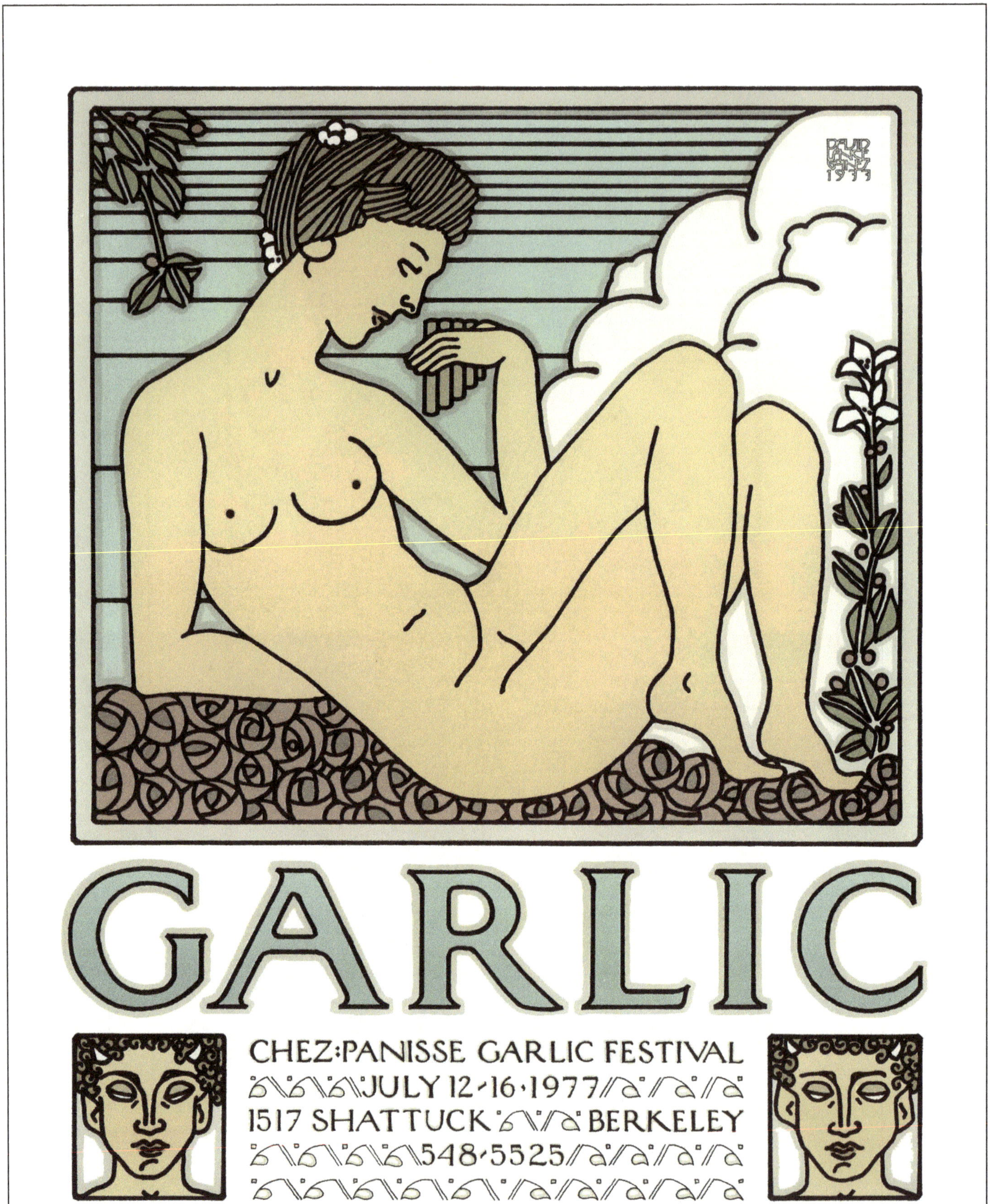

GARLIC

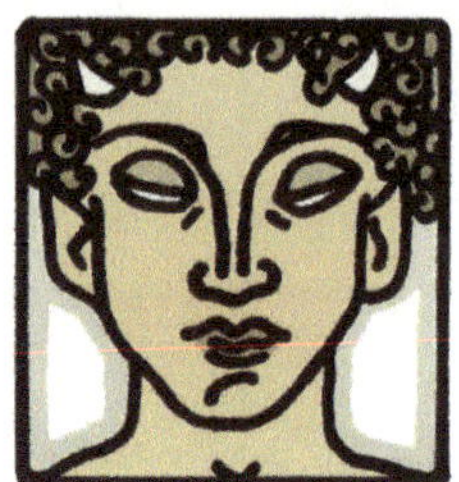

CHEZ:PANISSE GARLIC FESTIVAL
JULY 12-16-1977
1517 SHATTUCK BERKELEY
548-5525

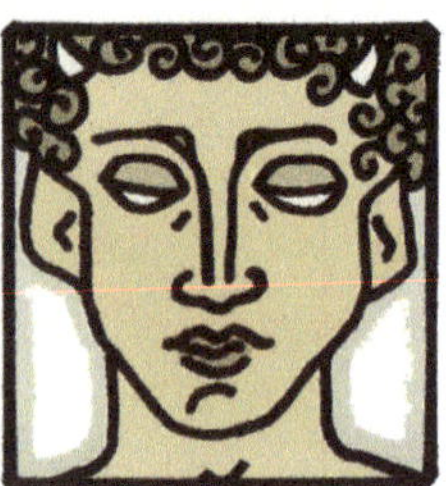

33. Garlic, 1977, 18" × 24"

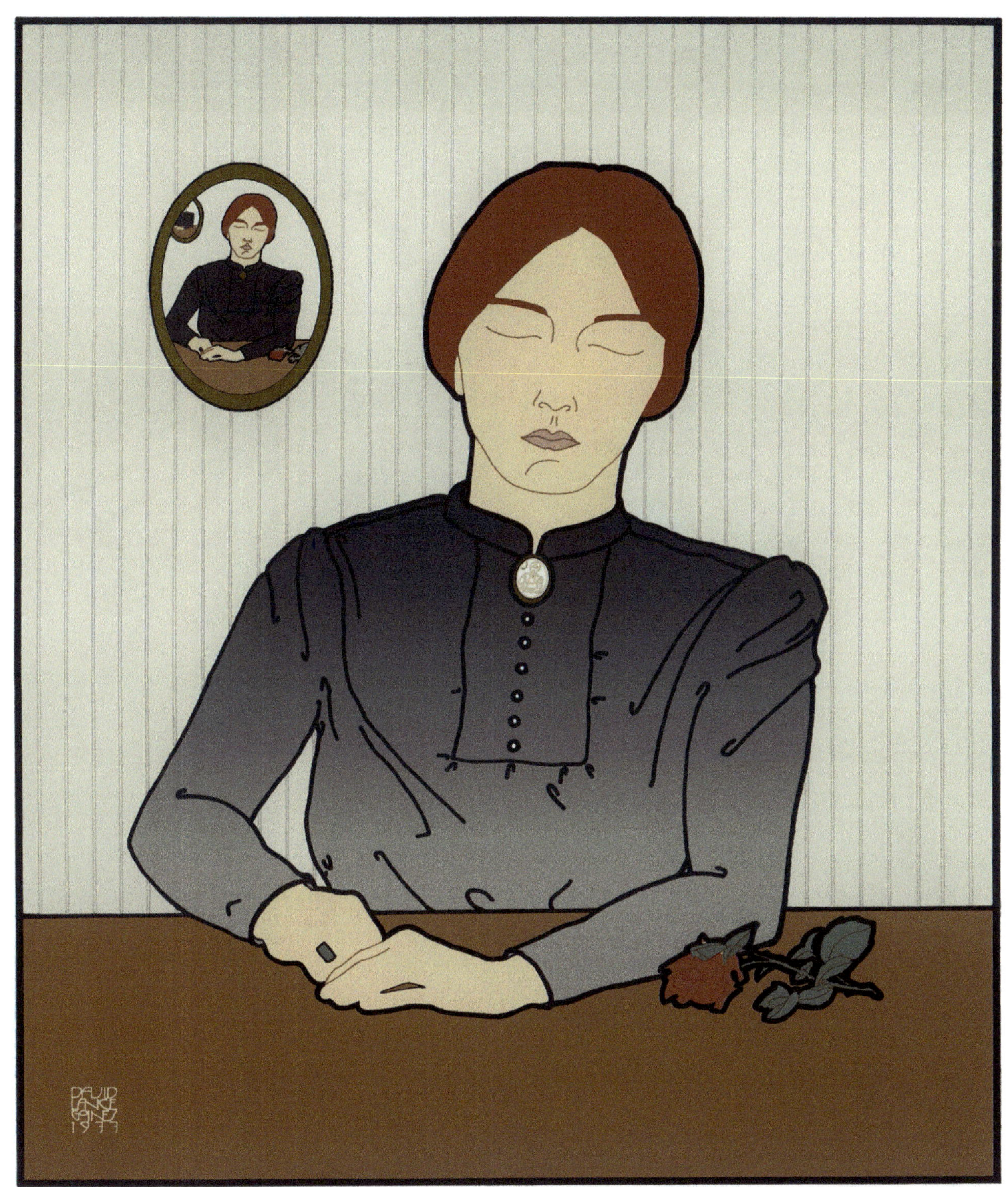

34. LETTER FROM AN UNKNOWN WOMAN, 1977, 18" × 24"

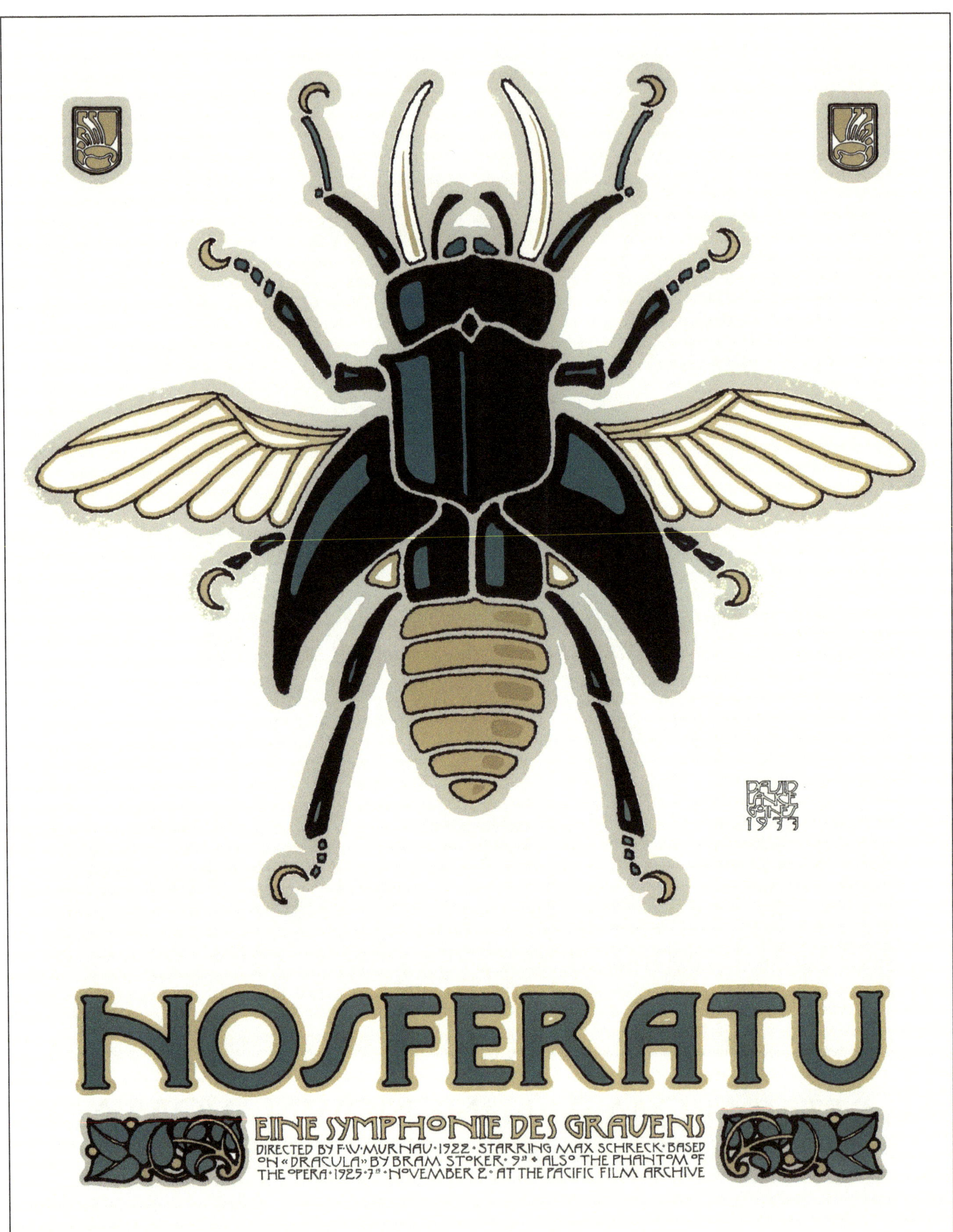

35. NOSFERATU, 1977, 18" × 24"

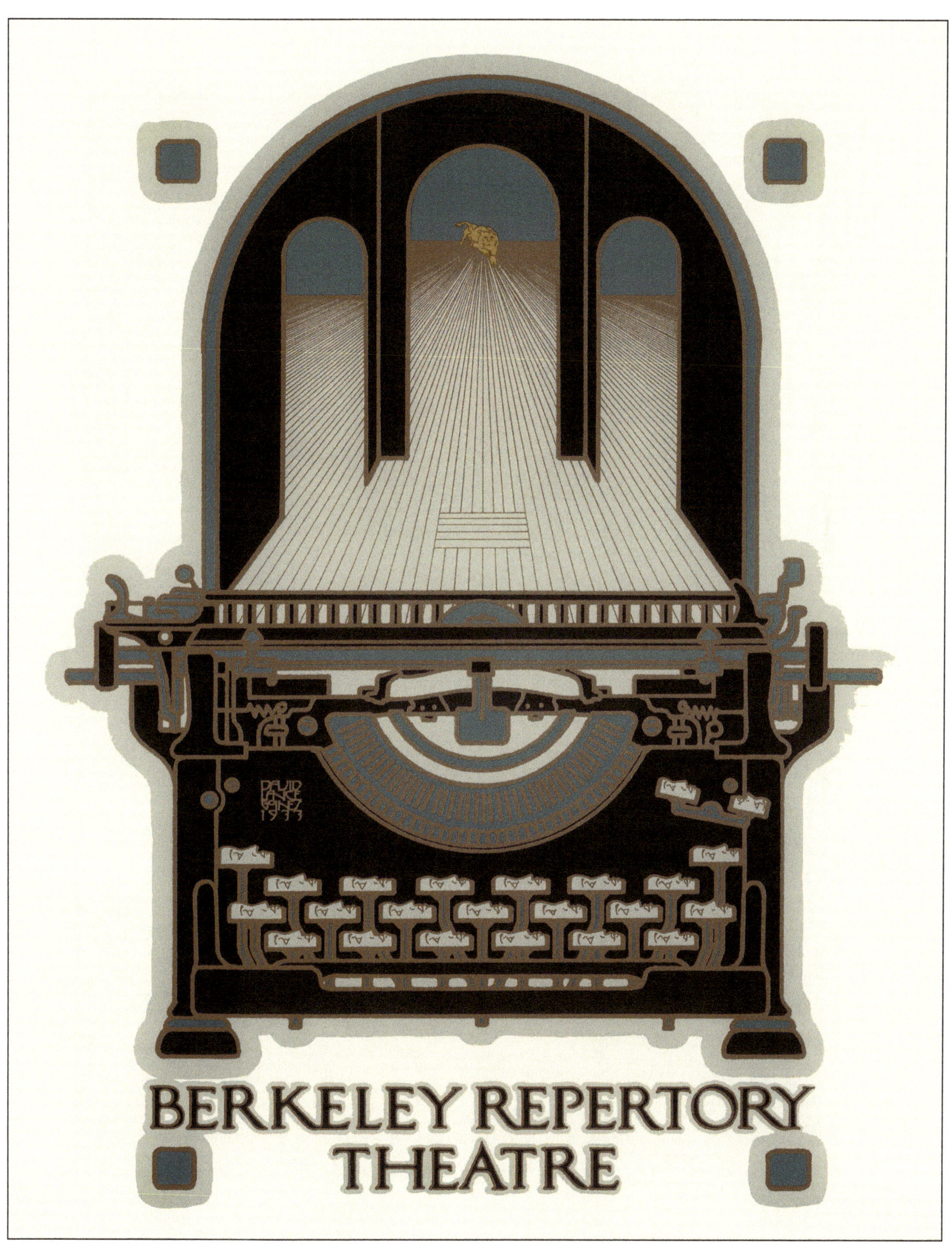

36. Berkeley Repertory Theatre, 1977, 18" × 24"

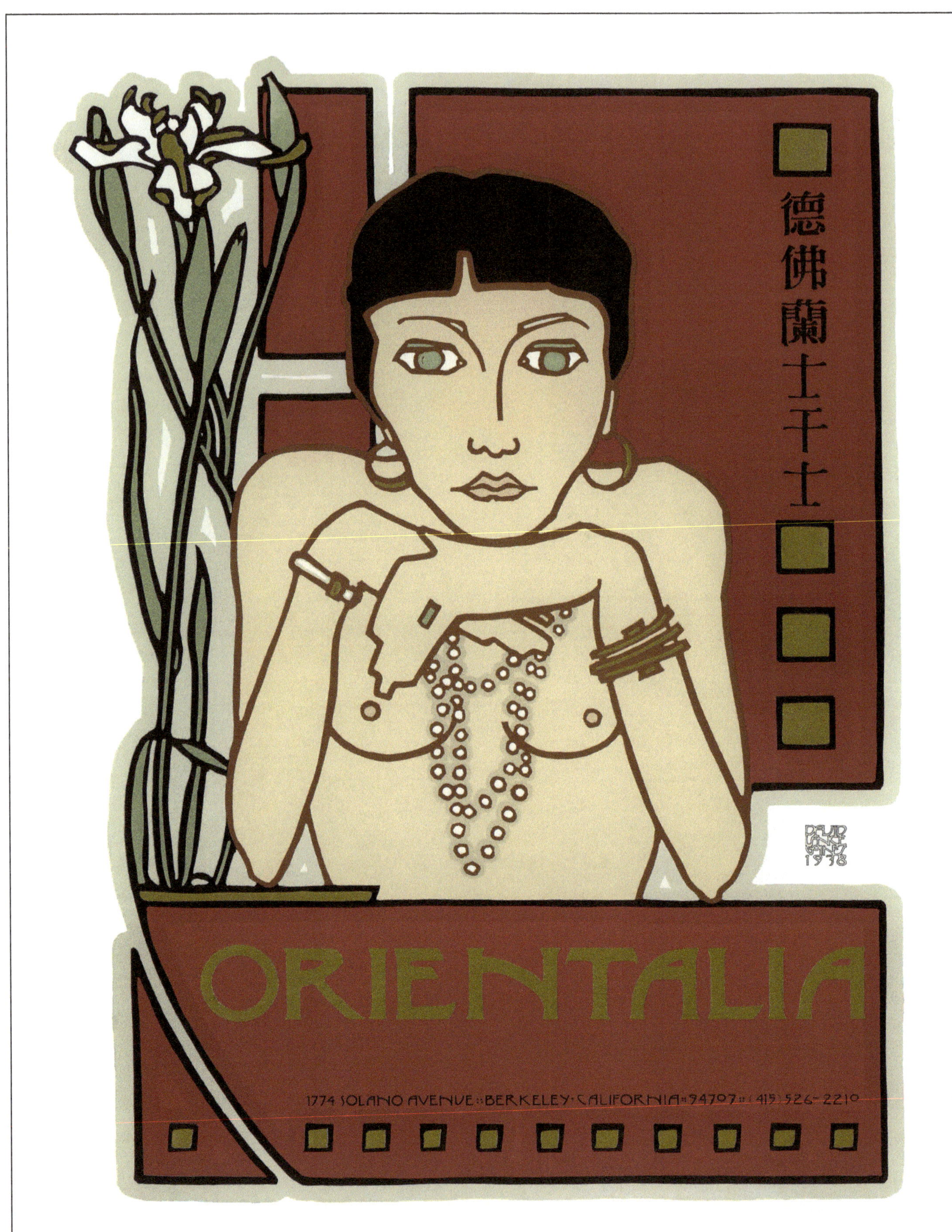

37. ORIENTALIA, 1978, 18" × 24"

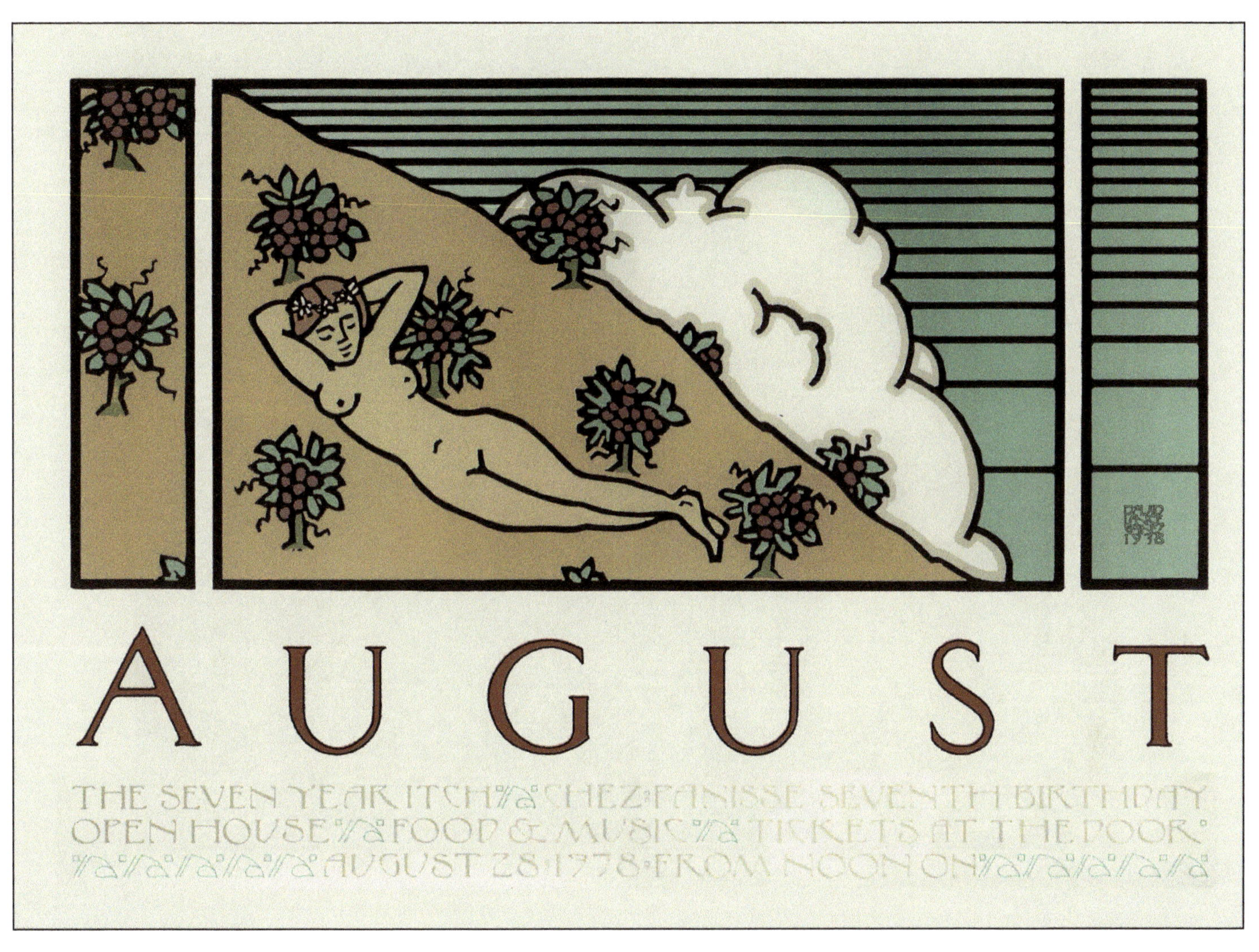

38. Chez Panisse Seventh Birthday (August), 1978, 24" × 18"

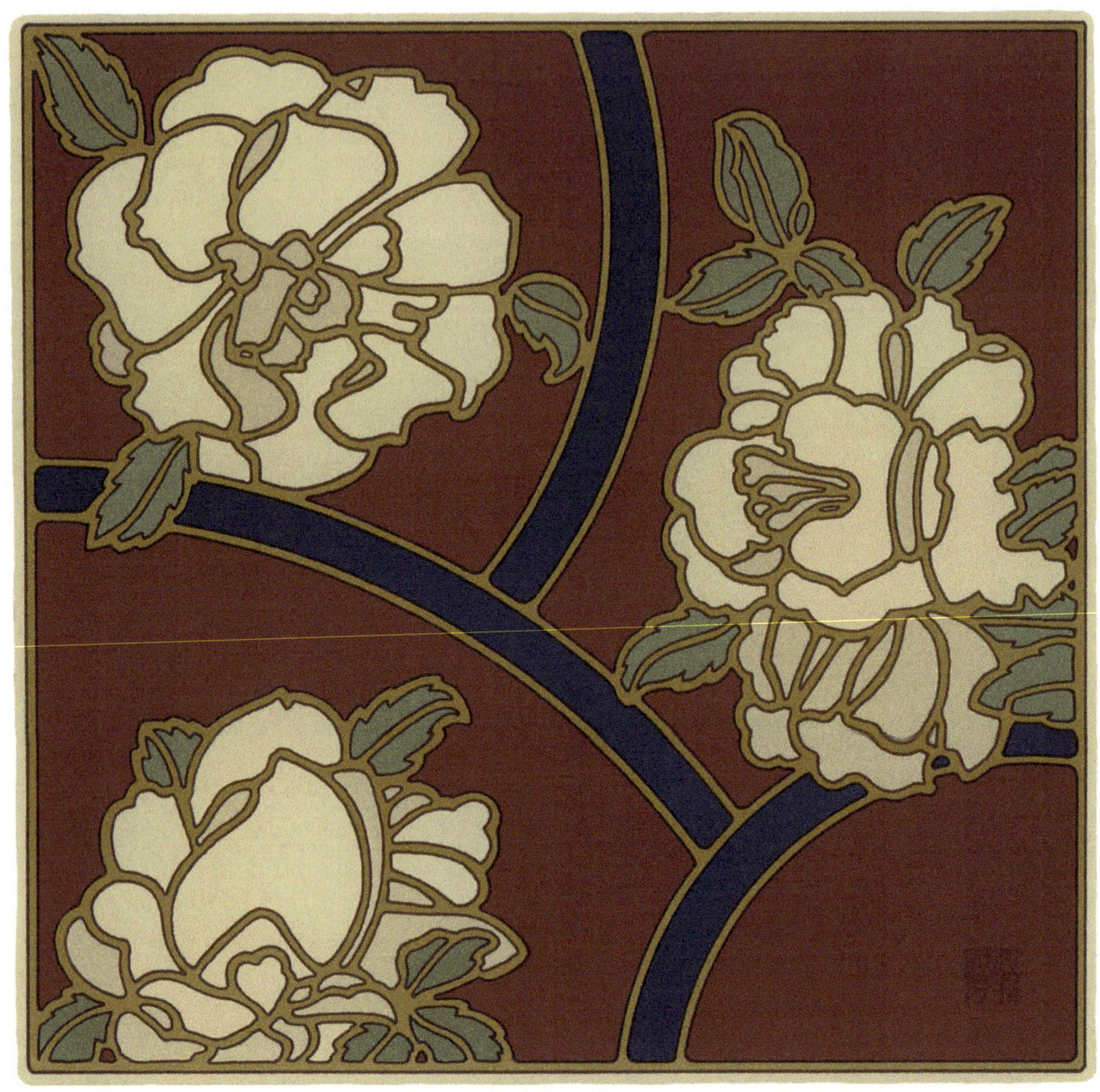

ASILOMAR

TWENTY · EIGHT

SEPTEMBER 22 - 24 · 1978

39. Asilomar, 1978, 18" × 24"

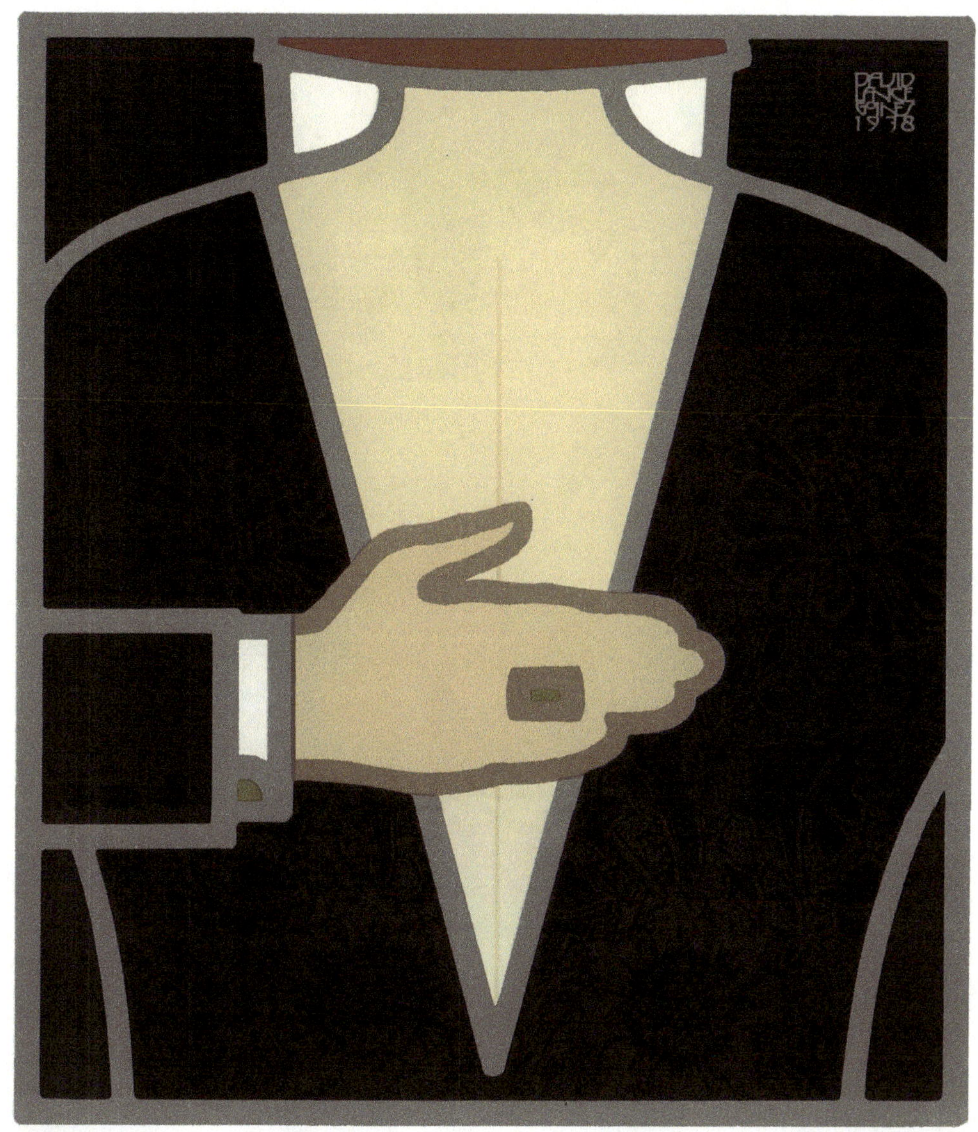

40. Dance, 1978, 16" × 24"

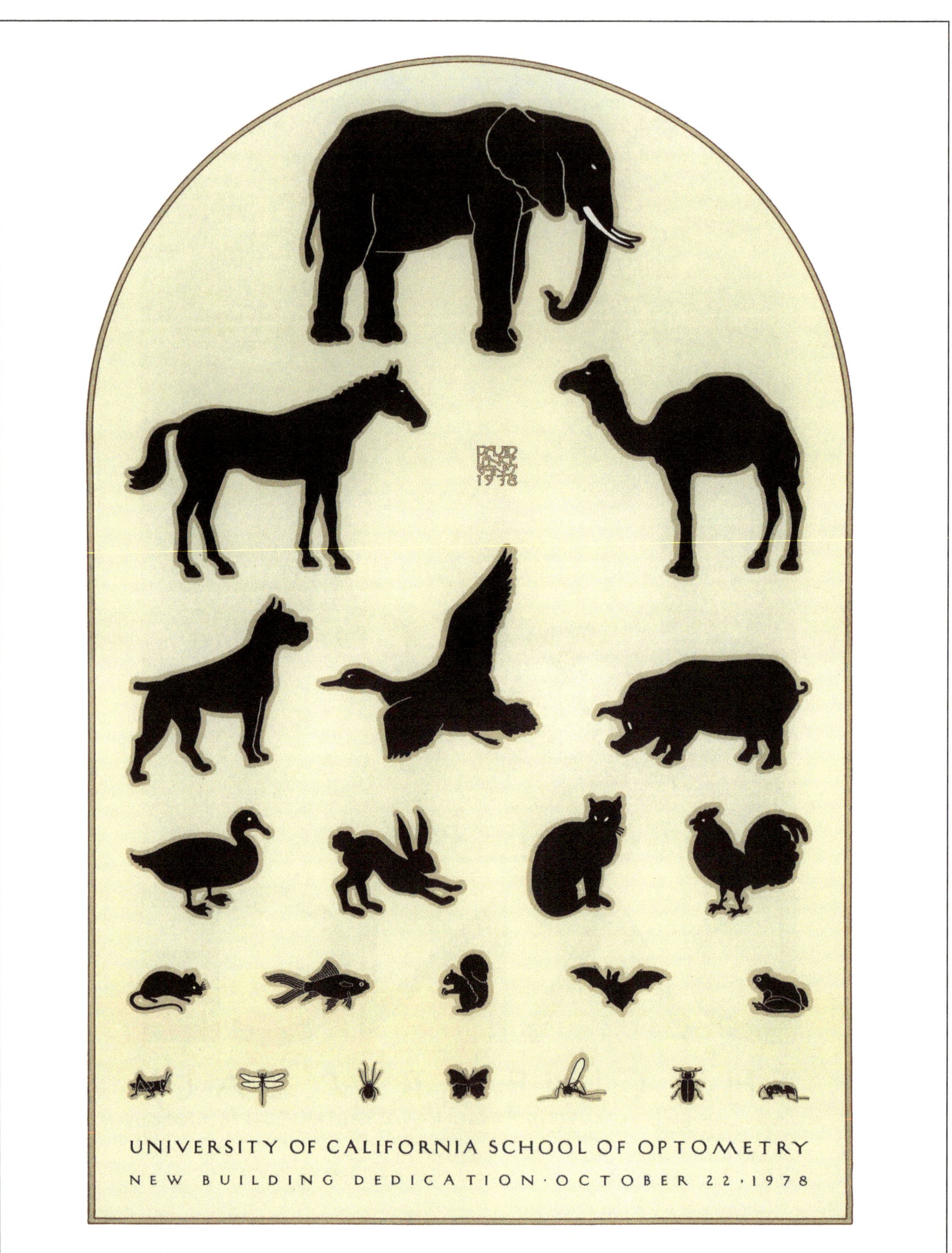

41. University of California School of Optometry, 1979, 16⅝" × 24"

RAVENS

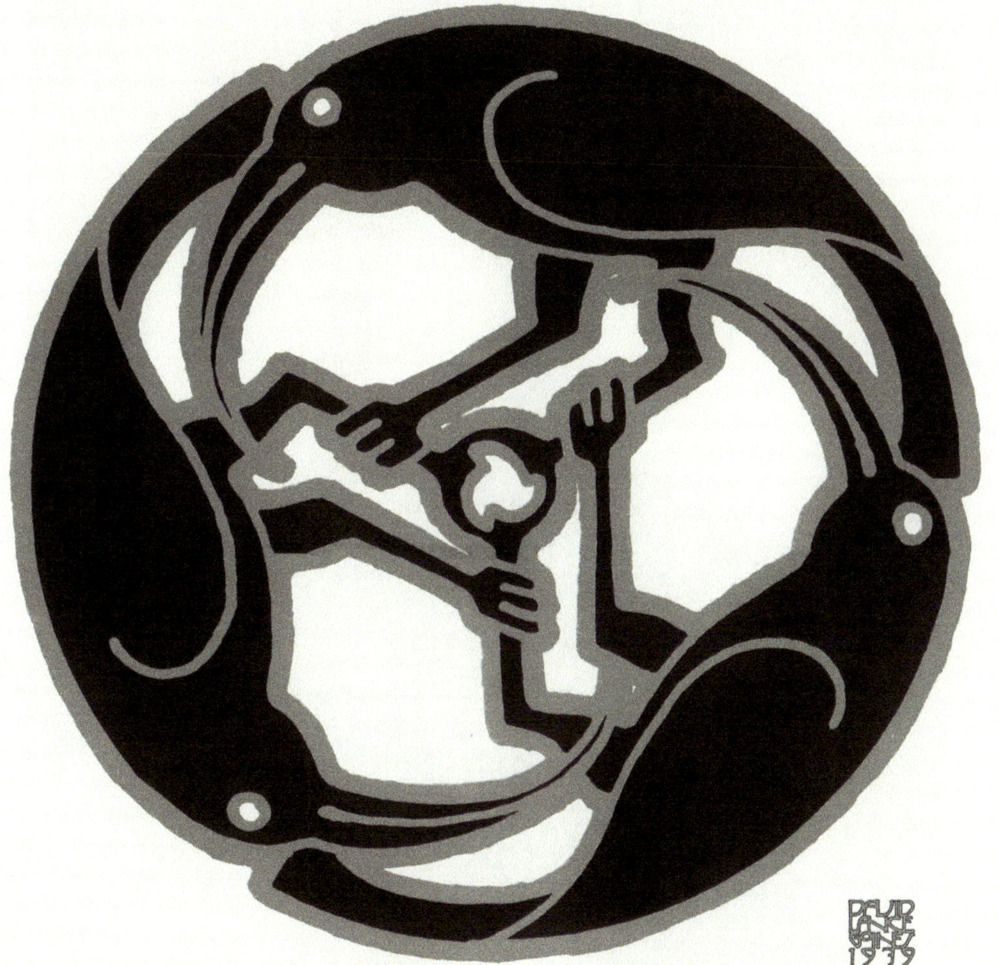

WOOD

WINERY

655 SUTTER STREET, SAN FRANCISCO, CALIFORNIA 94102 (415) 474-2700

42. RAVENSWOOD WINERY, 1979, 16" × 24"

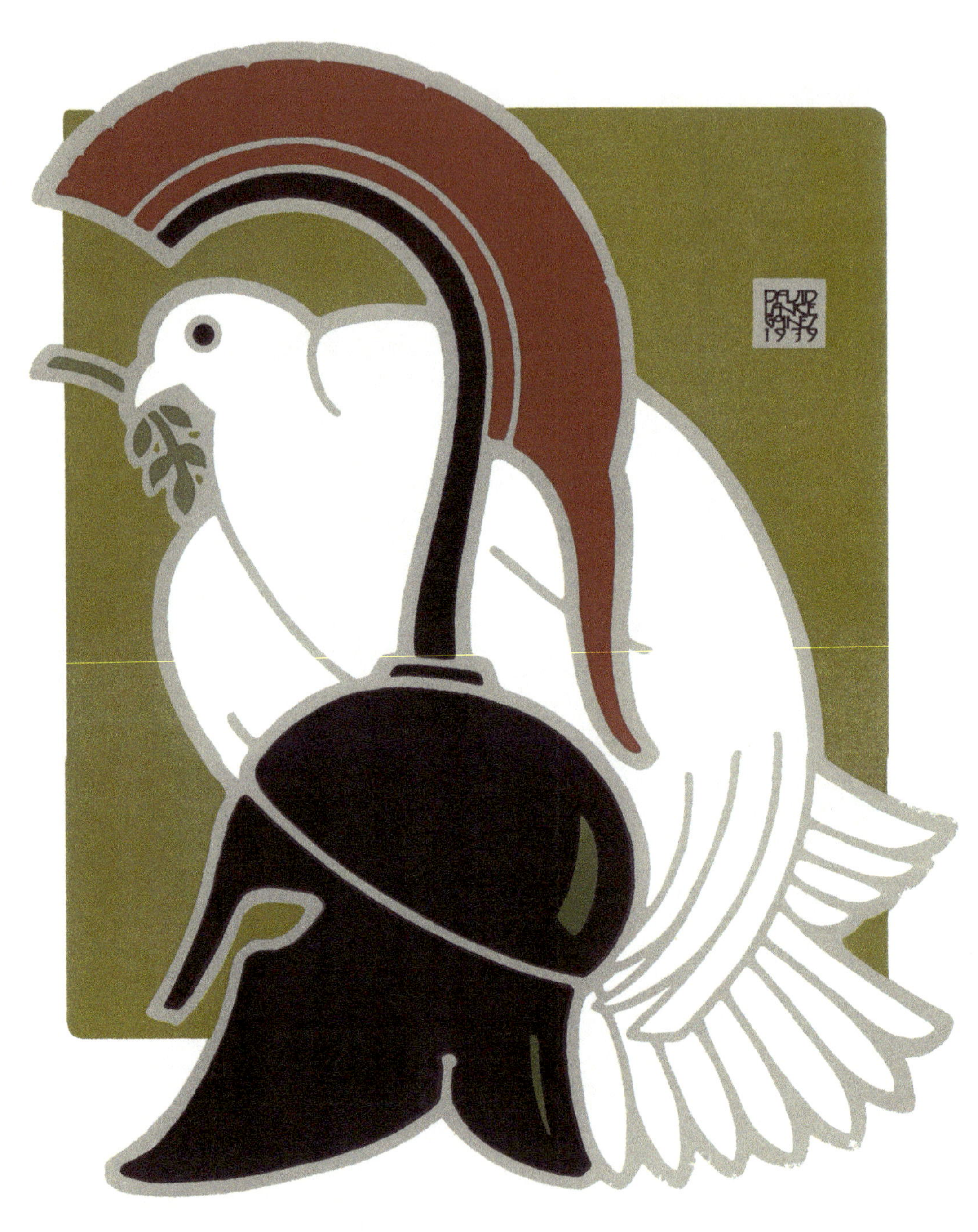

INTERNATIONAL
H O U S E
B E R K E L E Y · C A L I F O R N I A
1 9 3 0 - 1 9 8 0

43. International House, 1979, 16" × 24"

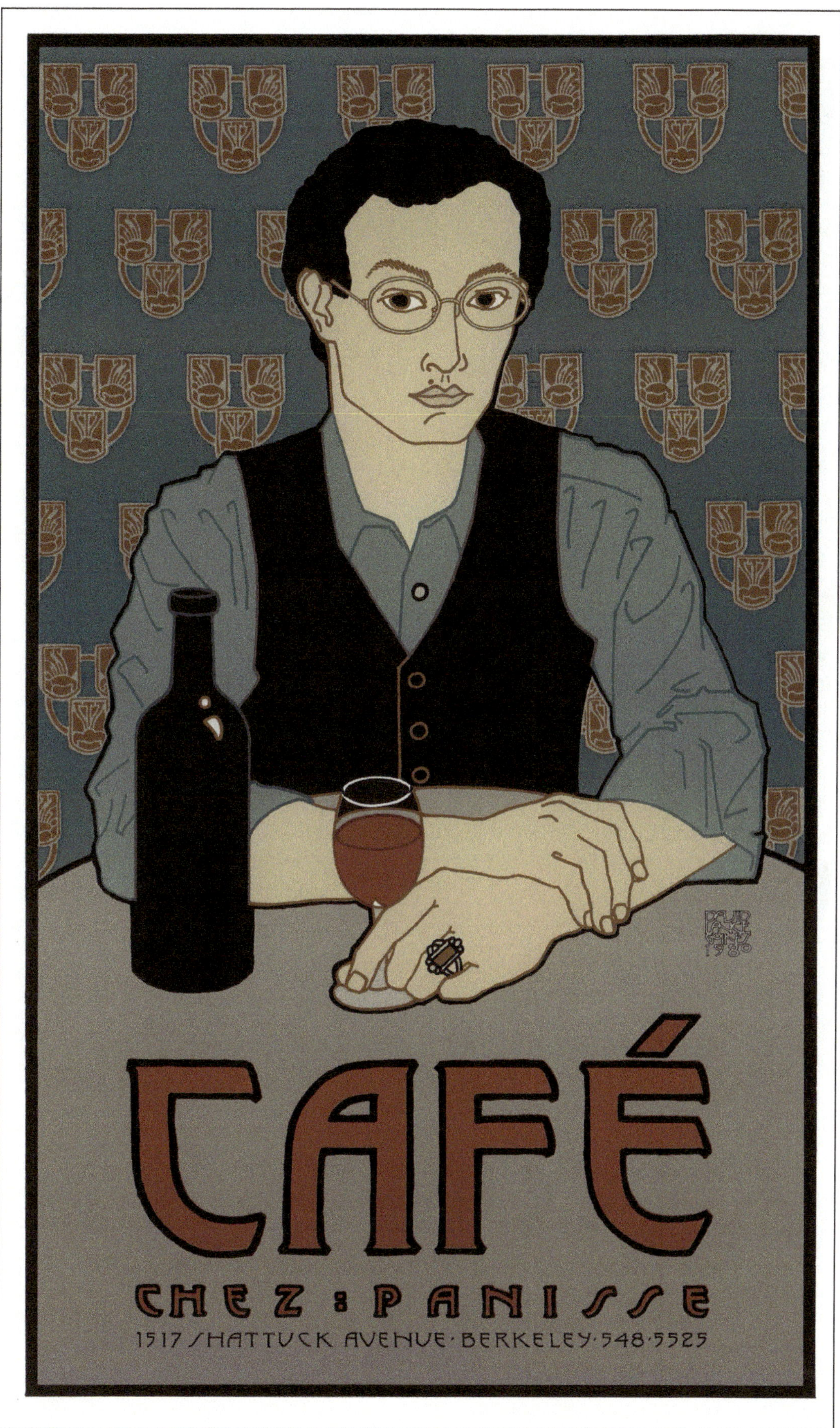

44. Café Chez Panisse, 1980, 14⅝" × 24"

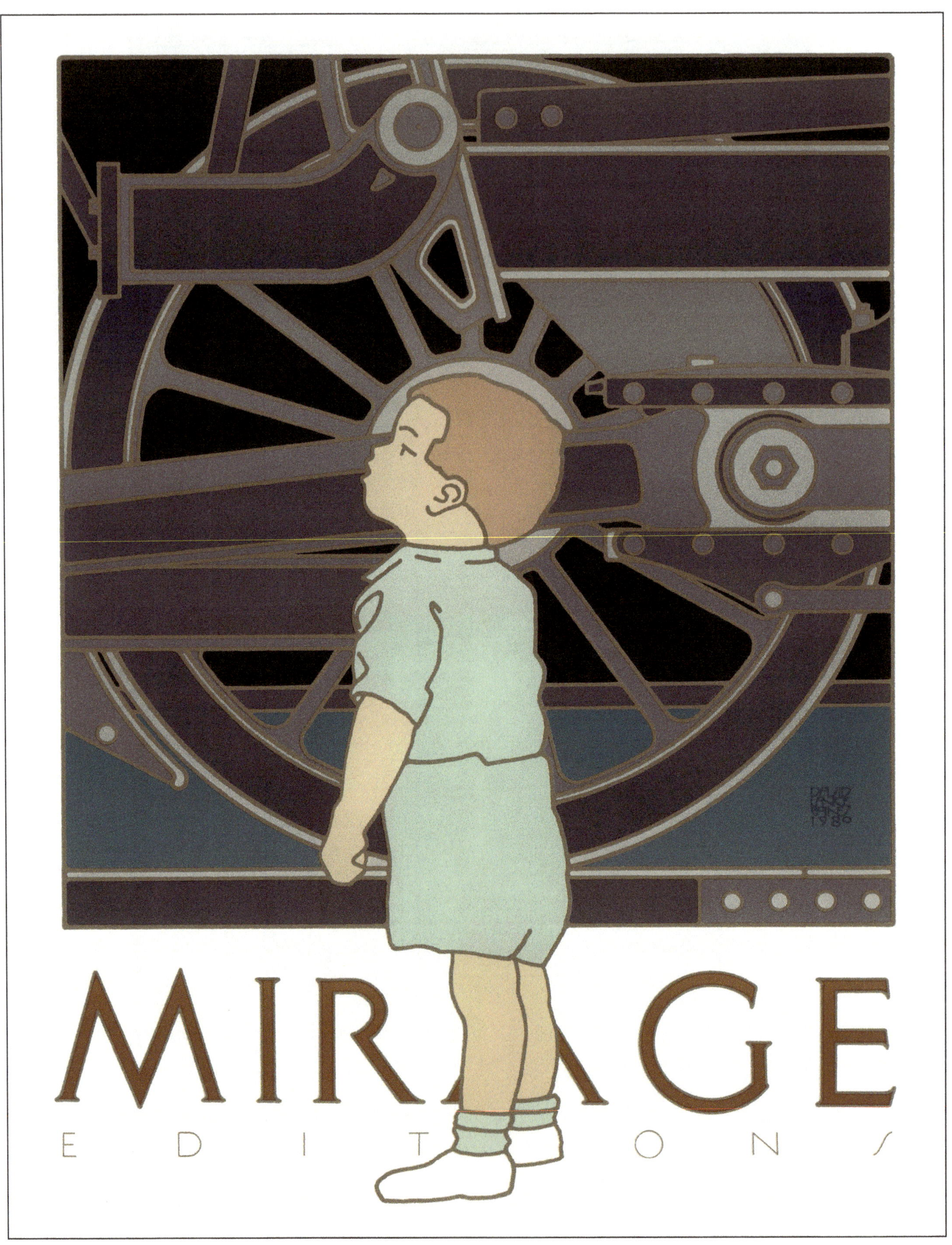

45. Mirage (Boy and Train), 1980, 18" × 24"

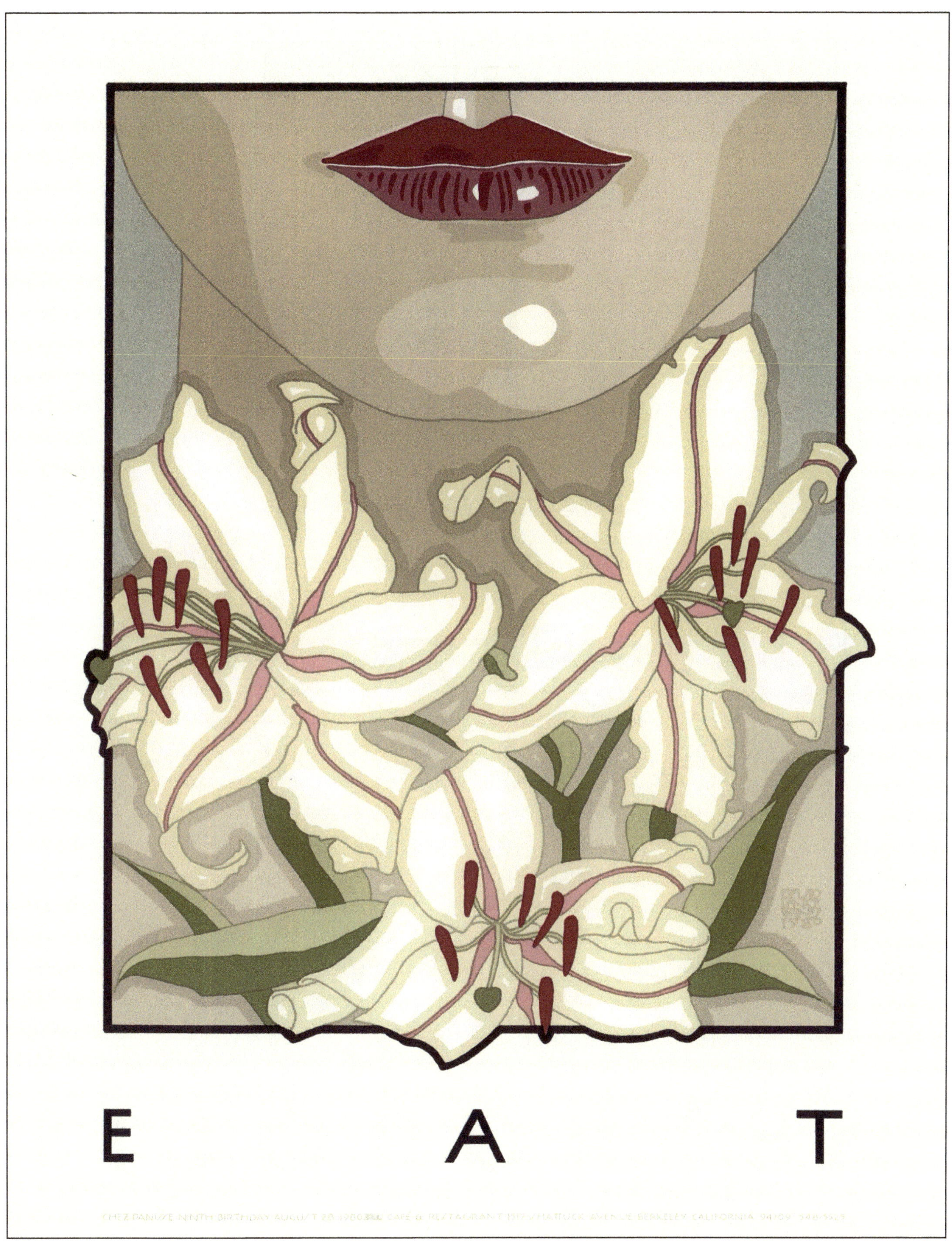

46. Eat, 1980, 16⅞" × 24"

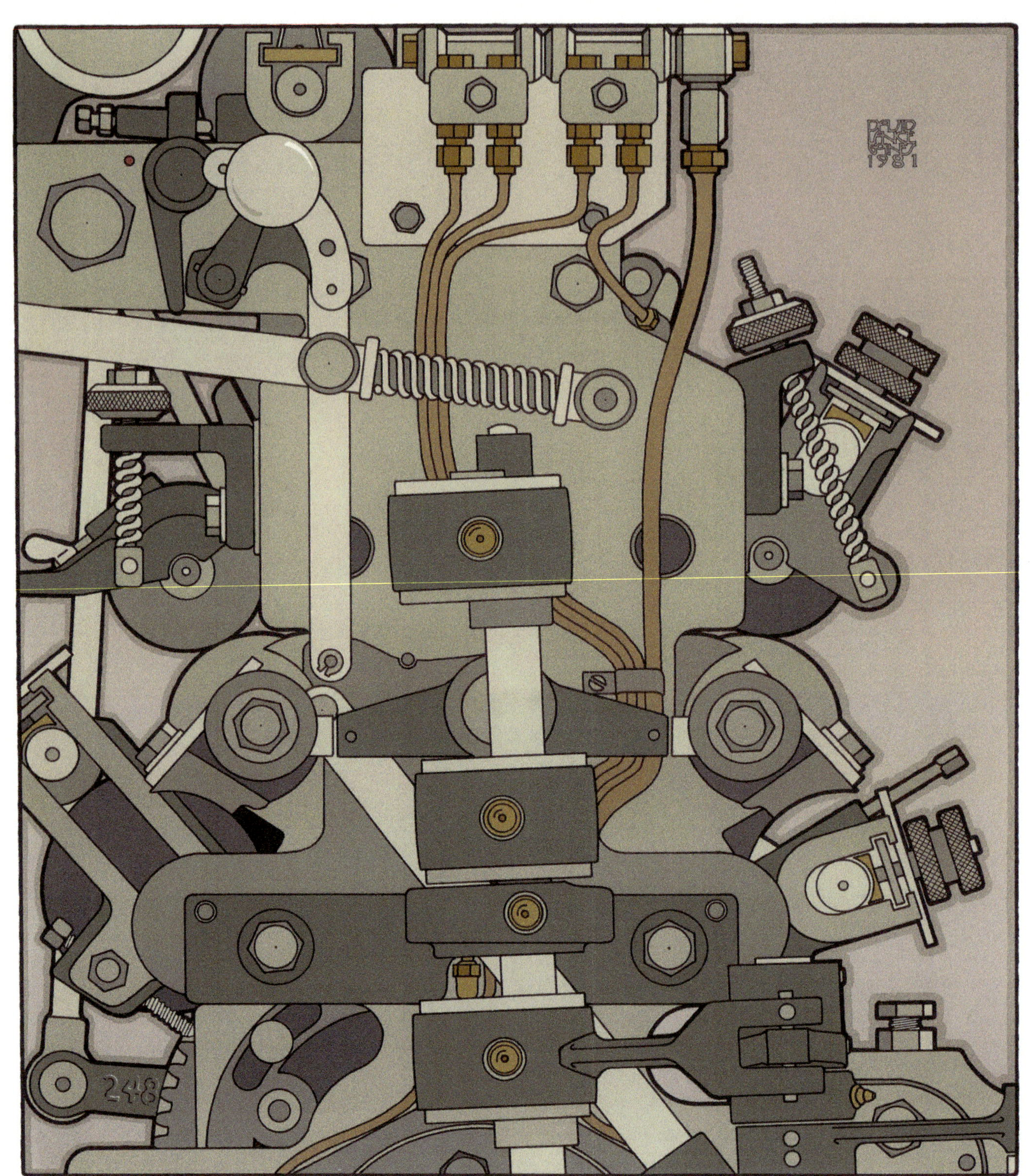

47. METROPOLIS, 1981, 18" × 24"

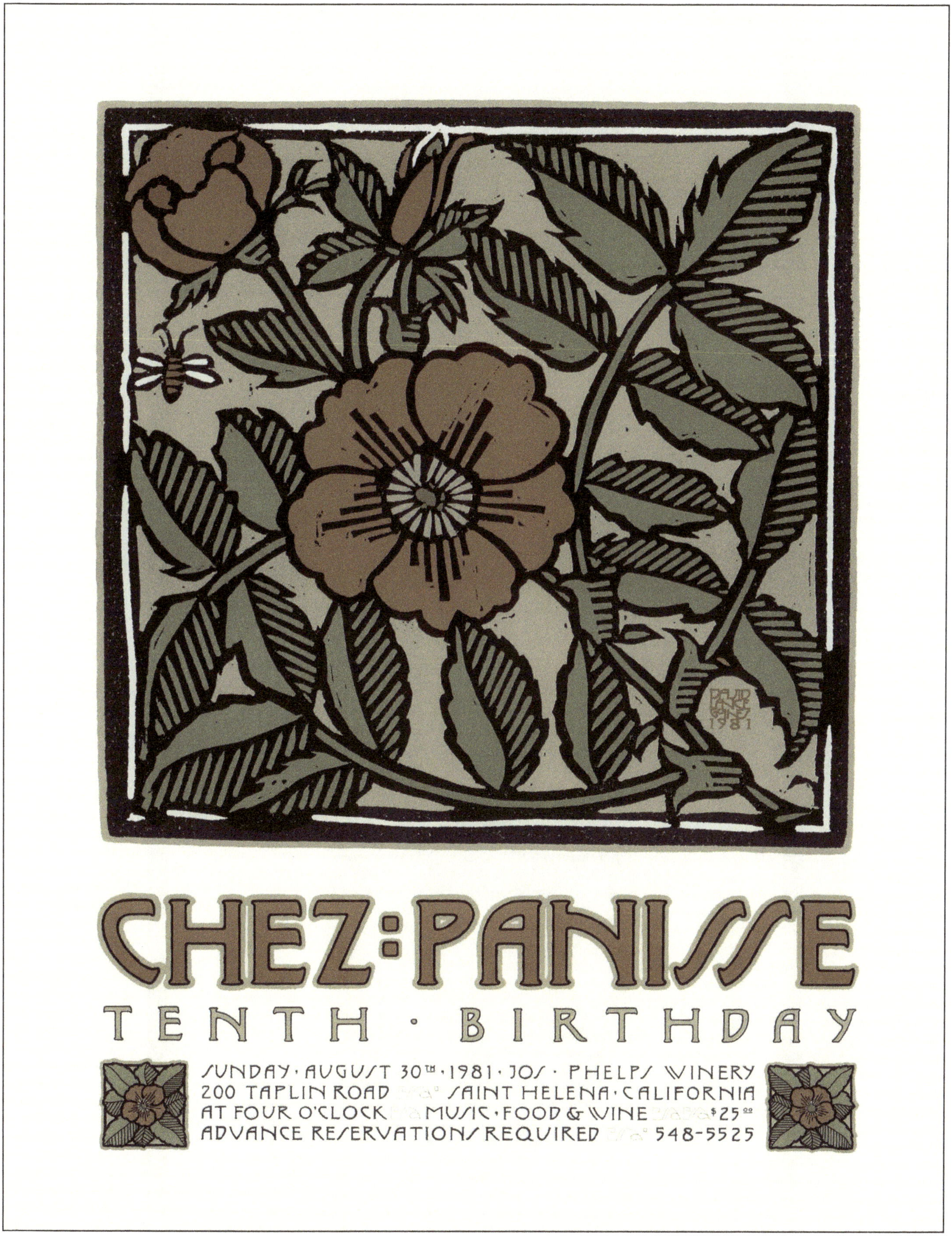

CHEZ:PANISSE

TENTH · BIRTHDAY

SUNDAY · AUGUST 30TH · 1981 · JOS · PHELPS WINERY
200 TAPLIN ROAD SAINT HELENA · CALIFORNIA
AT FOUR O'CLOCK MUSIC · FOOD & WINE $25.00
ADVANCE RESERVATIONS REQUIRED 548-5525

48. Chez Panisse Tenth Birthday, 1981, 18" × 24"

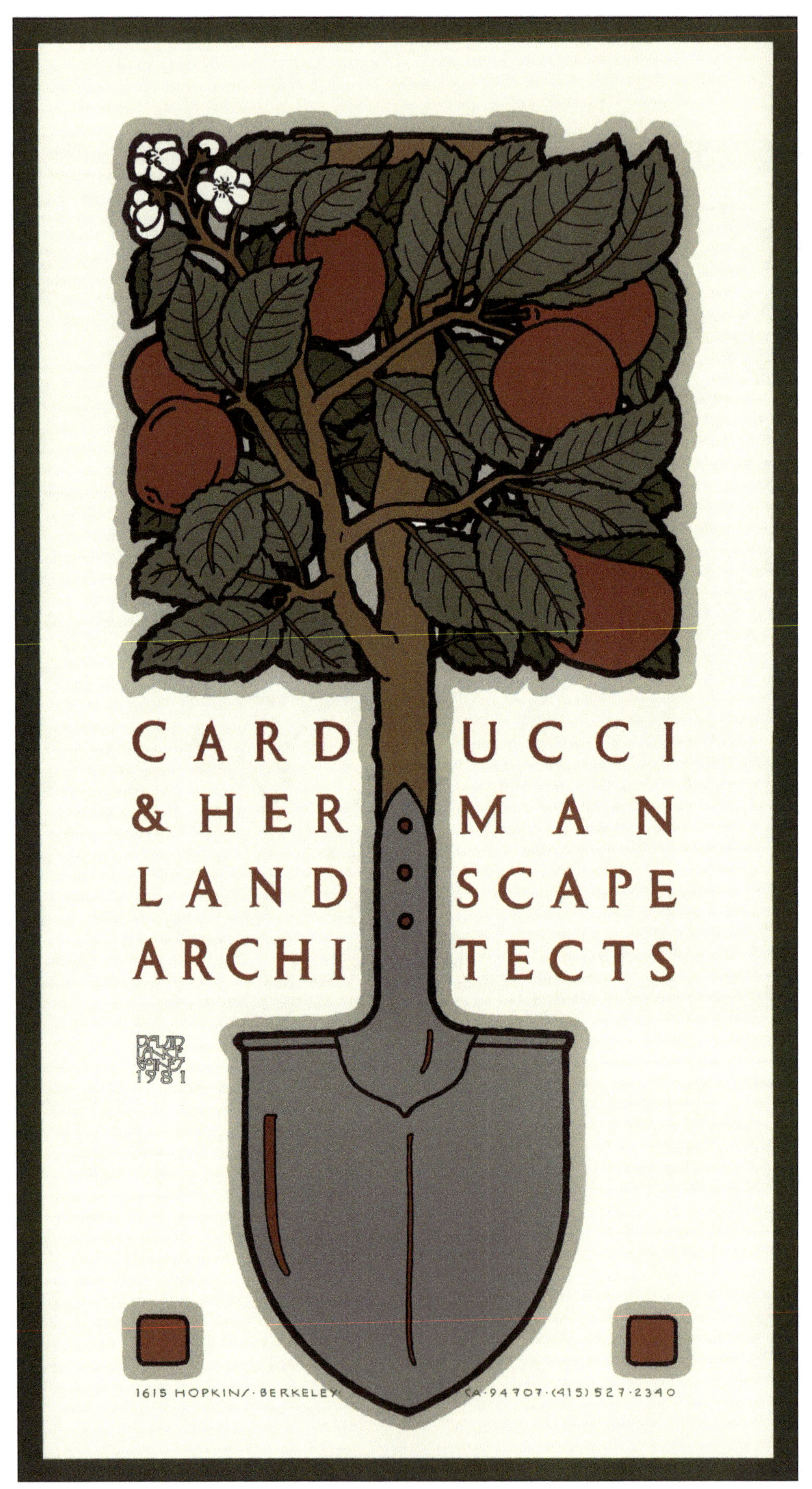

49. Carducci & Herman Landscape Architects, 1981, 12¾" × 24"

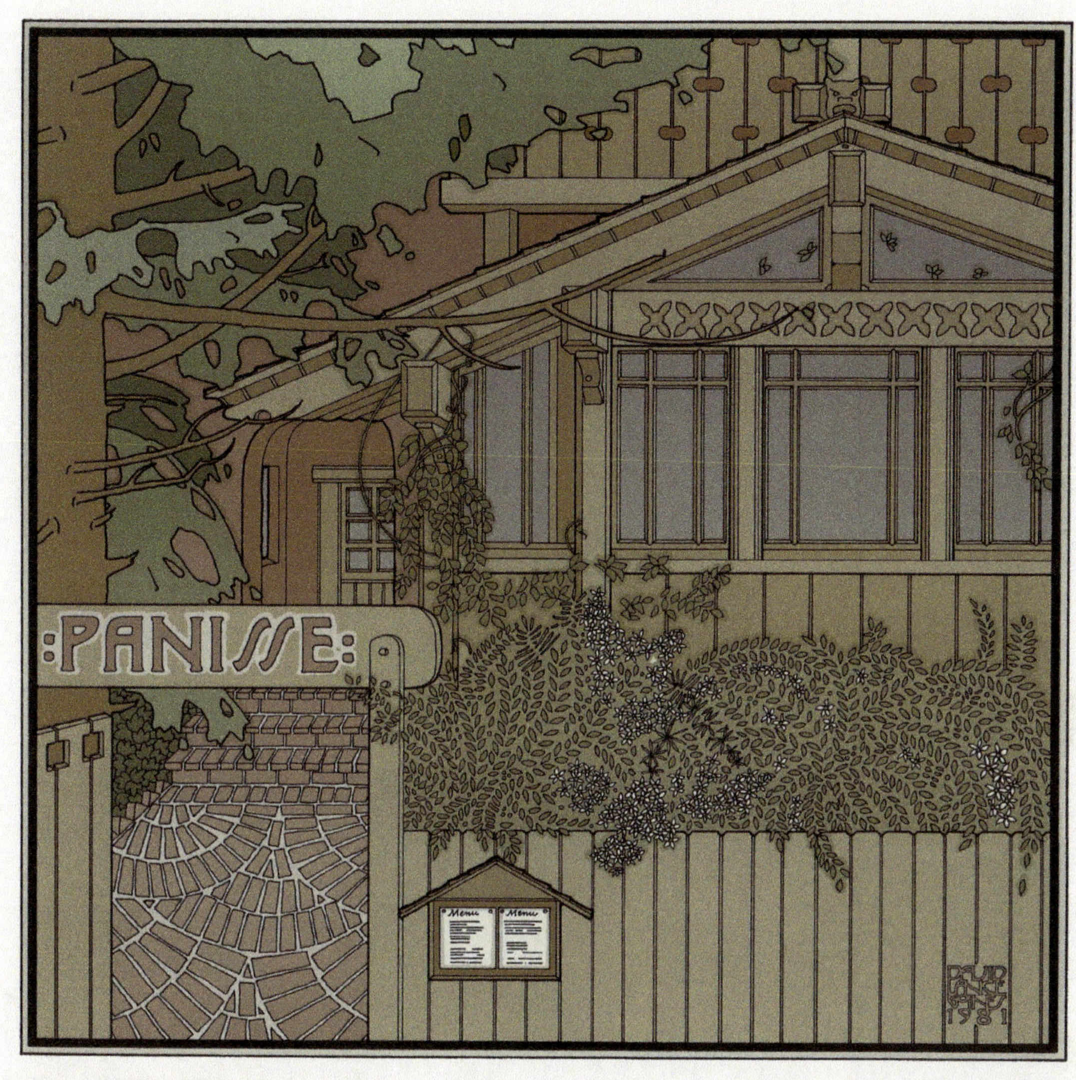

50. Chez Panisse Menu Cookbook, 1981, 15½" × 24"

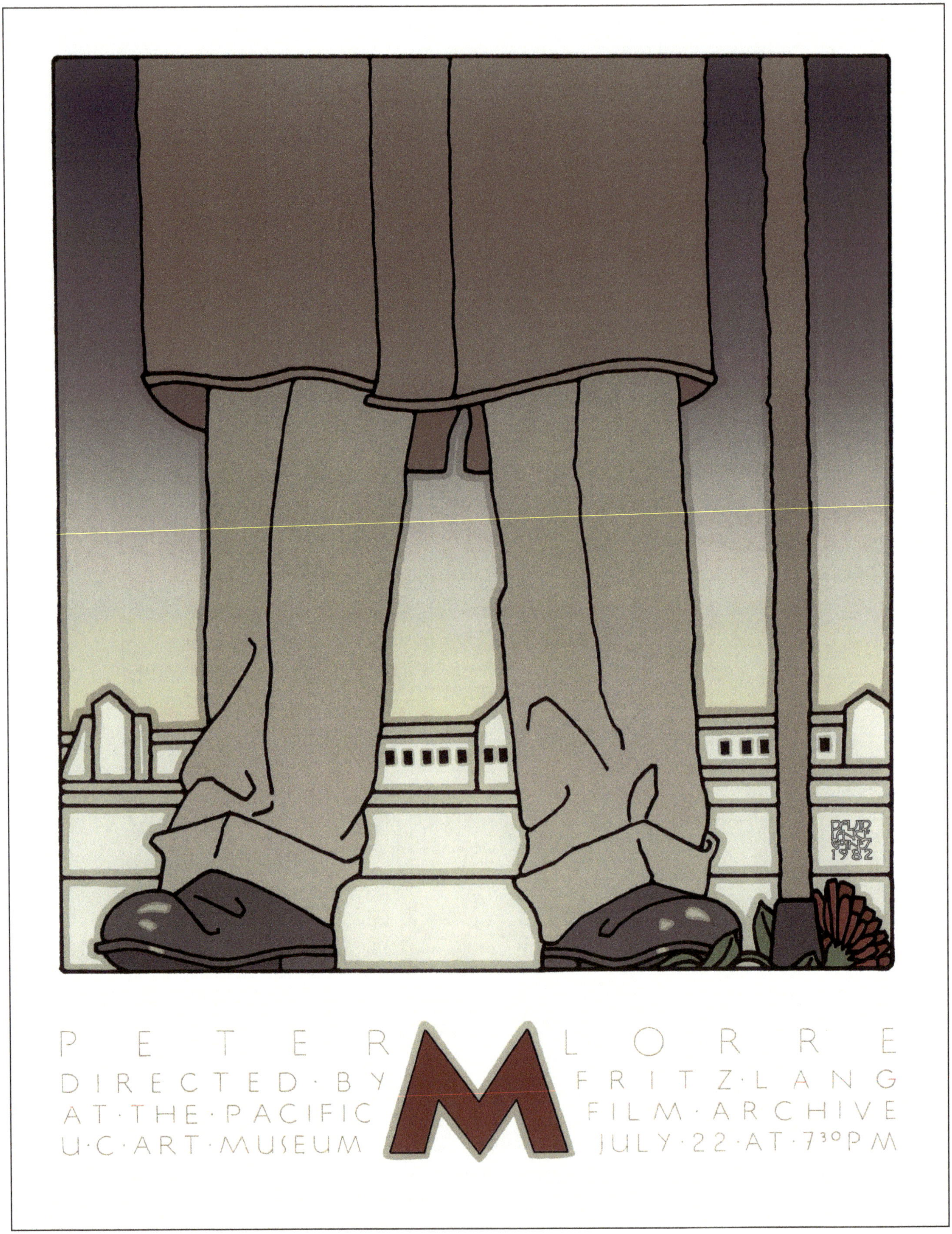

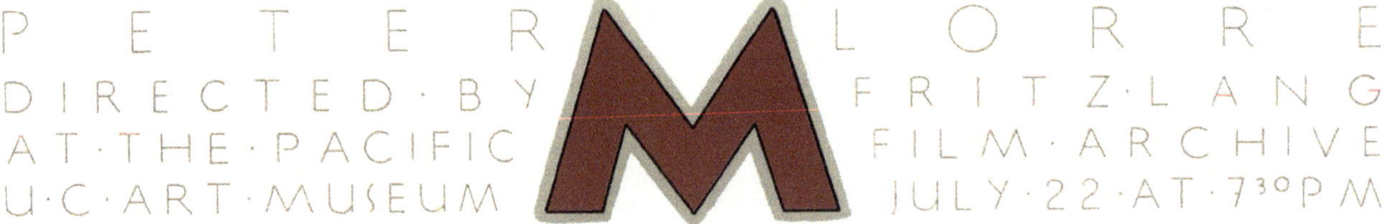

51. M, 1982, 18" × 24"

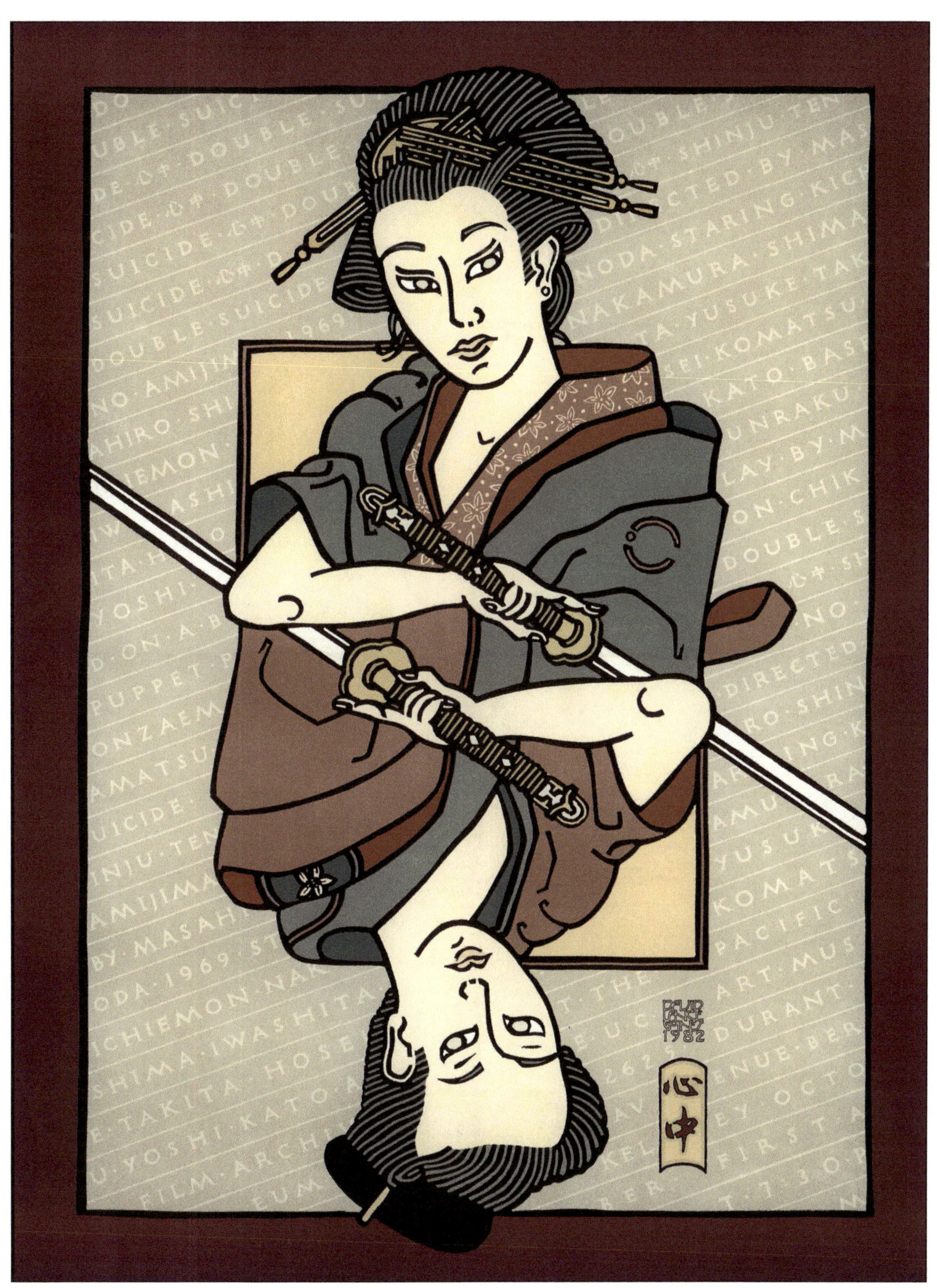

52. Double Suicide, 1982, 17⅝" × 24"

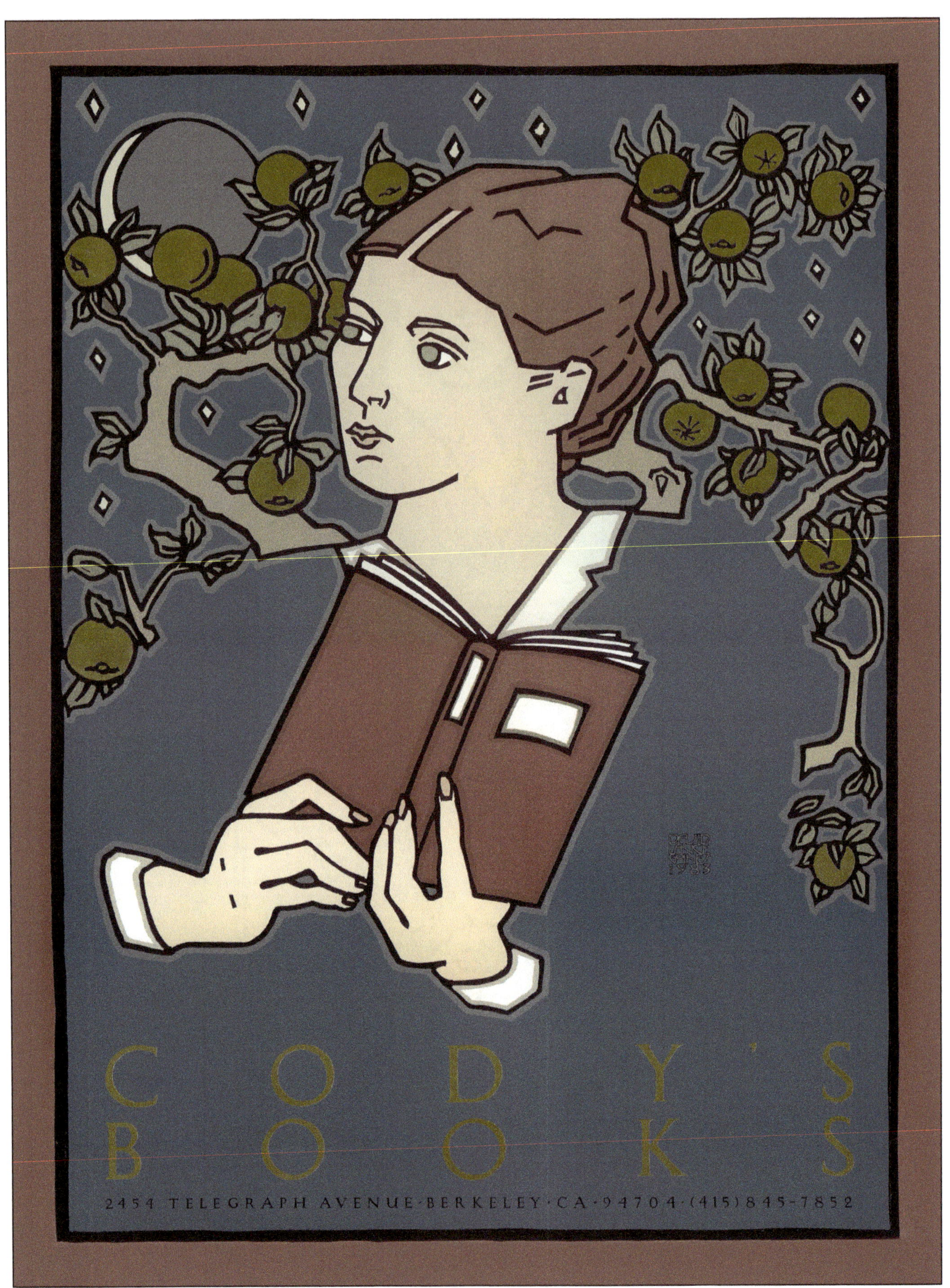

53. Cody's Books, 1983, 17½" × 24"

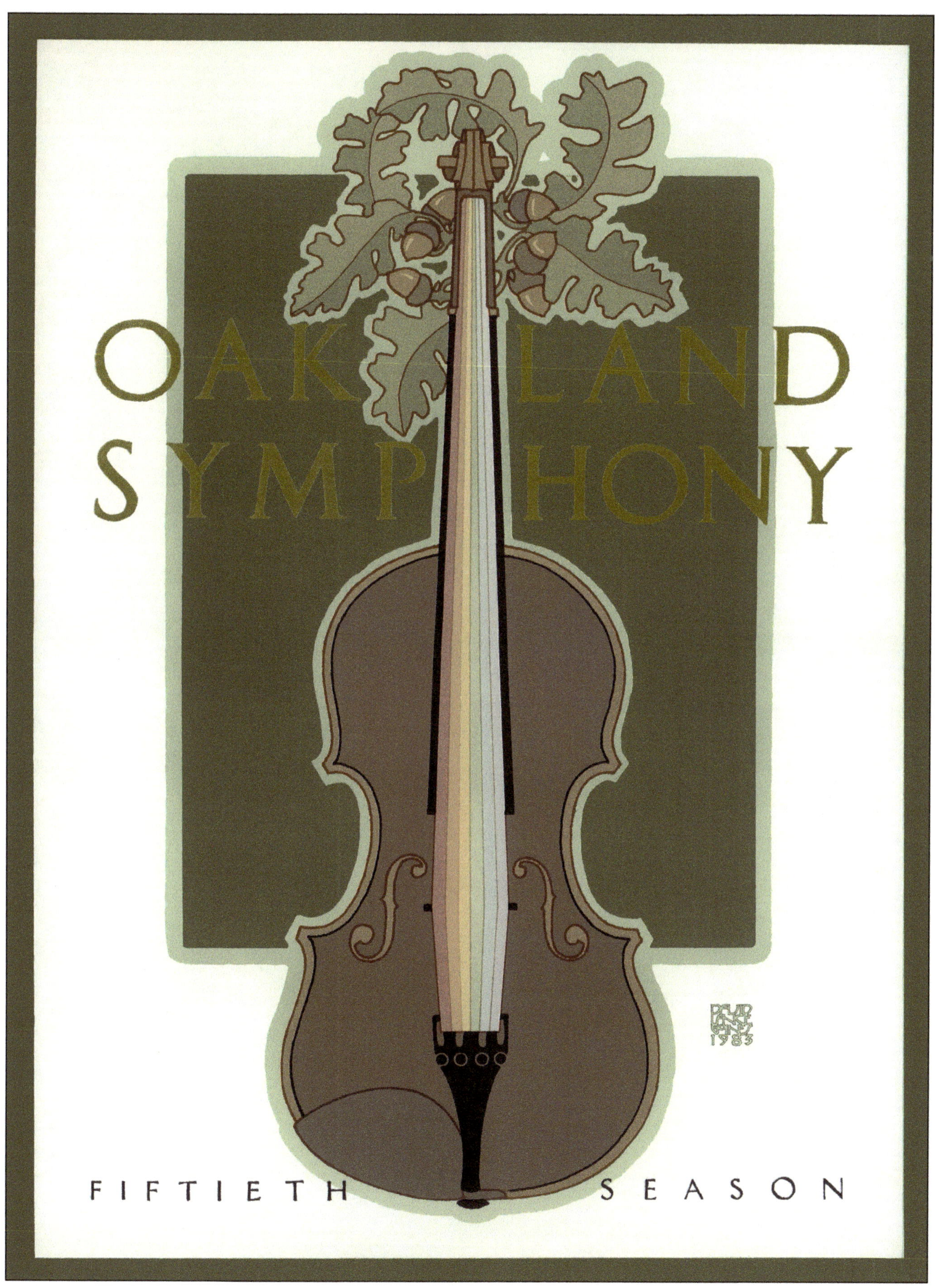

54. Oakland Symphony, 1983, 17⅜" × 24"

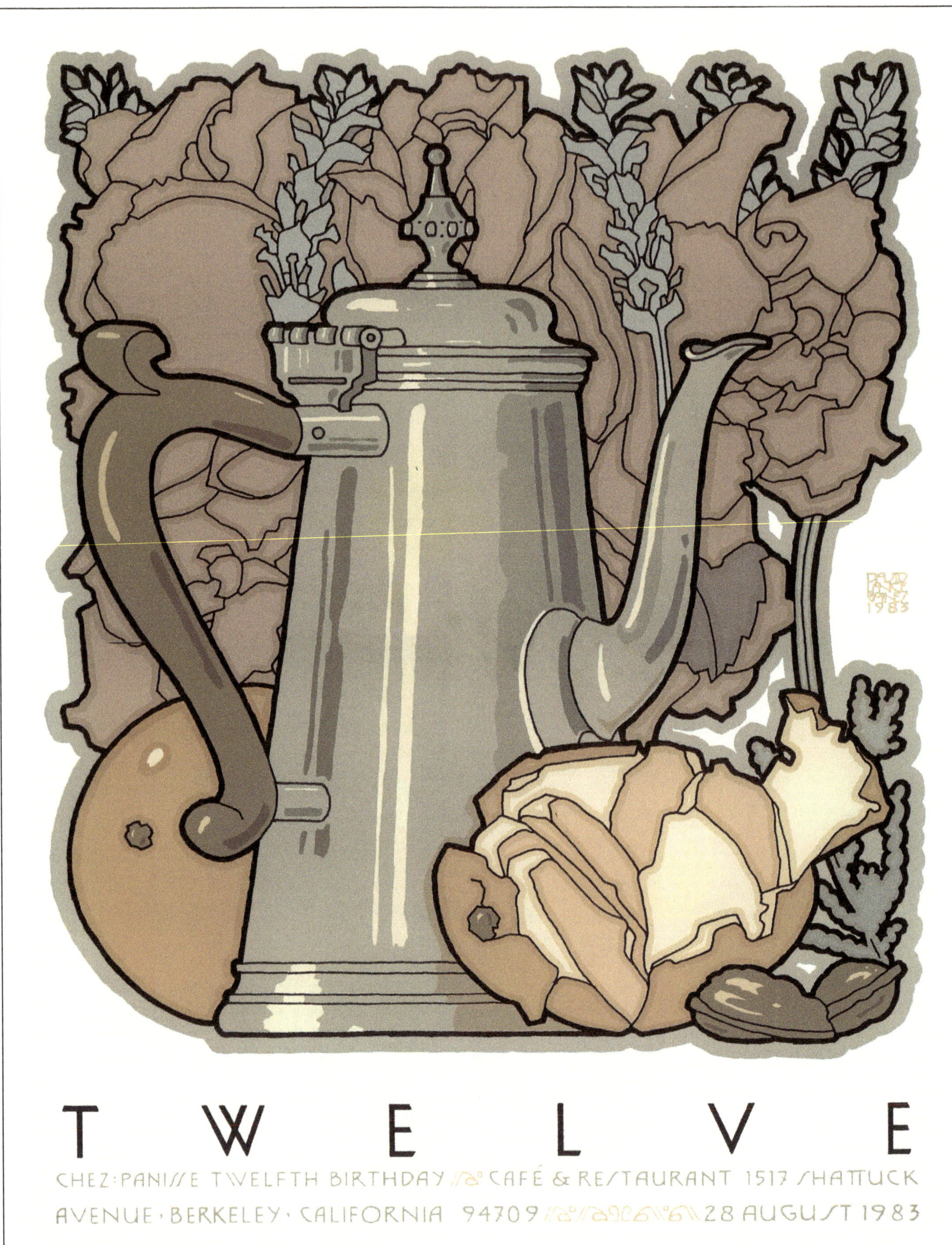

55. TWELVE (CHEZ PANISSE TWELFTH BIRTHDAY), 1983, 17¾" × 24"

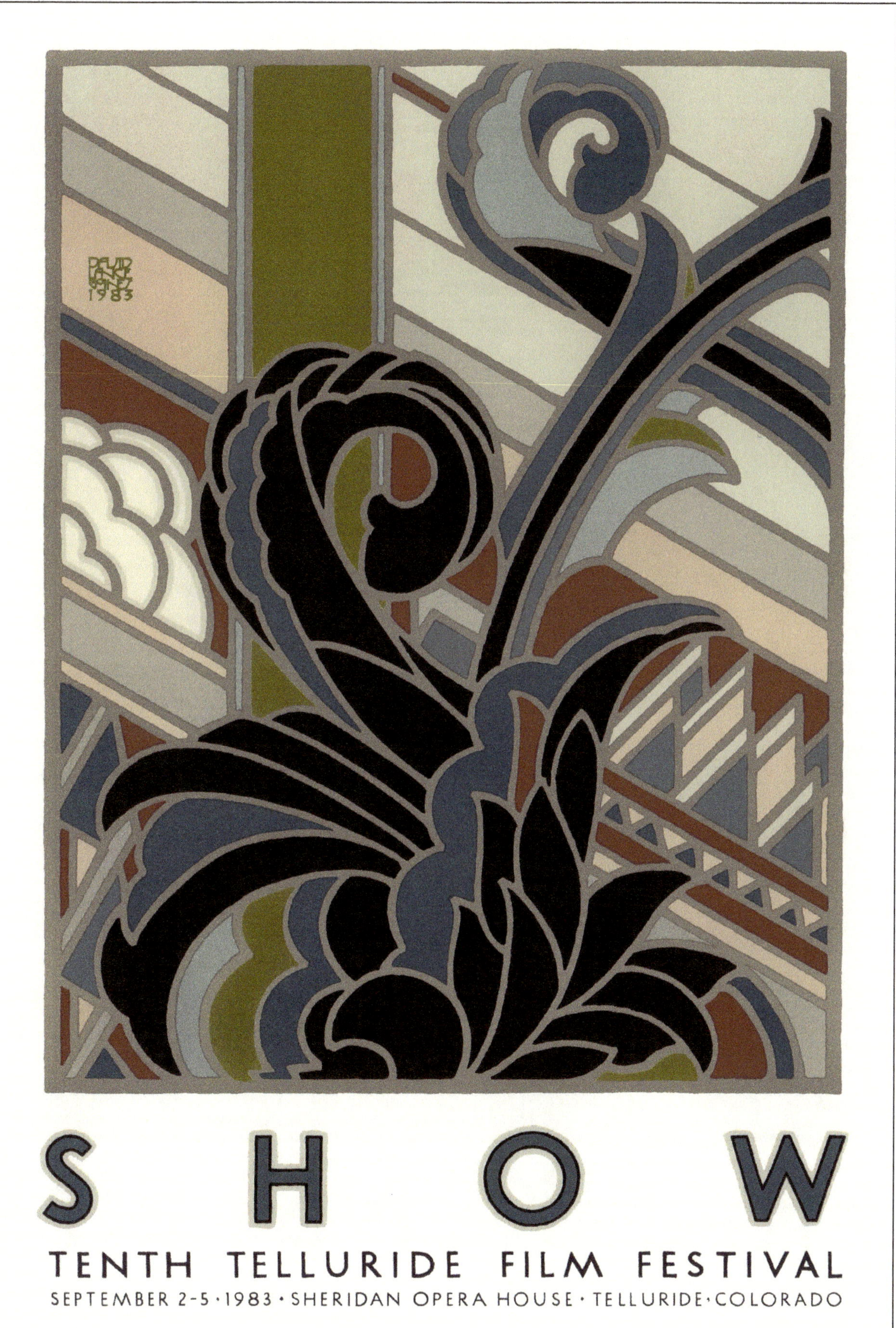

56. Show (Tenth Telluride Film Festival), 1983, 16" × 24"

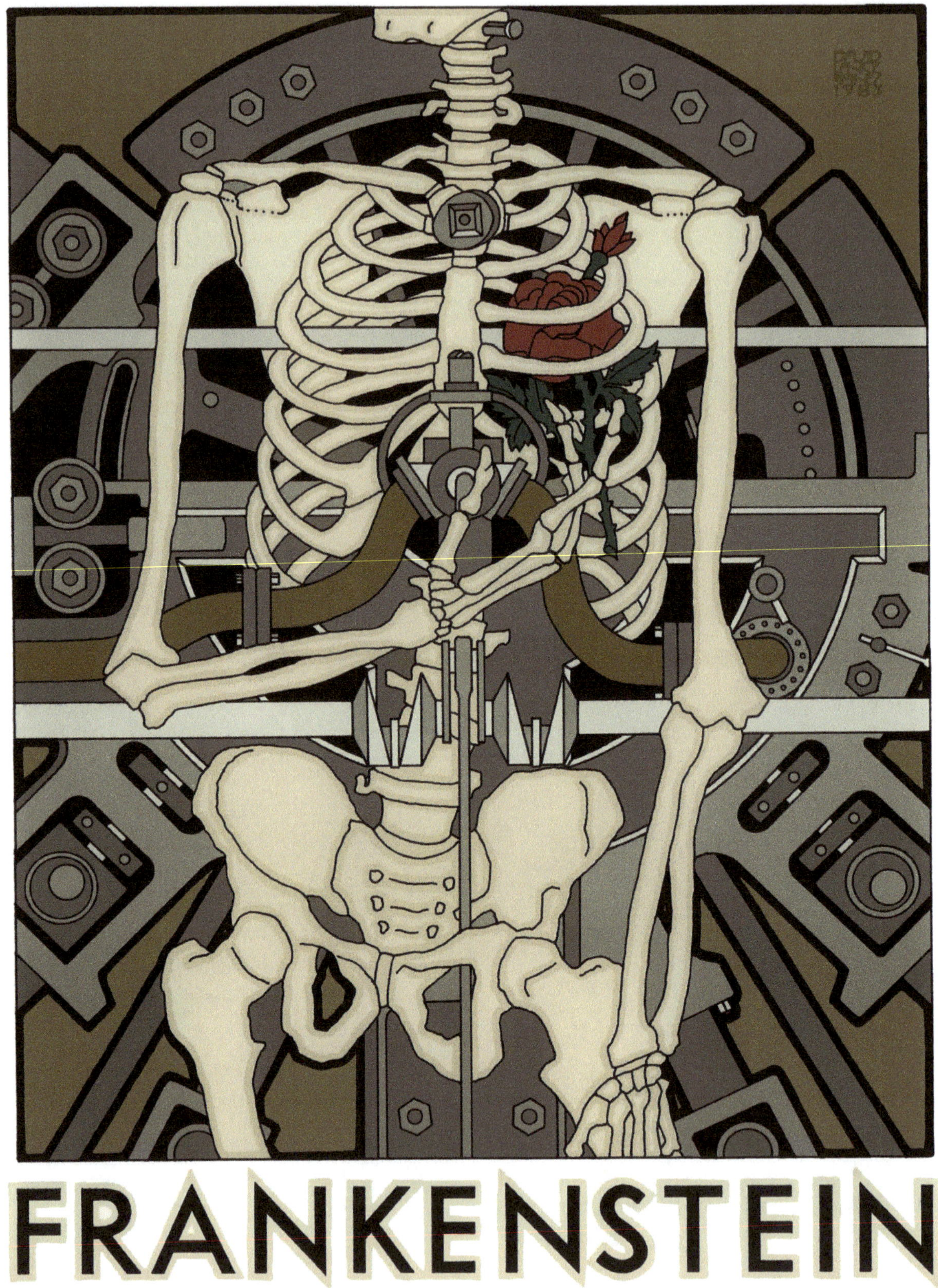

57. Frankenstein, 1983, 17⅛" × 24"

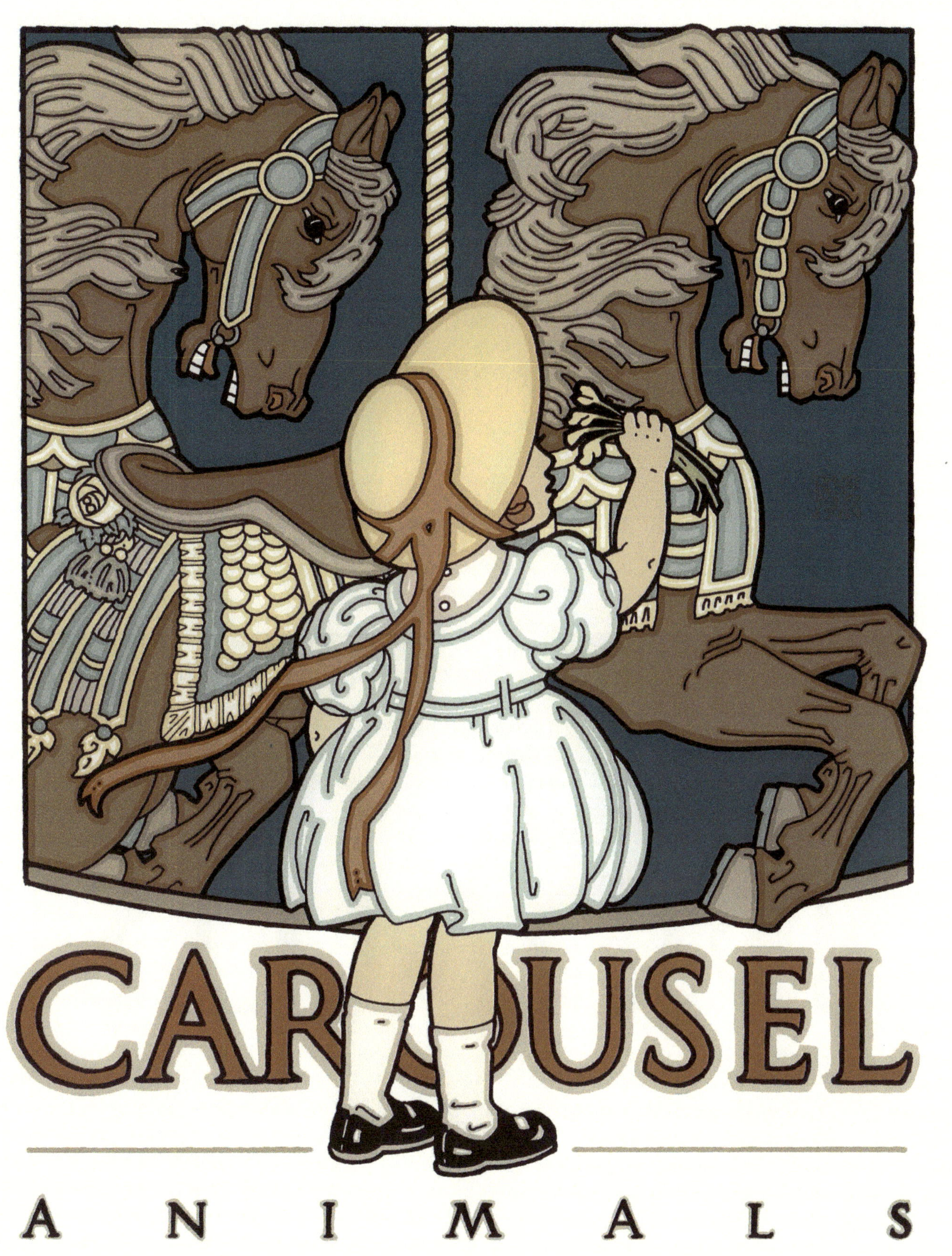

58. Carousel Animals, 1984, 17¾" × 24"

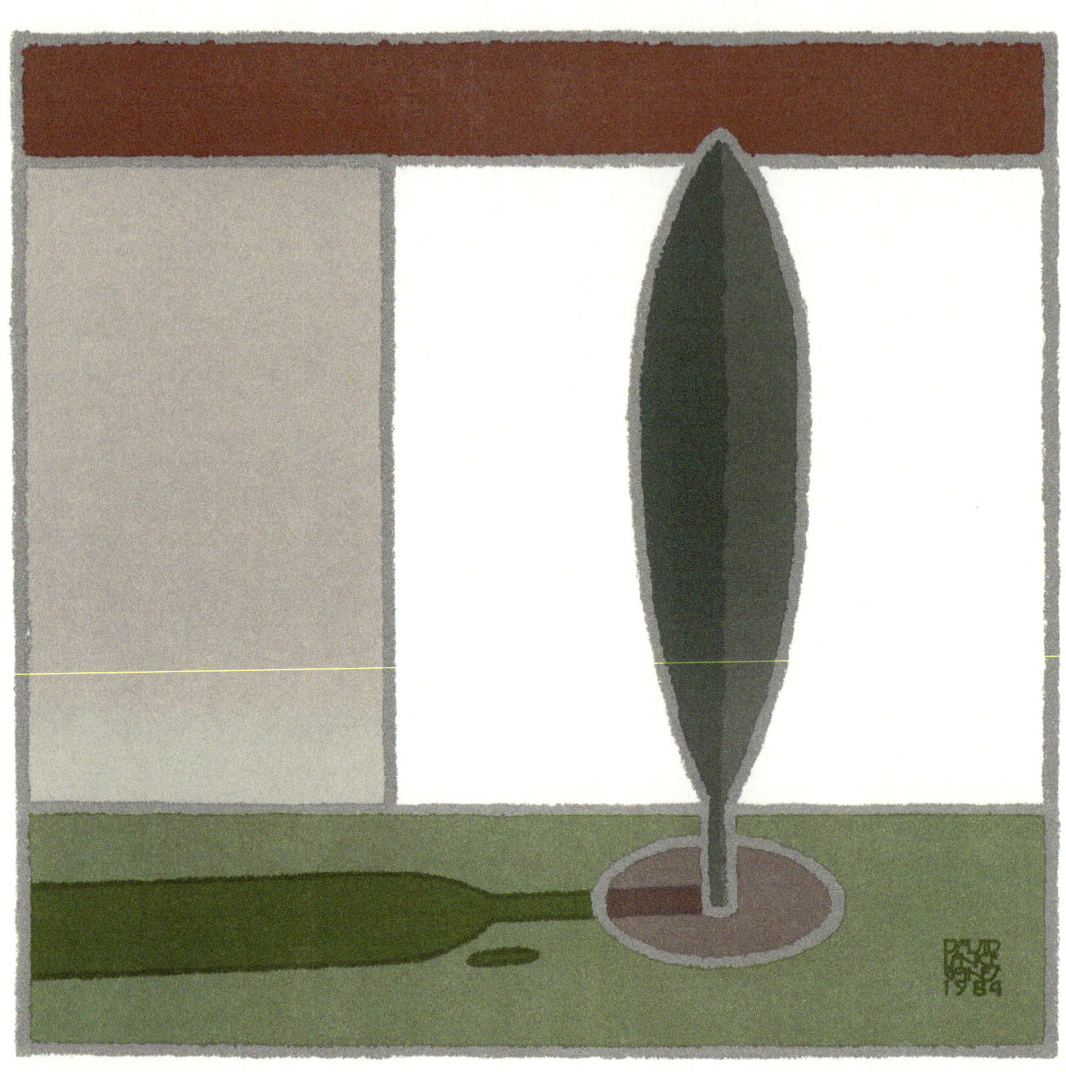

DOMUS

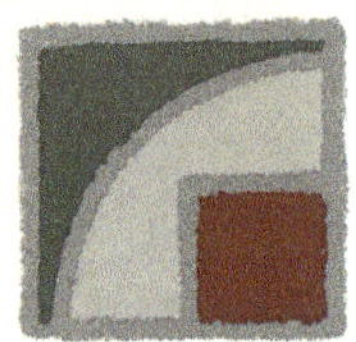

THE CARPET CENTER
THIRTY-FIFTH ANNIVERSARY
SEVENTH & PARKER · BERKELEY

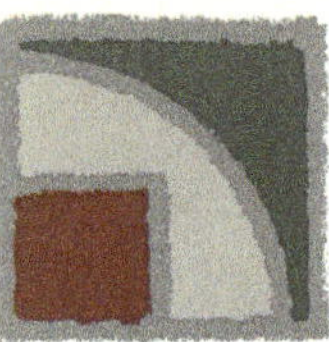

59. Domus, 1984, 18" × 24"

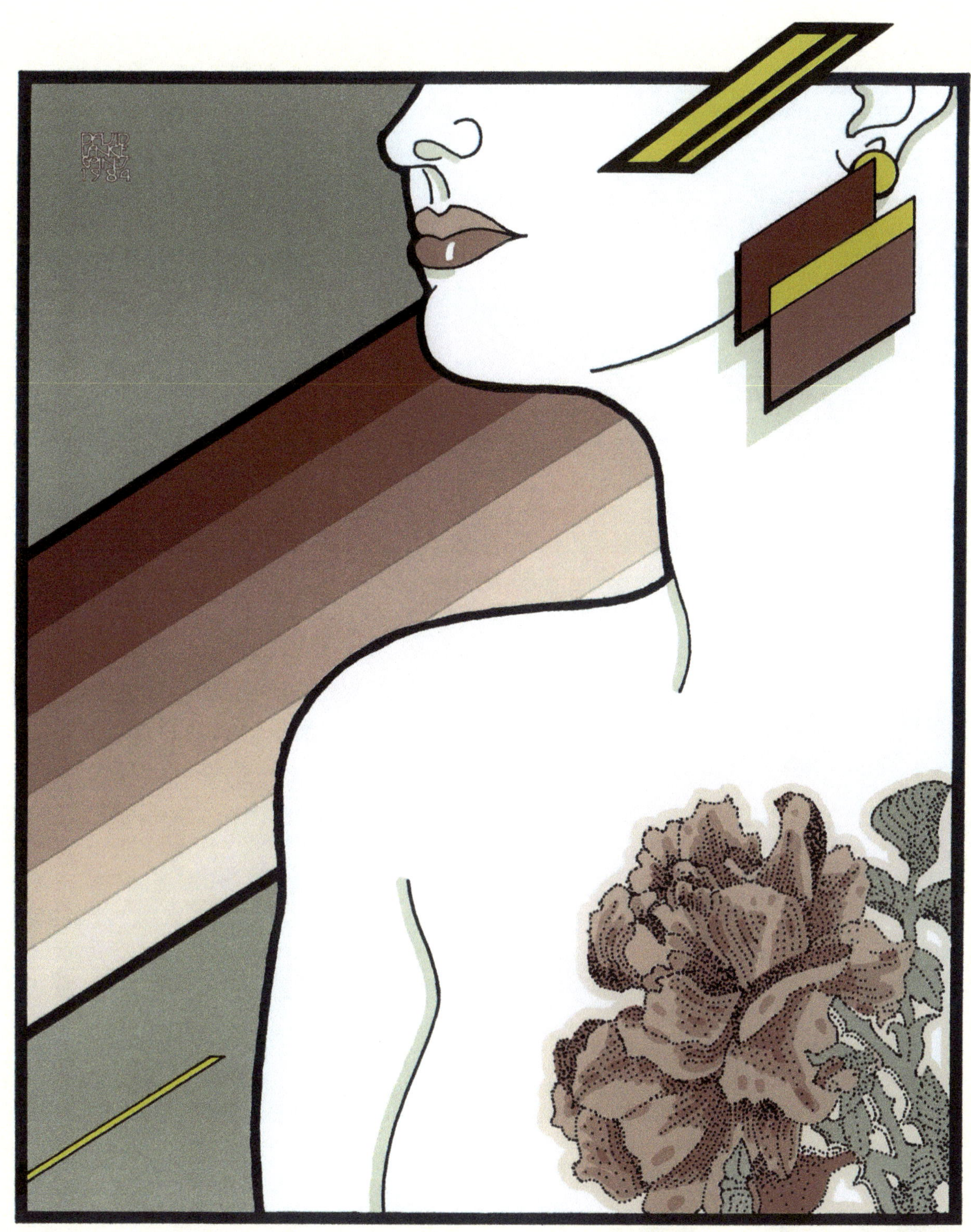

60. Thirteen (Chez Panisse Thirteenth Anniversary), 1984, 18" × 24"

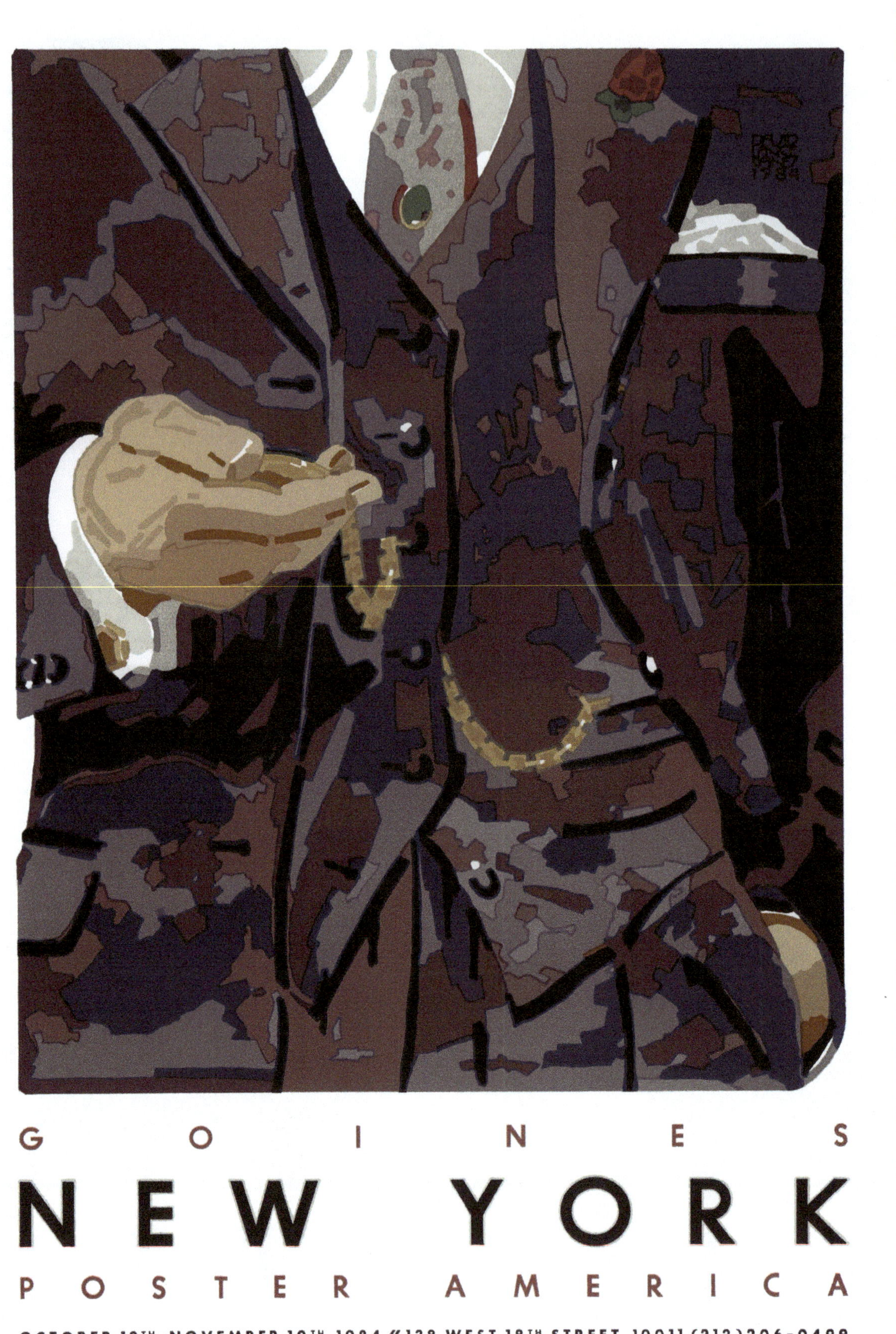

61. New York (Goines Show at Poster America), 1984, 16" × 24"

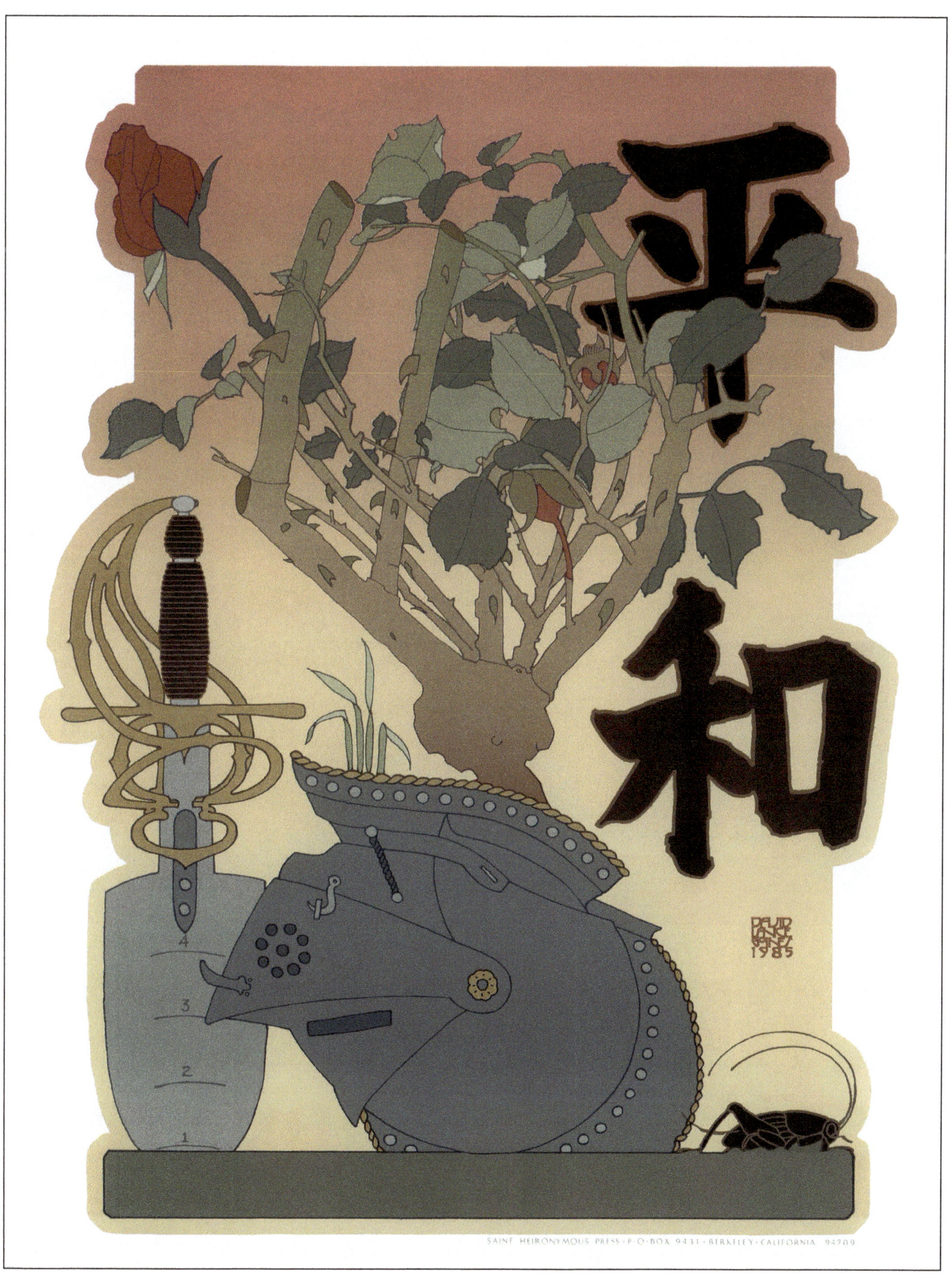

62. Heiwa, 1985, 17¾" × 24"

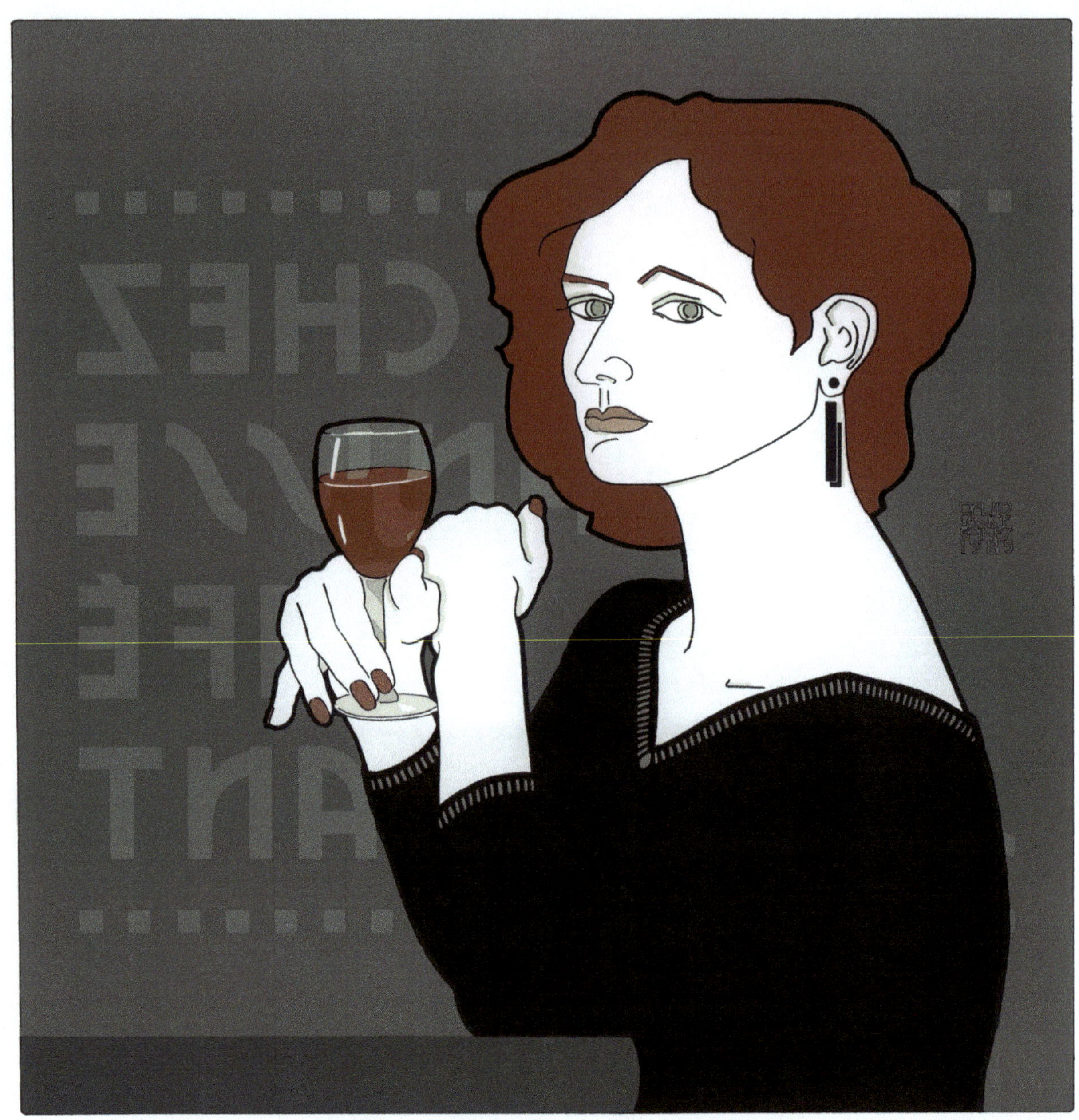

63. Chez Panisse Red-Haired Lady, 1985, 17½" × 24"

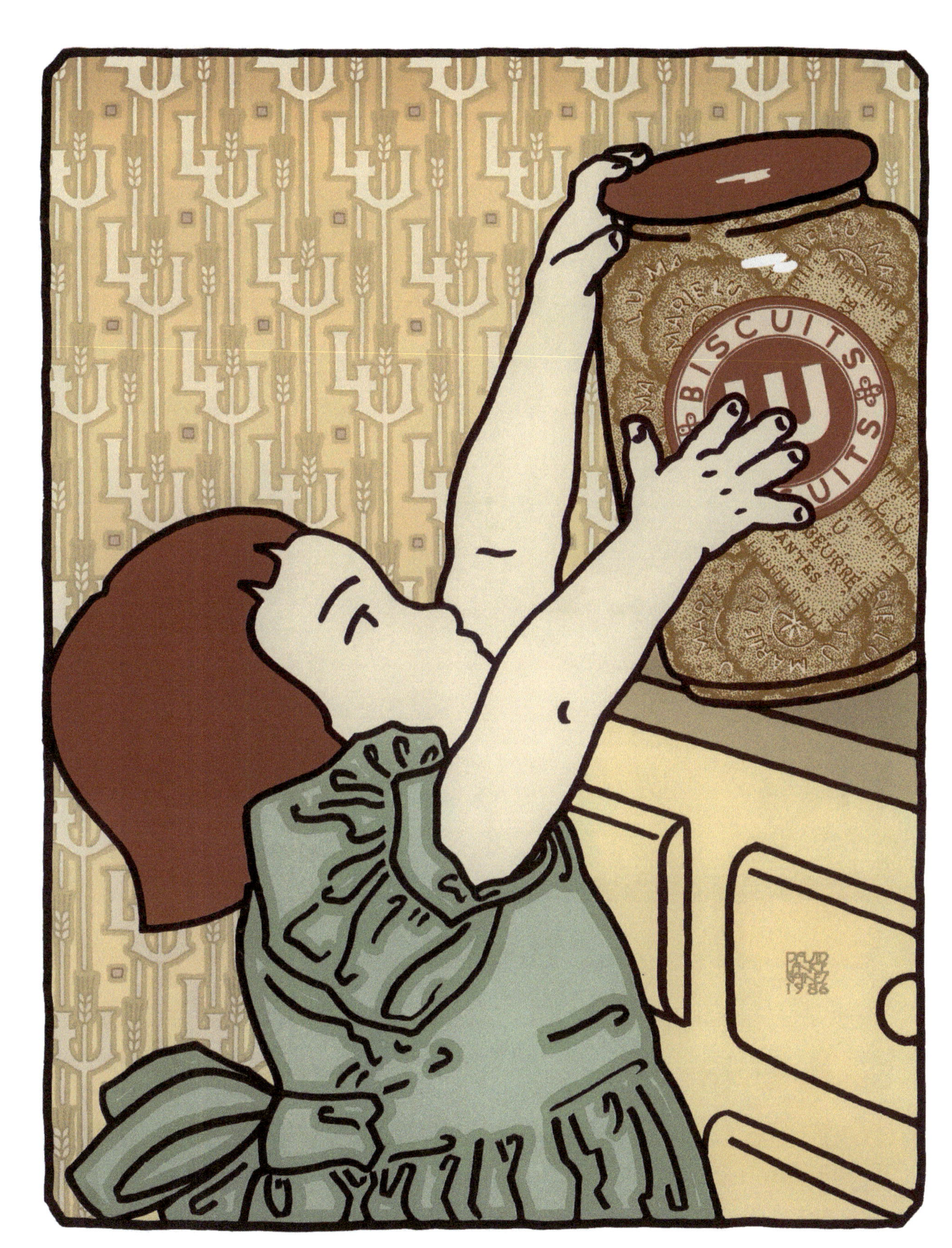

64. Biscuits Lefevre Utile (Lu), 1986, 18" × 24"

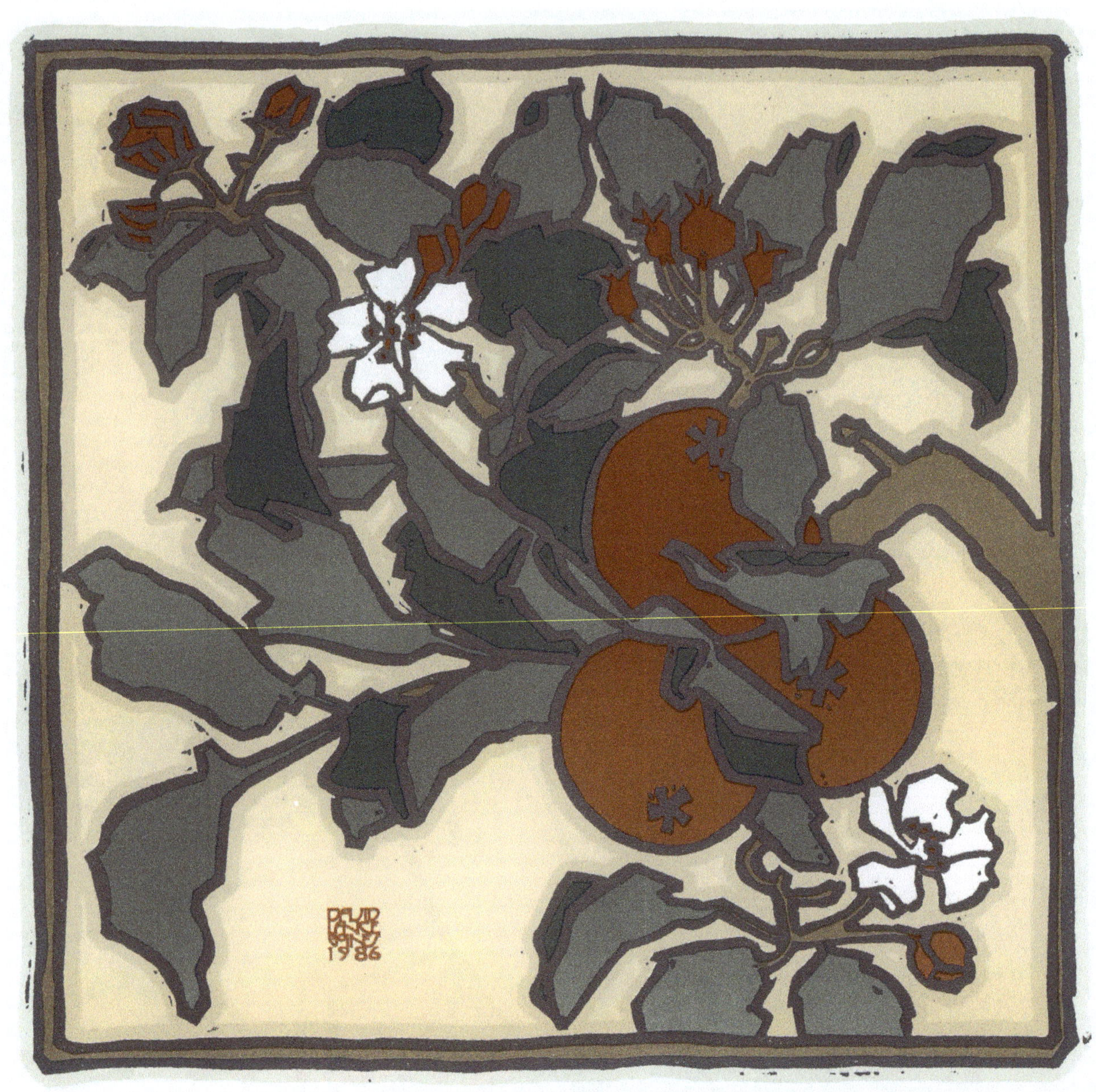

65. Chez Panisse Fifteenth Birthday, 1986, 18" × 24"

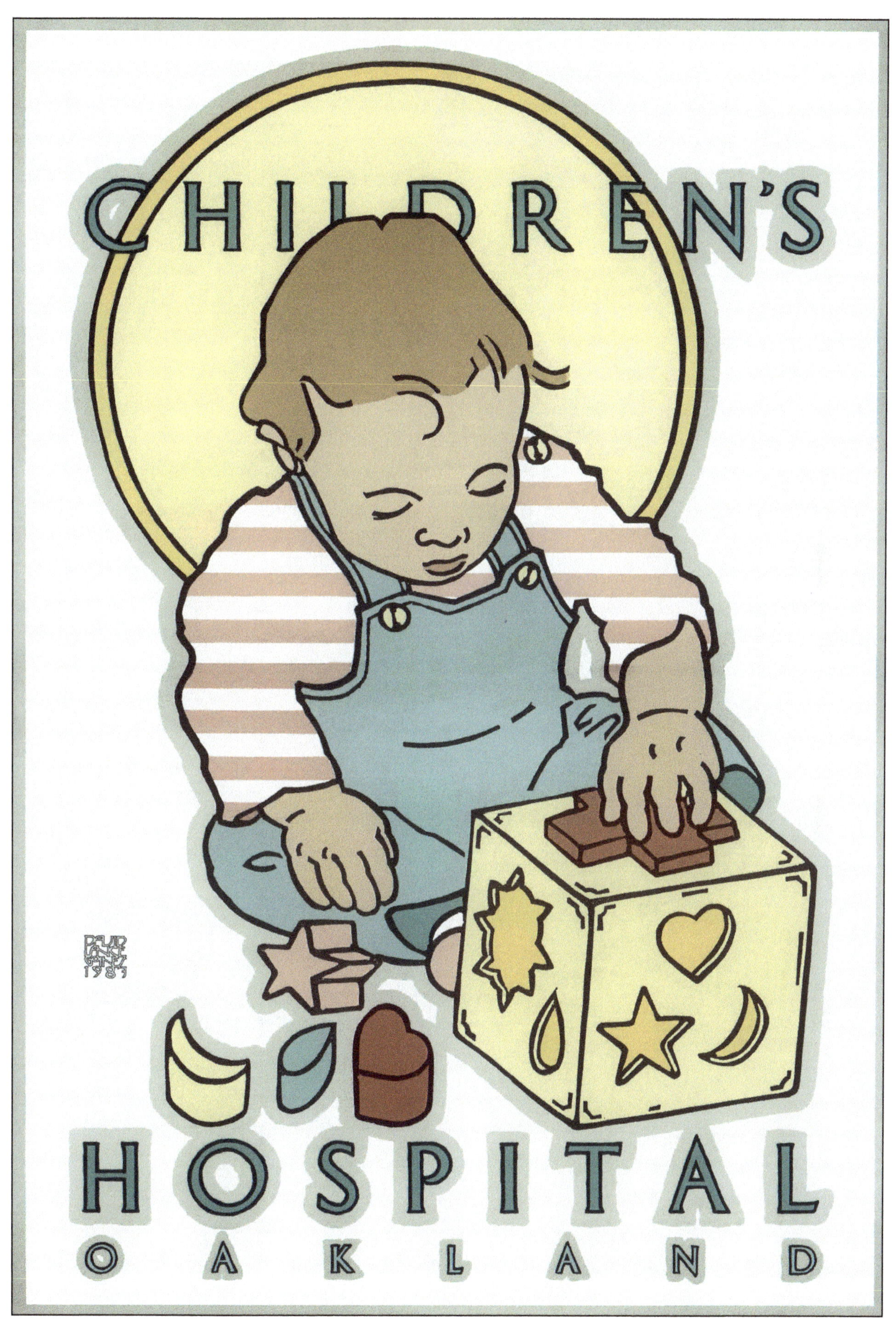

66. Children's Hospital, Oakland, 1987, 16" × 24"

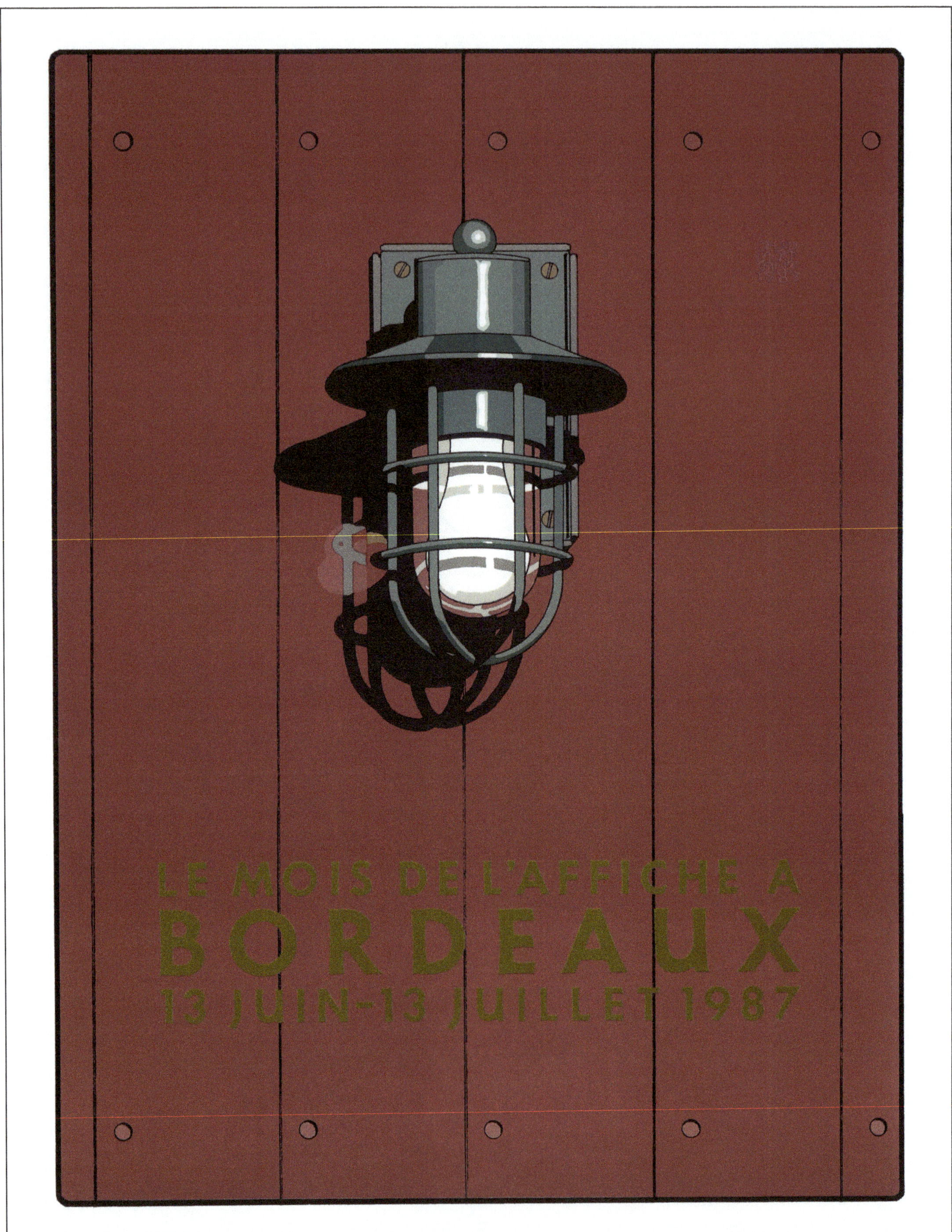

67. Bordeaux, 1987, 18" × 24"

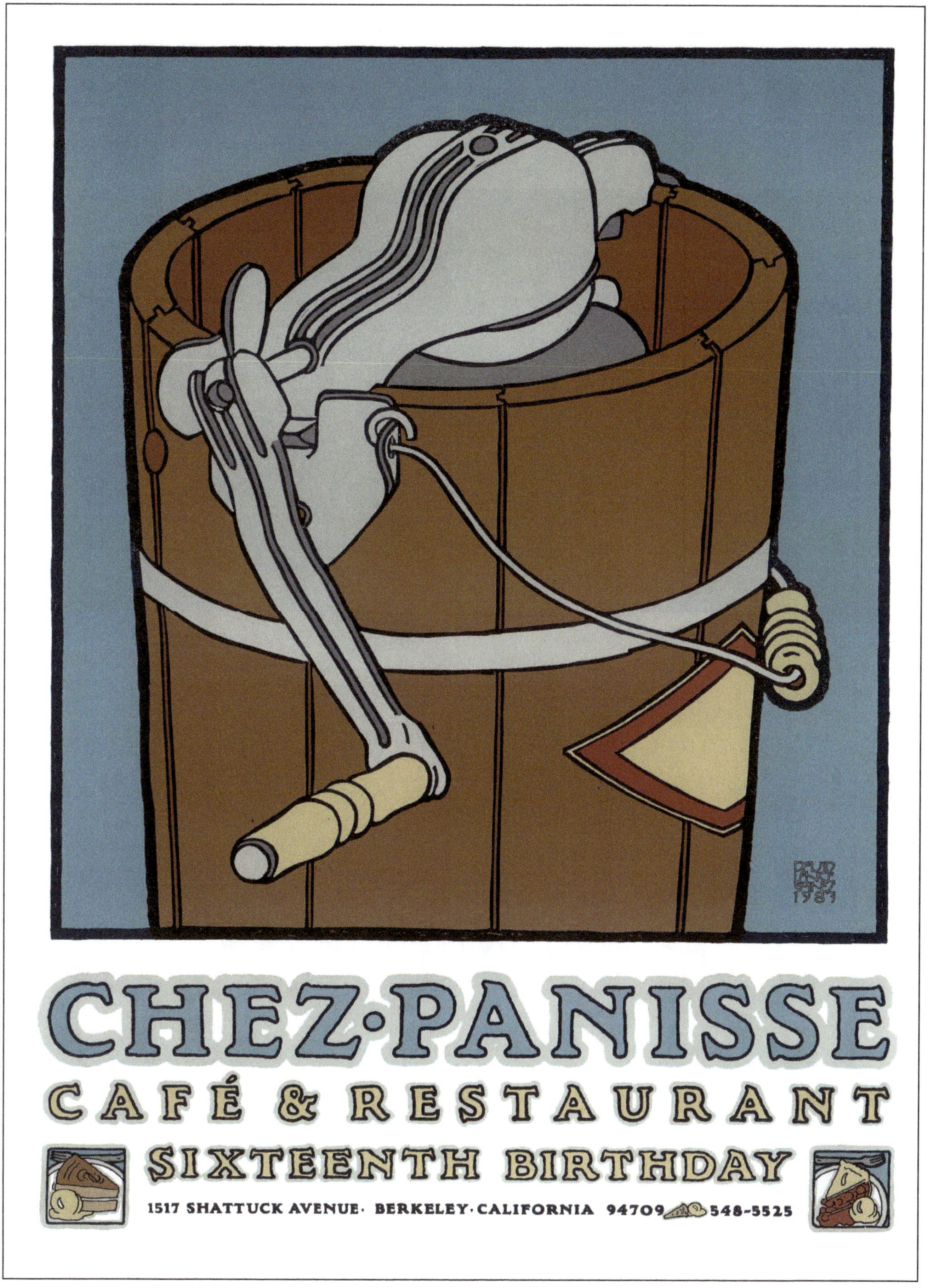

CHEZ·PANISSE

CAFÉ & RESTAURANT

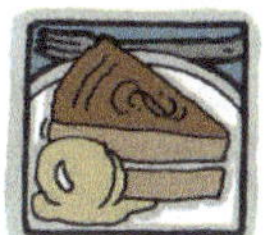

SIXTEENTH BIRTHDAY

1517 SHATTUCK AVENUE· BERKELEY·CALIFORNIA 94709 548-5525

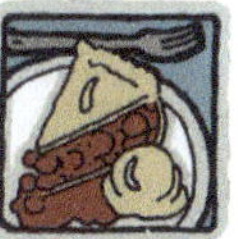

68. Chez Panisse Sixteenth Birthday, 1987, 17" × 24"

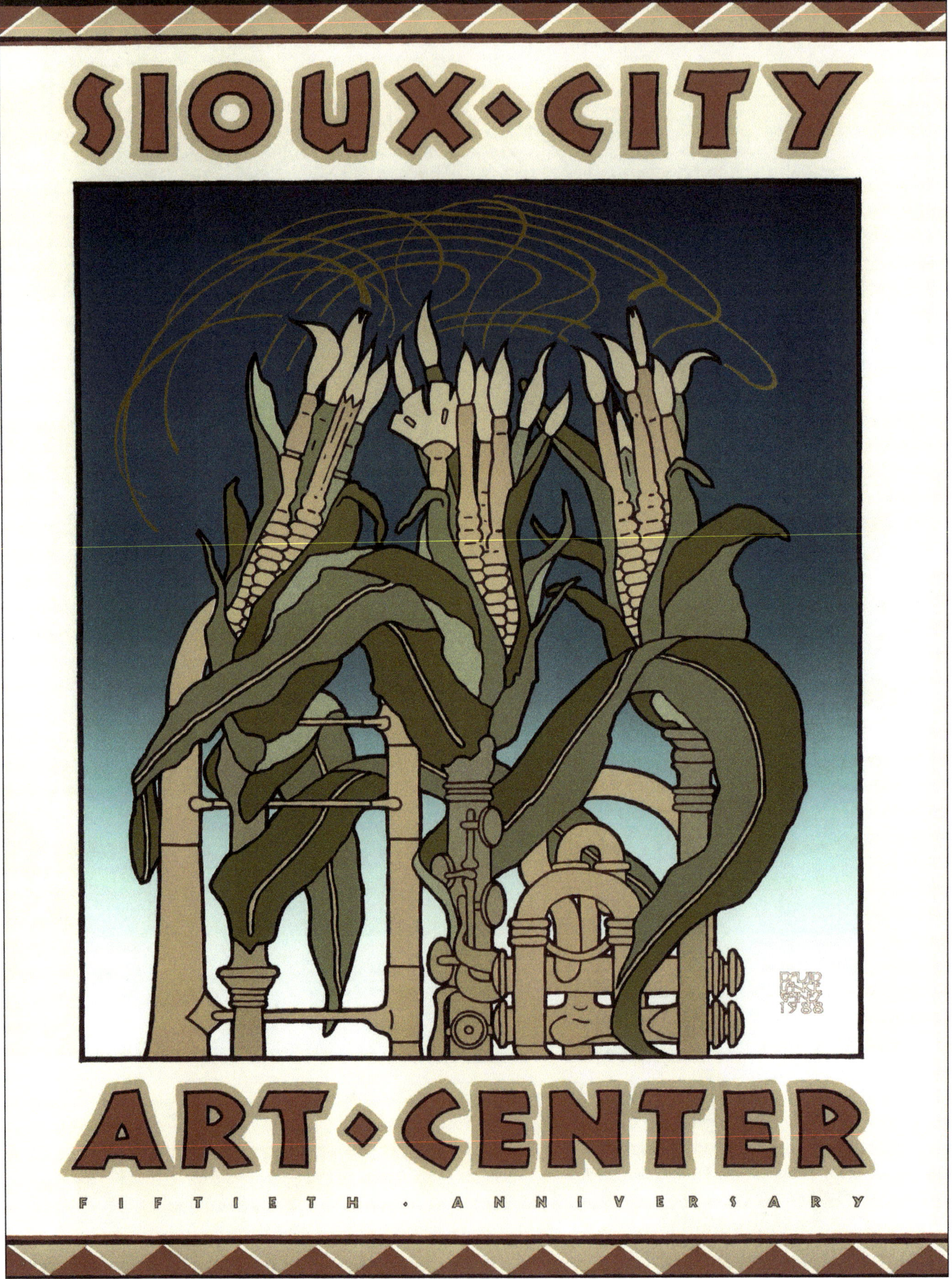

69. Sioux City Art Center, 1988, 17⅜" × 24"

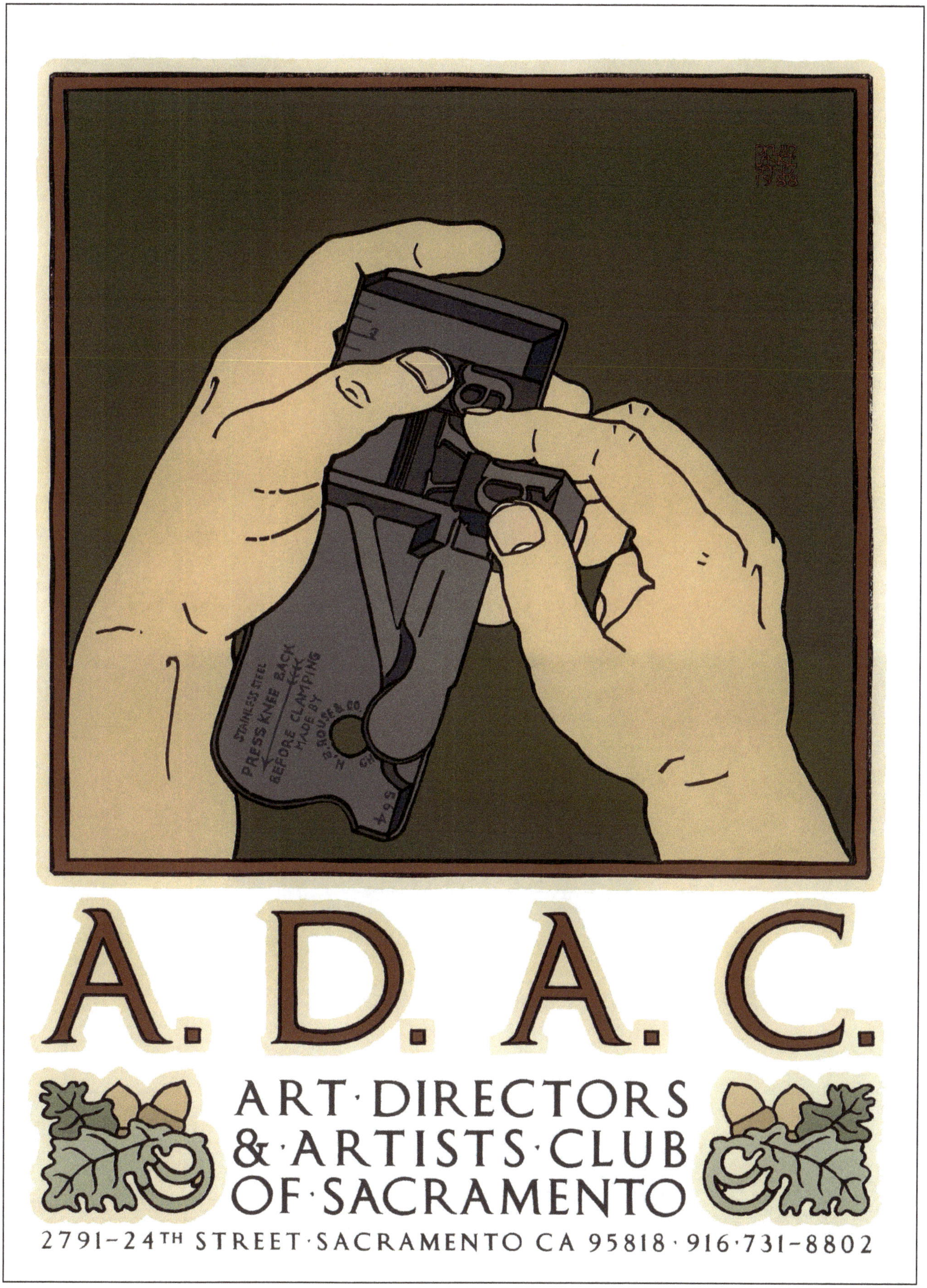

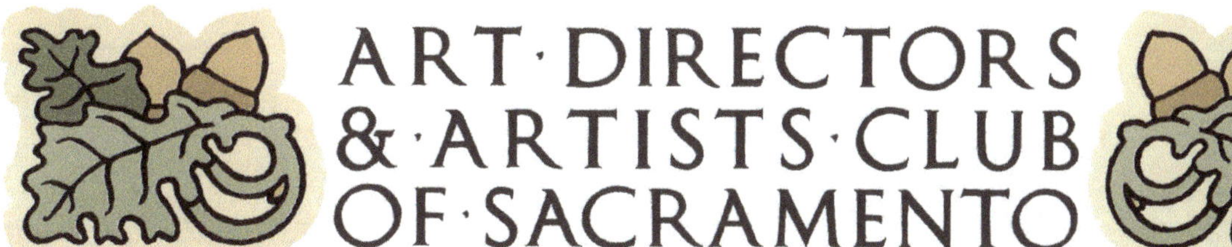

70. A.D.A.C., 1988, 17⅛" × 24"

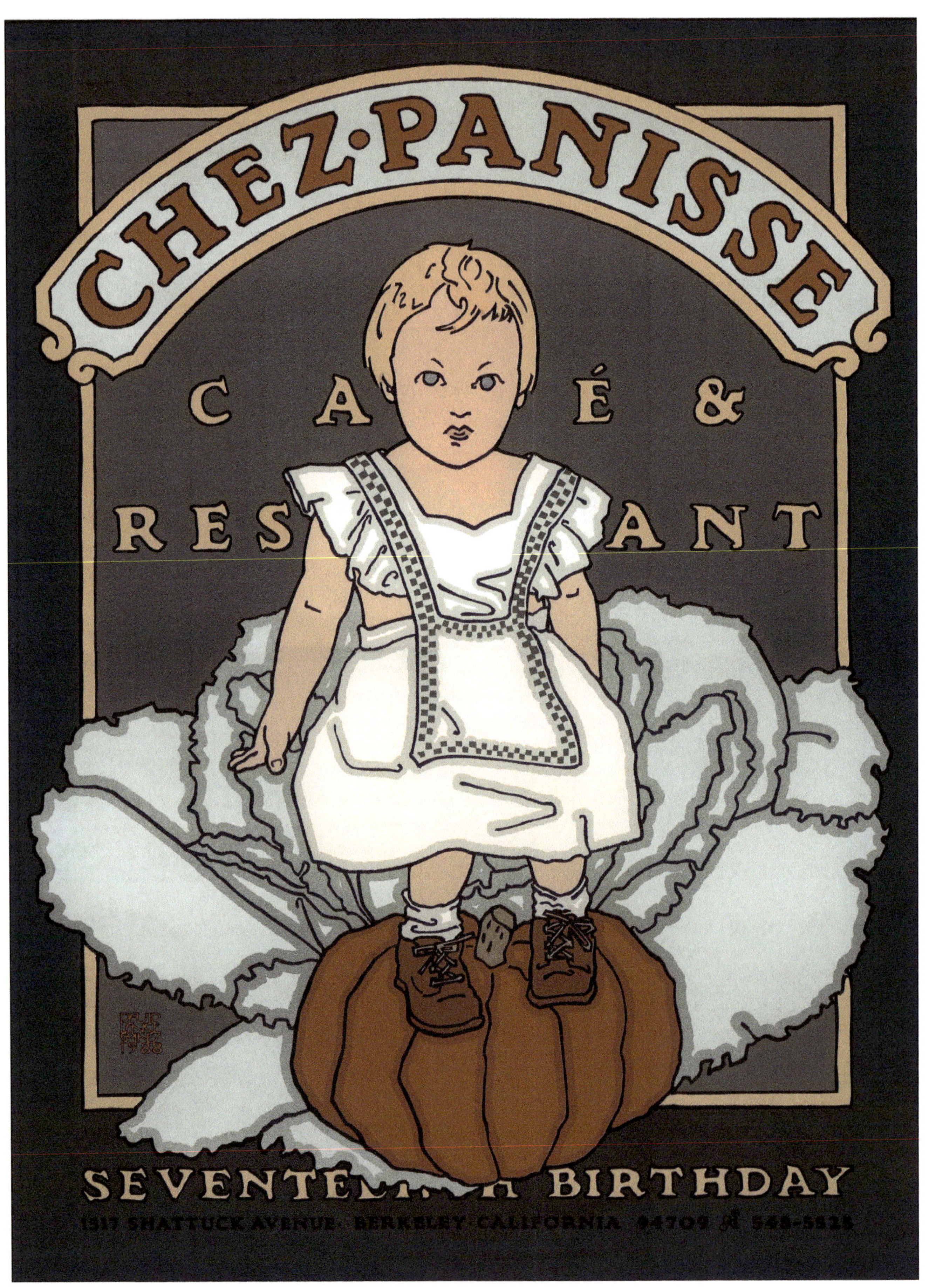

71. Chez Panisse Seventeenth Birthday, 1988, 17⅛" × 24"

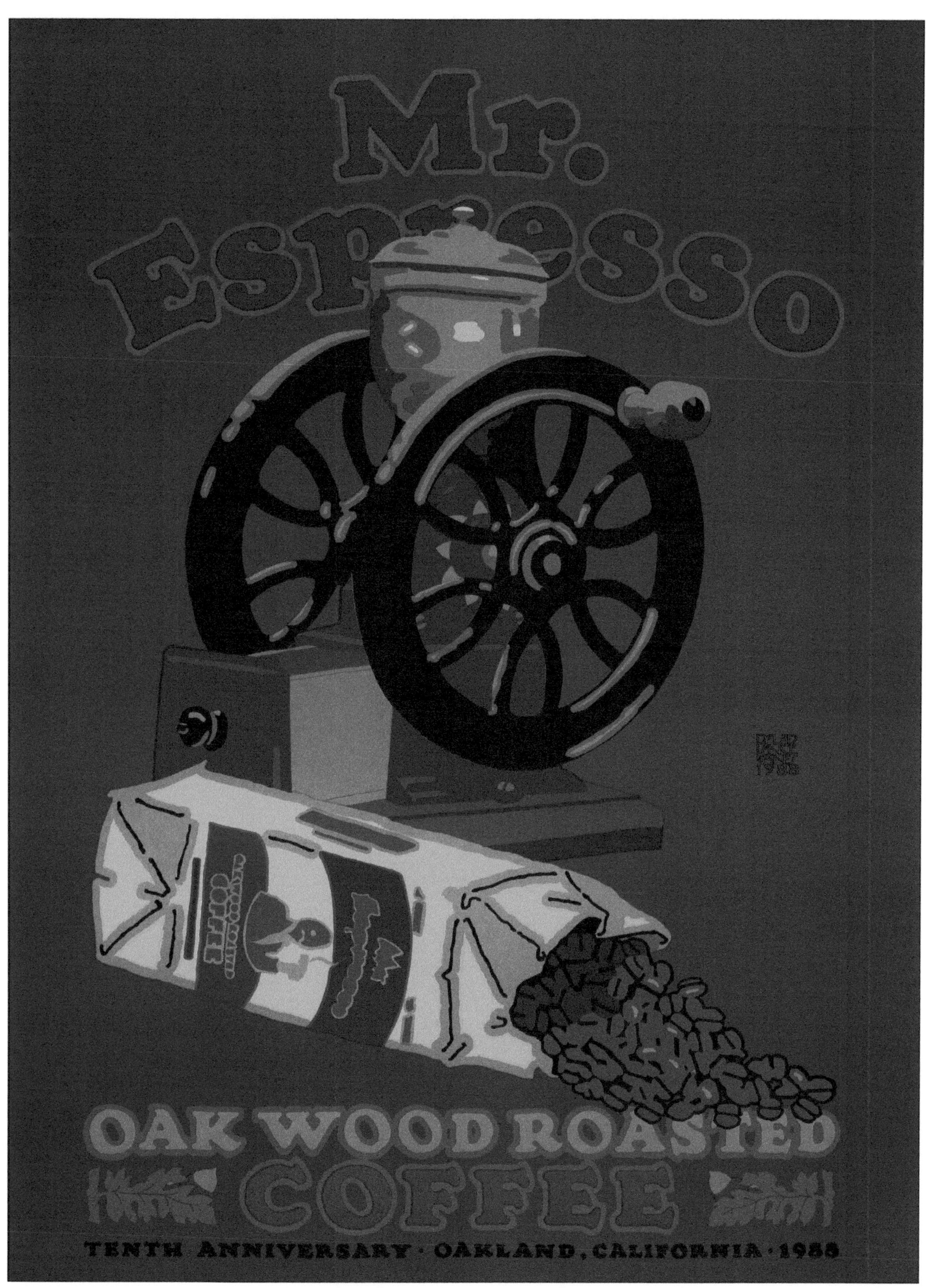

72. Mr. Espresso, 1988, 17" × 24"

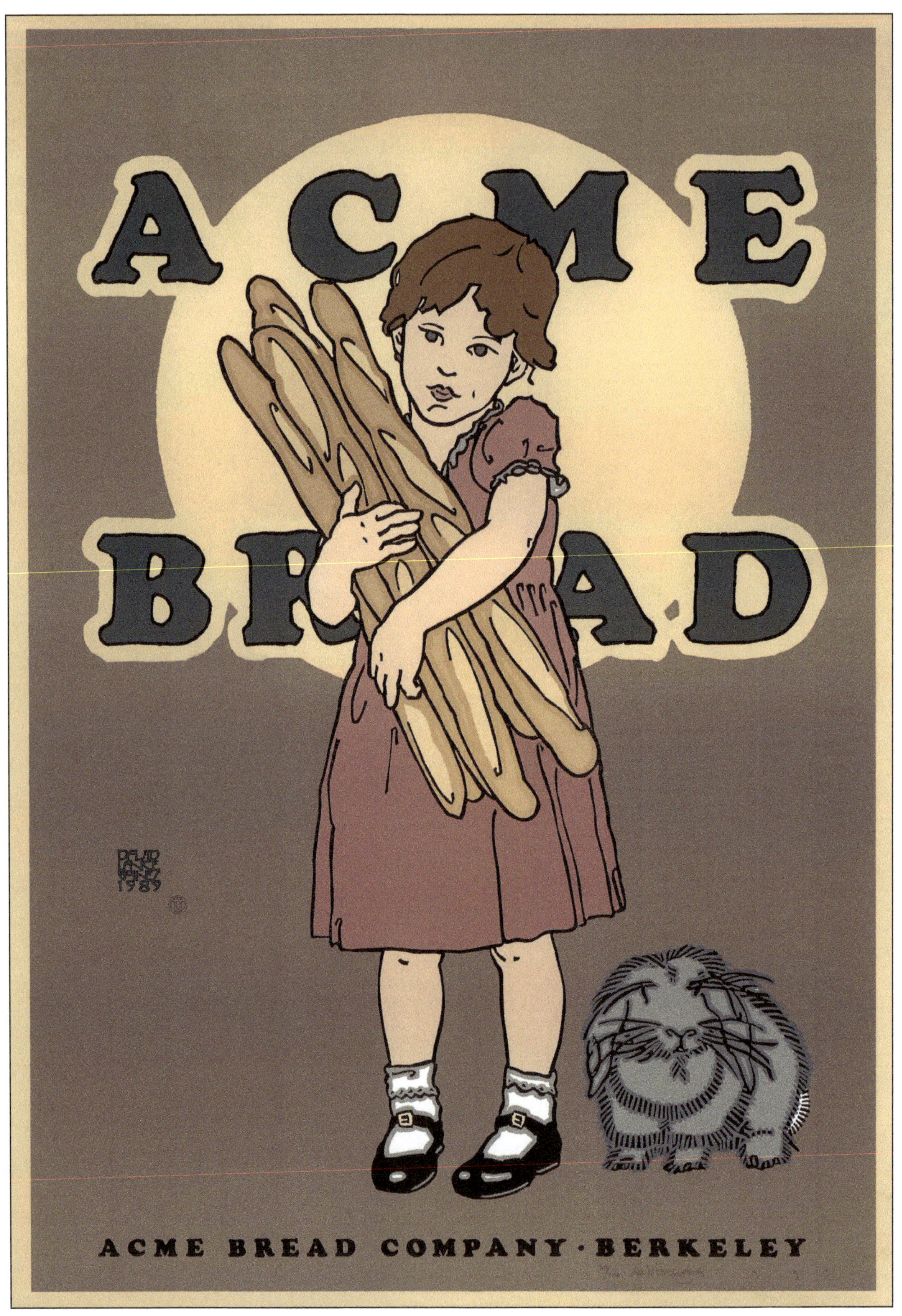

73. Acme Bread, 1989, 16" × 24"

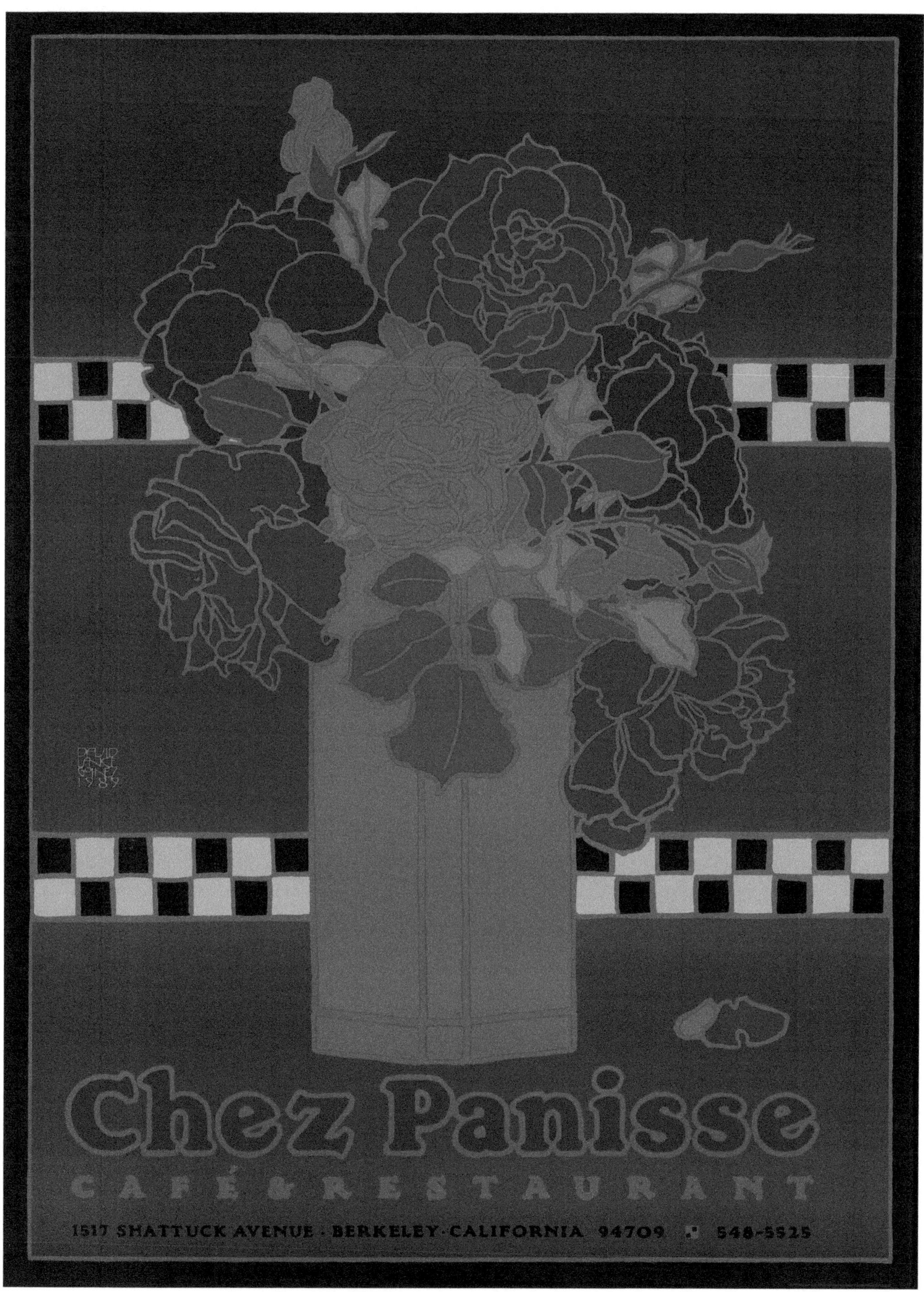

74. Chez Panisse, 1989, 17" × 24"

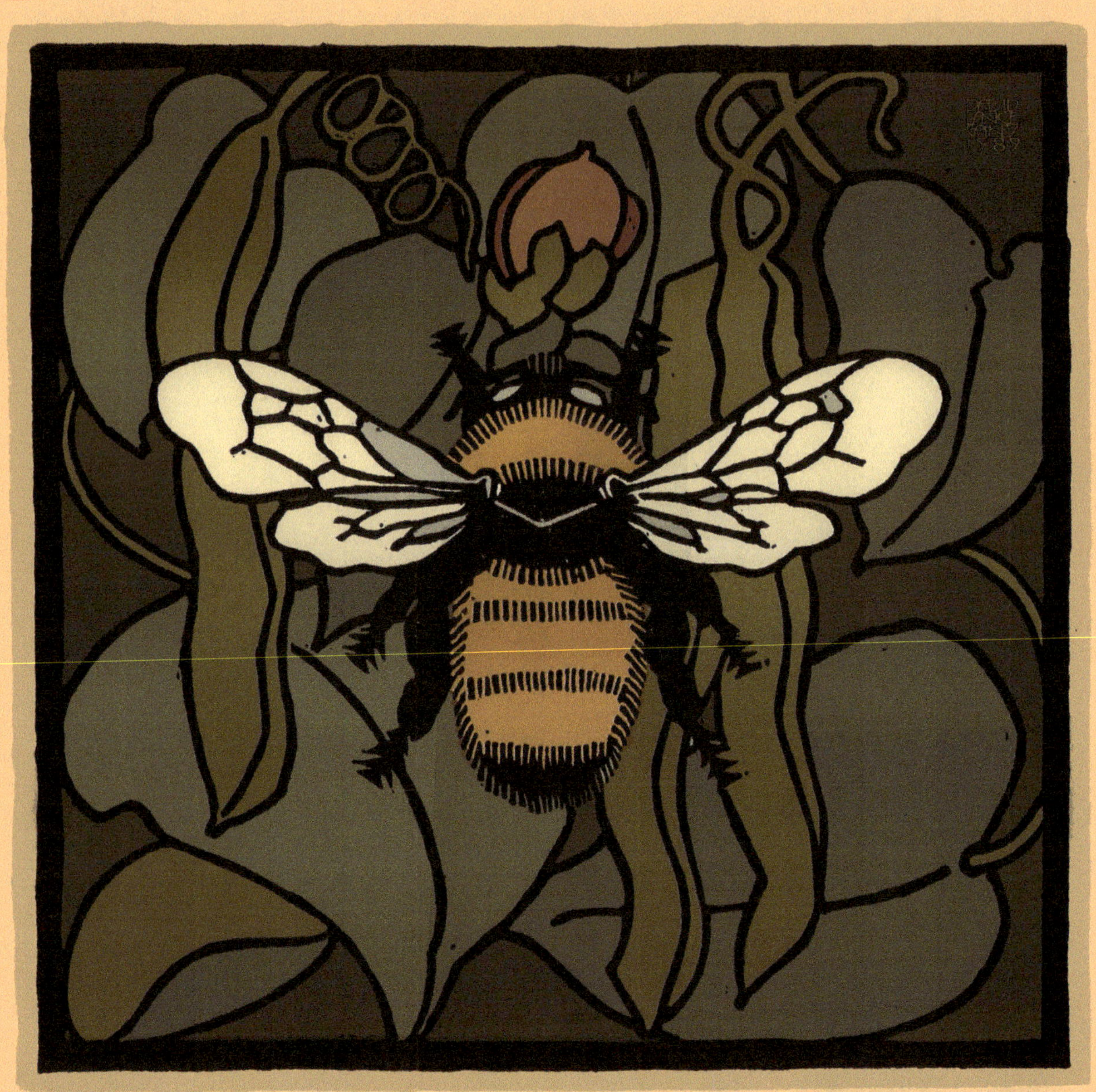

75. Goines: Twenty-One Years of Work, 1989, 17" × 24"

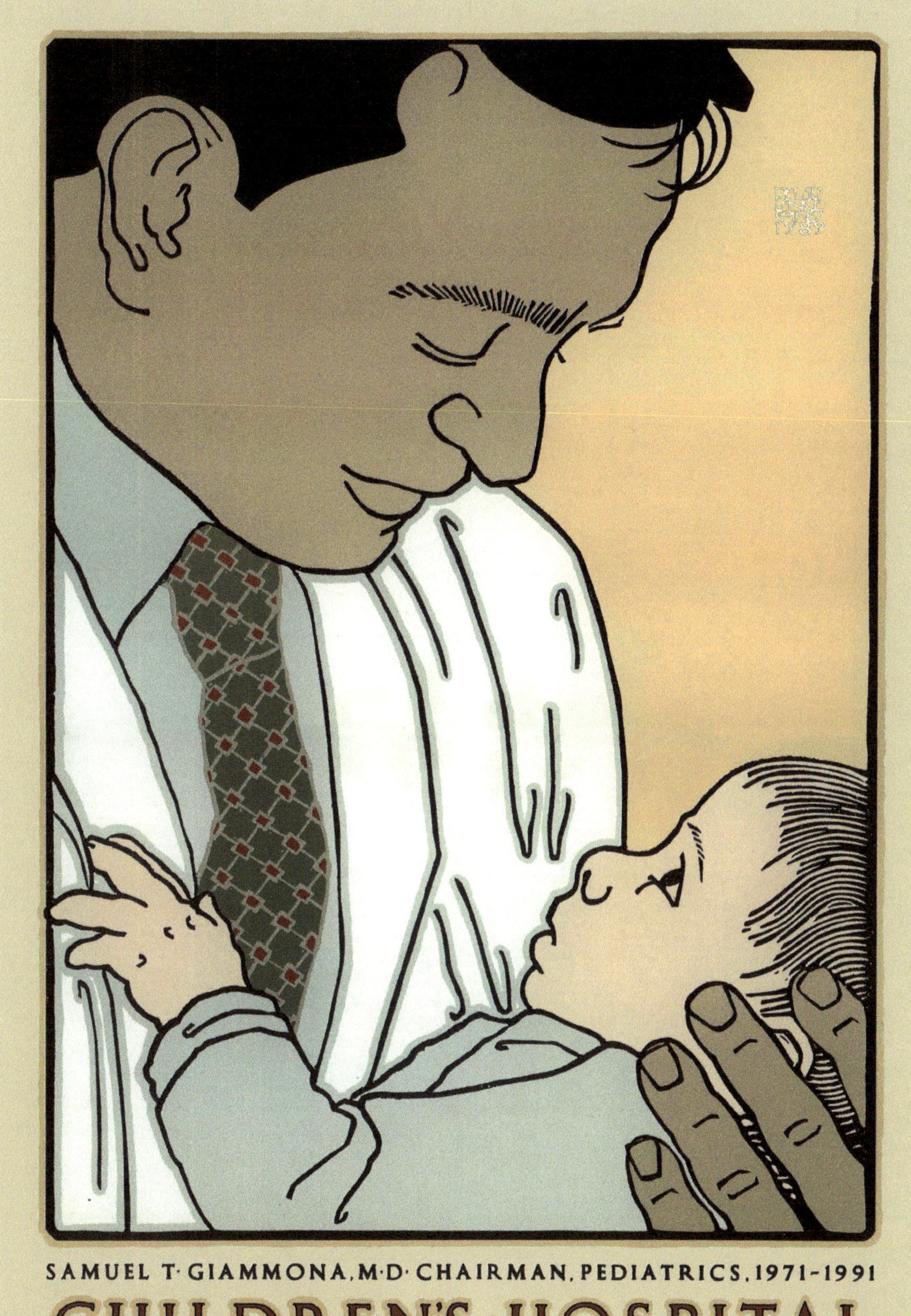

76. Children's Hospital, San Francisco, 1989, 15" × 24"

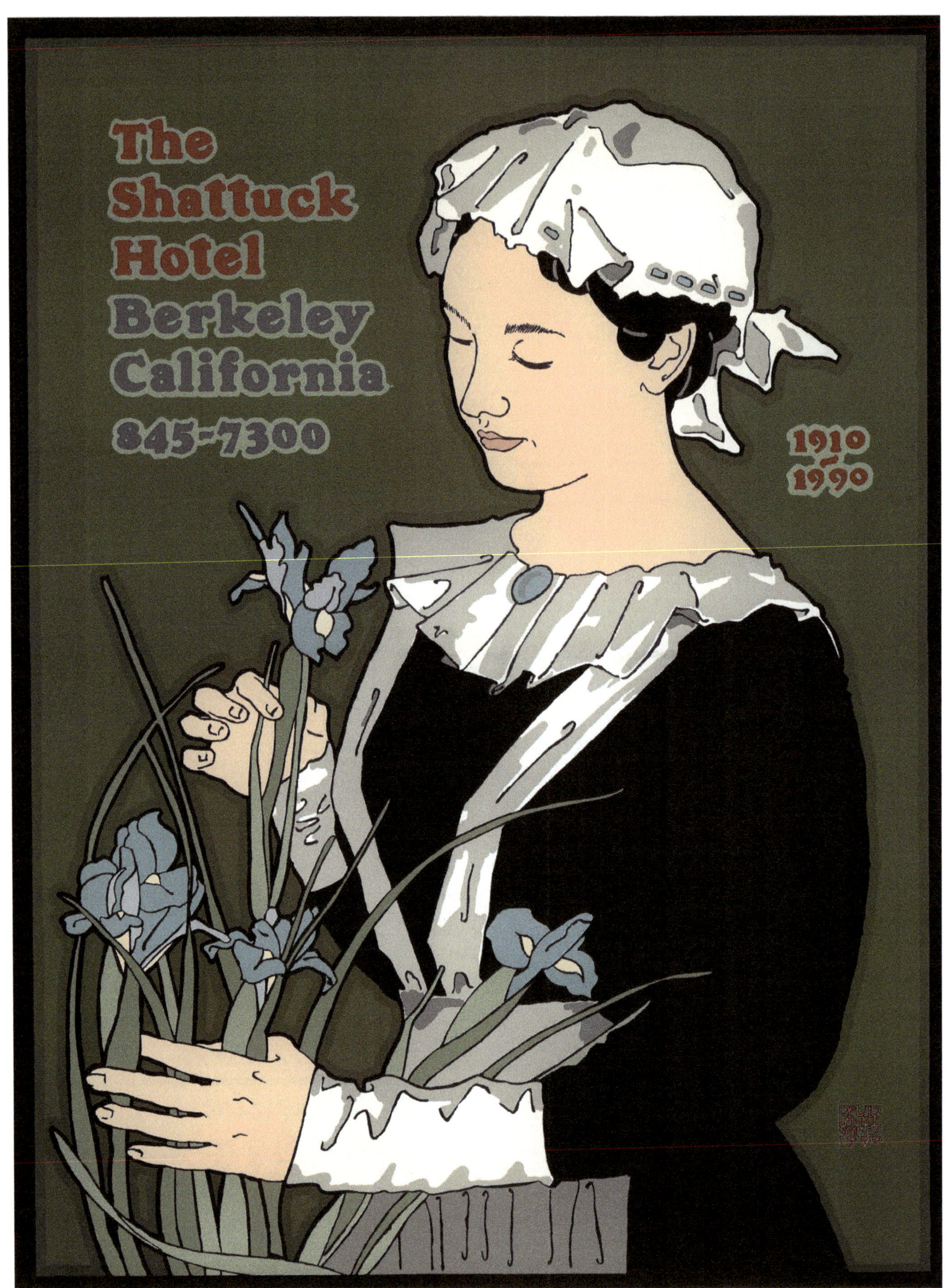

77. Shattuck Hotel, 1990, 17⅜" × 24"

CURTIS

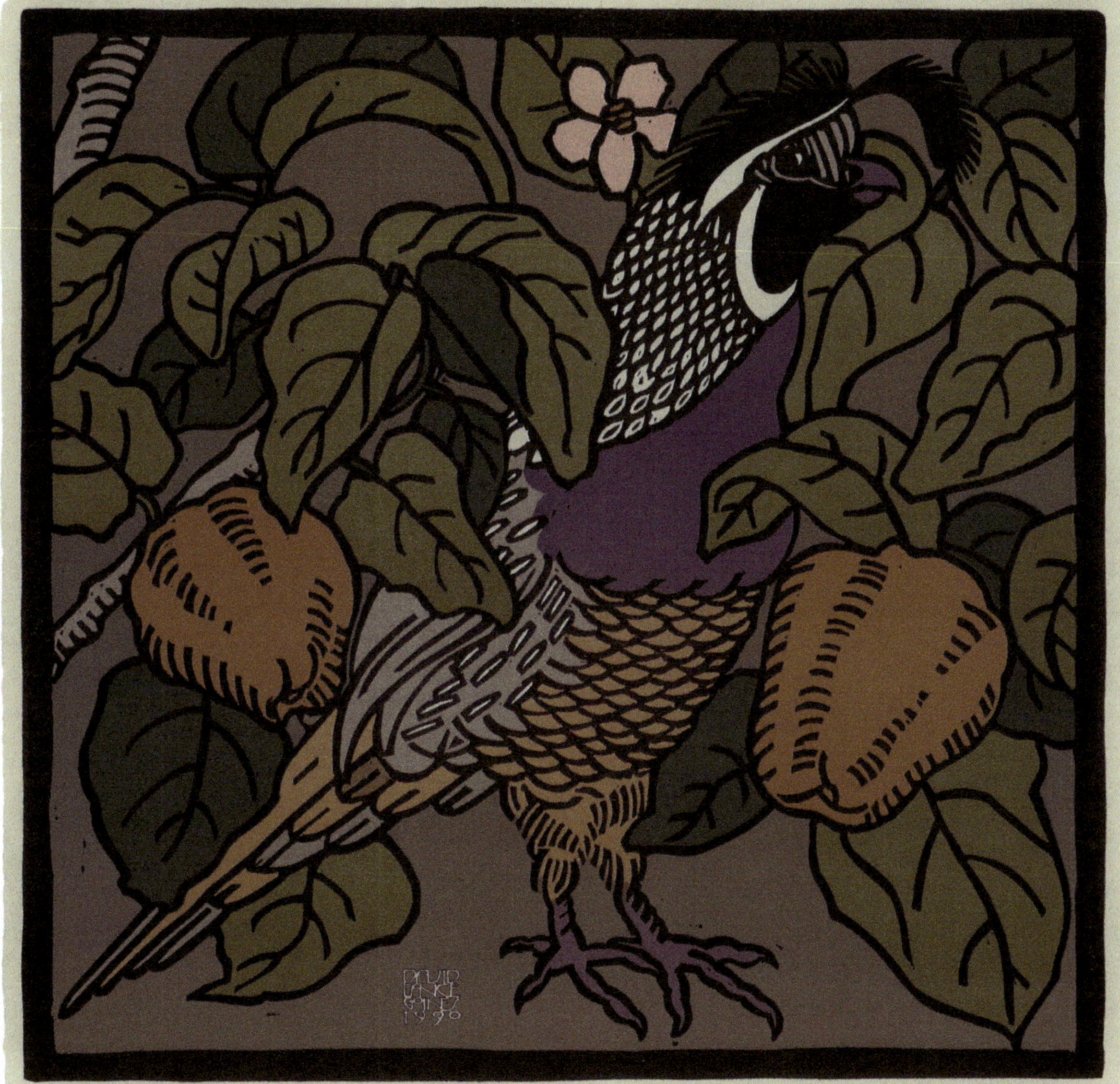

GRADATIONS

CURTIS GRADATIONS OFFERS A SELECTION OF LUXURIOUS COVER PAPERS WITH A 50% COTTON CONTENT. THEY ARE SUITABLE FOR OFFSET LITHOGRAPHY, ENGRAVING, EMBOSSING, FOIL STAMPING AND DIE CUTTING. BECAUSE THEY ARE MANUFACTURED TO ARCHIVAL STANDARDS, THEY ARE APPROPRIATE FOR LIMITED EDITION BOOKS, ART PRINTS AND HIGH-QUALITY PUBLICATIONS WHERE PERMANENCE IS A REQUIREMENT.

JAMES RIVER CORPORATION, CURTIS GRADATIONS COVER, CREAM TINT, BASIS 80

78. Curtis Gradations, 1990, 17 5/16" × 24"

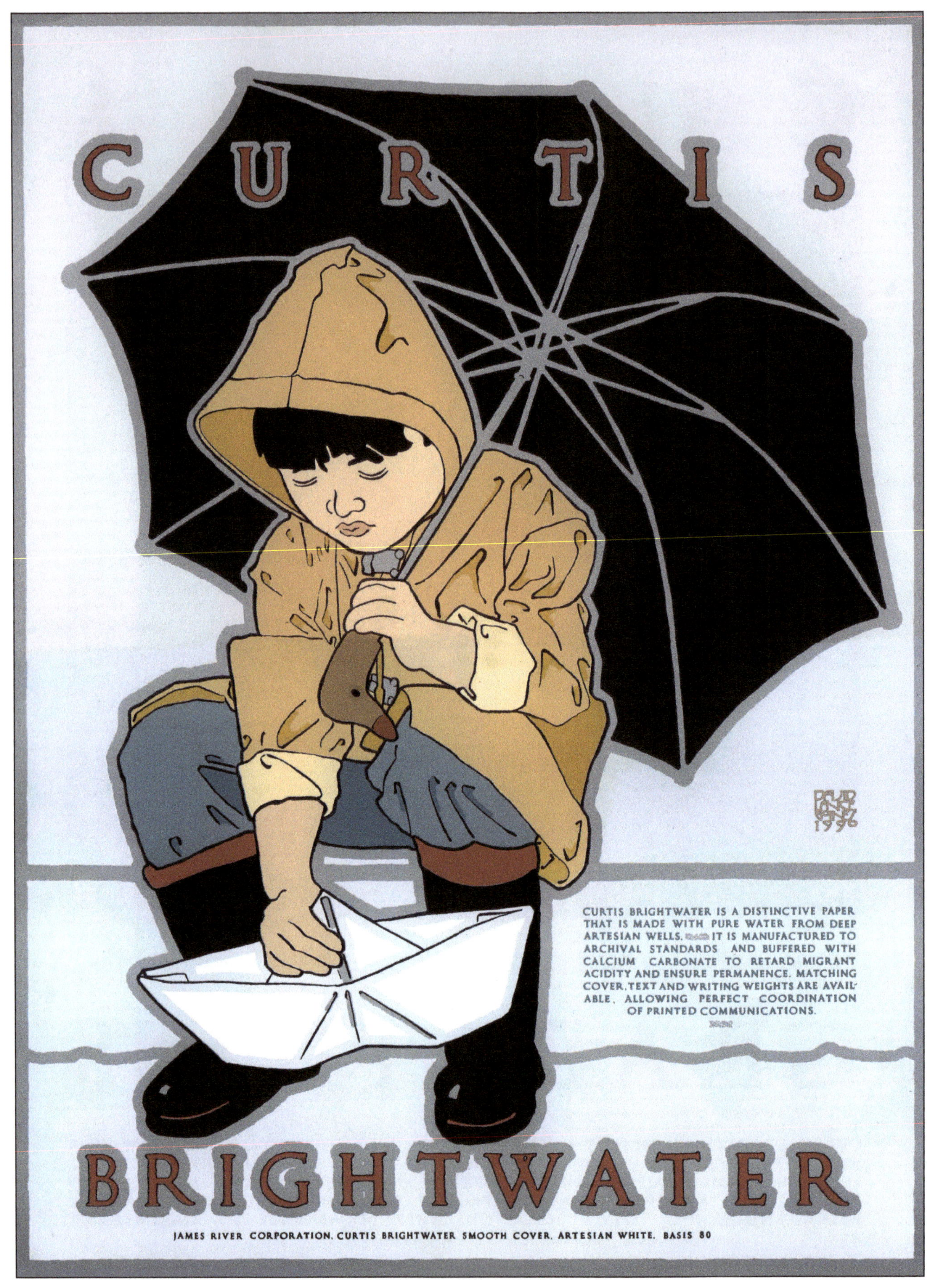

79. Curtis Brightwater, 1990, 17" × 24"

EARTH'S

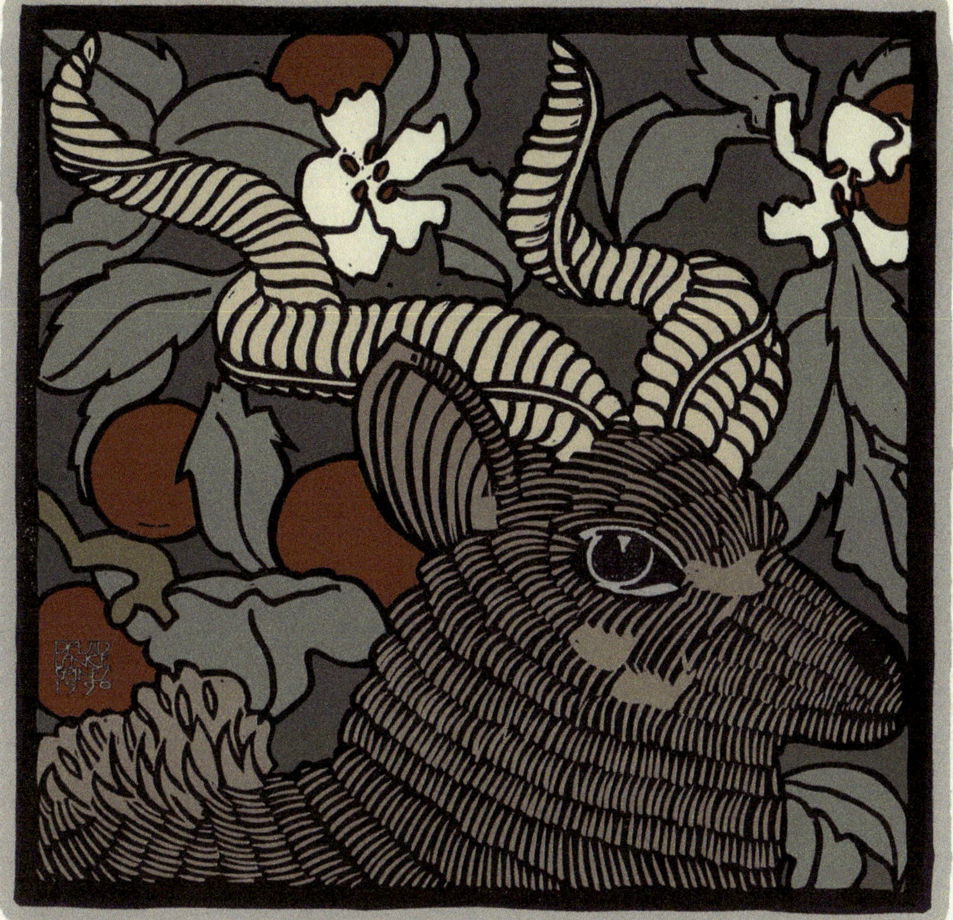

TEN COMMANDMENTS

I THOU SHALT LOVE AND HONOR THE EARTH
FOR IT BLESSES THY LIFE AND GOVERNS THY SURVIVAL.
II THOU SHALT KEEP EACH DAY SACRED TO THE EARTH
AND CELEBRATE THE TURNING OF ITS SEASONS.
III THOU SHALT NOT HOLD THYSELF ABOVE OTHER LIVING THINGS
NOR DRIVE THEM TO EXTINCTION.
IV THOU SHALT GIVE THANKS FOR THY FOOD
TO THE CREATURES AND PLANTS THAT NOURISH THEE.
V THOU SHALT LIMIT THY OFFSPRING
FOR MULTITUDES OF PEOPLE ARE A BURDEN UNTO THE EARTH.
VI THOU SHALT NOT KILL
NOR WASTE EARTH'S RICHES UPON WEAPONS OF WAR.
VII THOU SHALT NOT PURSUE PROFIT AT THE EARTH'S EXPENSE
BUT STRIVE TO RESTORE ITS DAMAGED MAJESTY.
VIII THOU SHALT NOT HIDE FROM THYSELF OR OTHERS
THE CONSEQUENCES OF THY ACTIONS UPON THE EARTH.
IX THOU SHALT NOT STEAL FROM FUTURE GENERATIONS
BY IMPOVERISHING OR POISONING THE EARTH.
X THOU SHALT CONSUME MATERIAL GOODS IN MODERATION
SO ALL MAY SHARE EARTH'S BOUNTY.

80. Earth's Ten Commandments, 1990, 16" × 24"

HARBOR

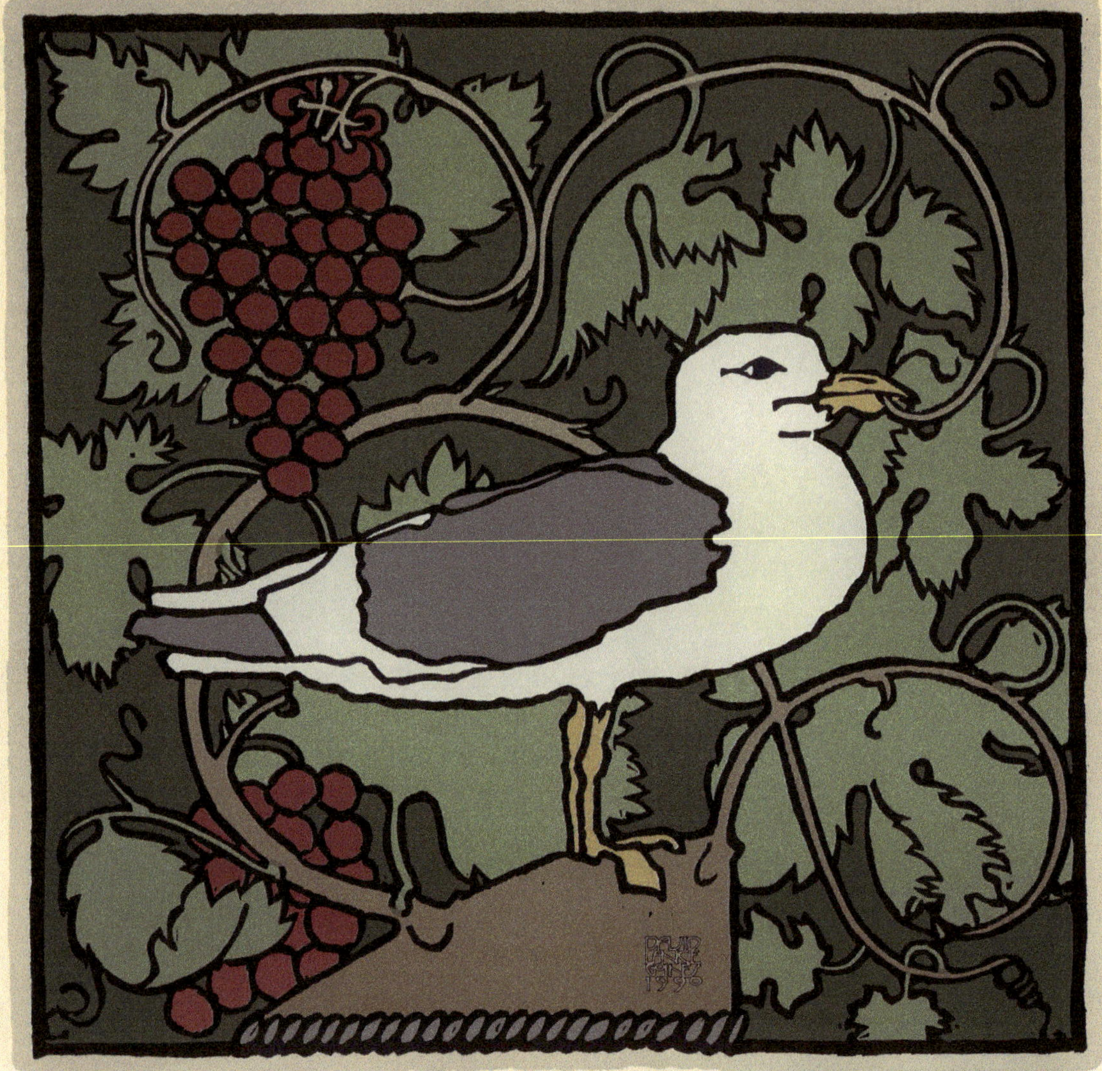

WINERY

1988

AMADOR COUNTY

ZINFANDEL

PRODUCED AND BOTTLED BY HARBOR WINERY
WEST SACRAMENTO, CALIFORNIA

81. HARBOR WINERY, 1990, 16⅜" × 24"

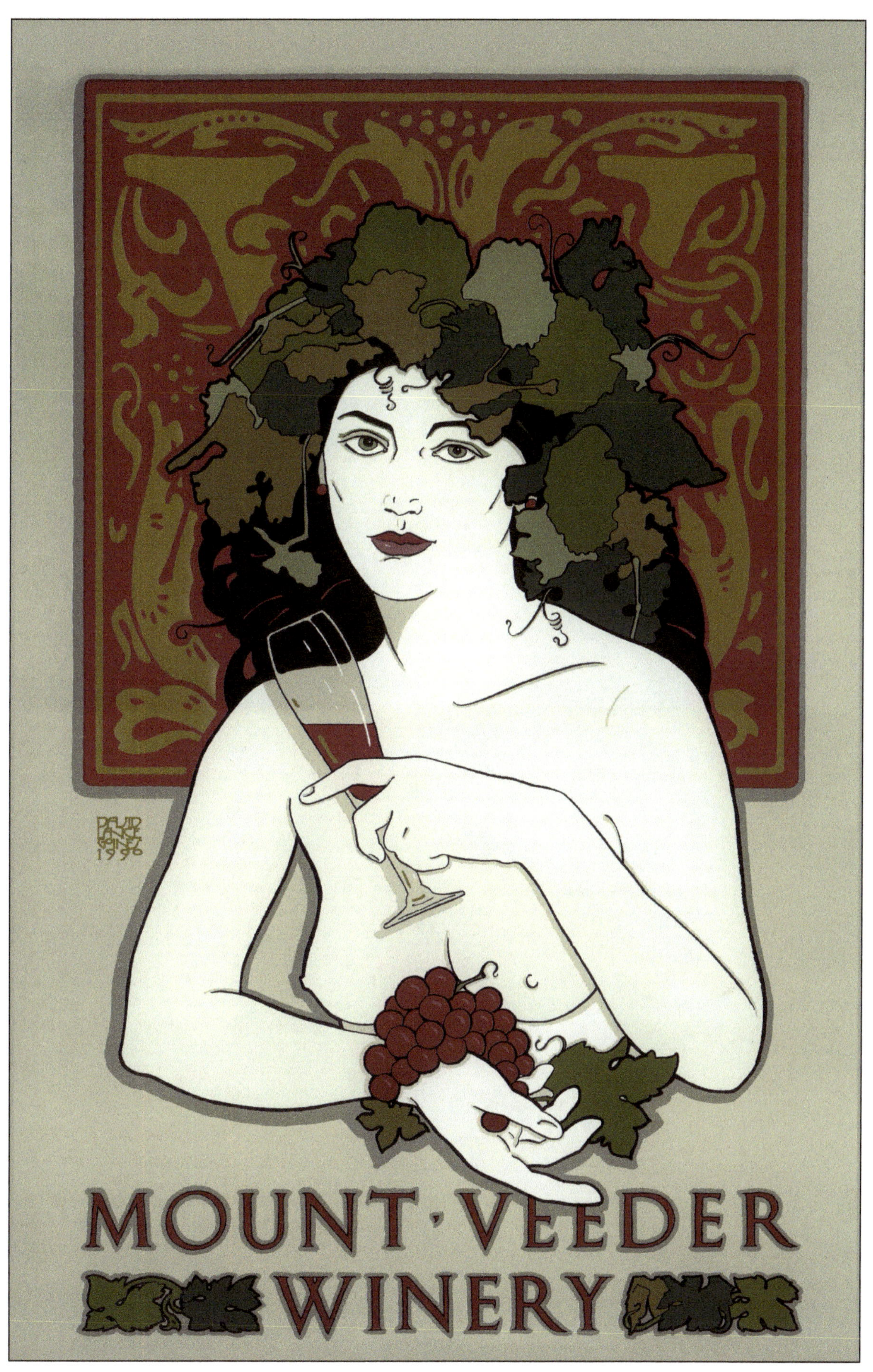

82. Mount Veeder Winery, 1990, 15 1/16" × 24"

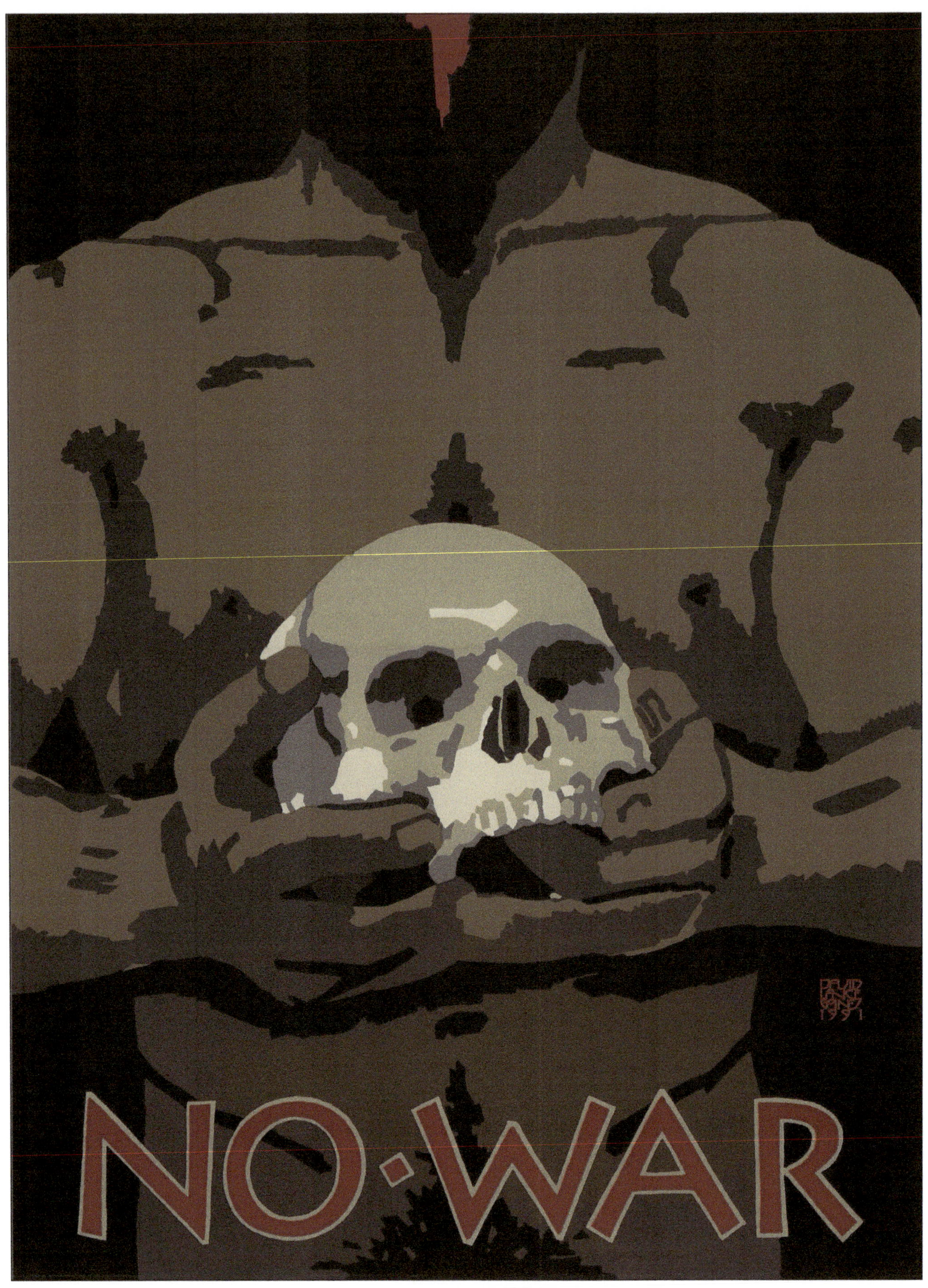

83. No War, 1991, 17" × 24"

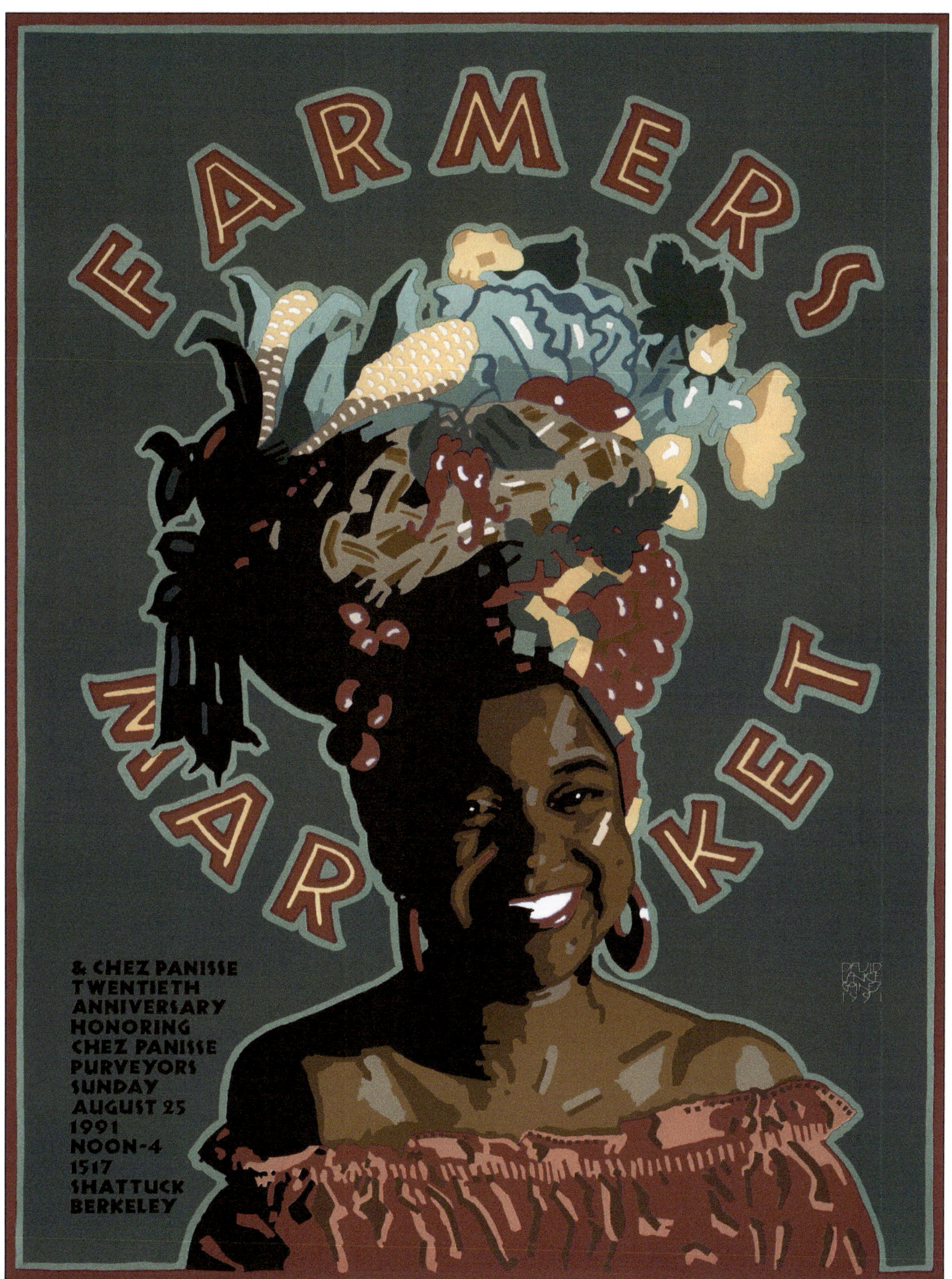

84. Farmers Market (Chez Panisse Twentieth Anniversary), 1991, 17⅝" × 24"

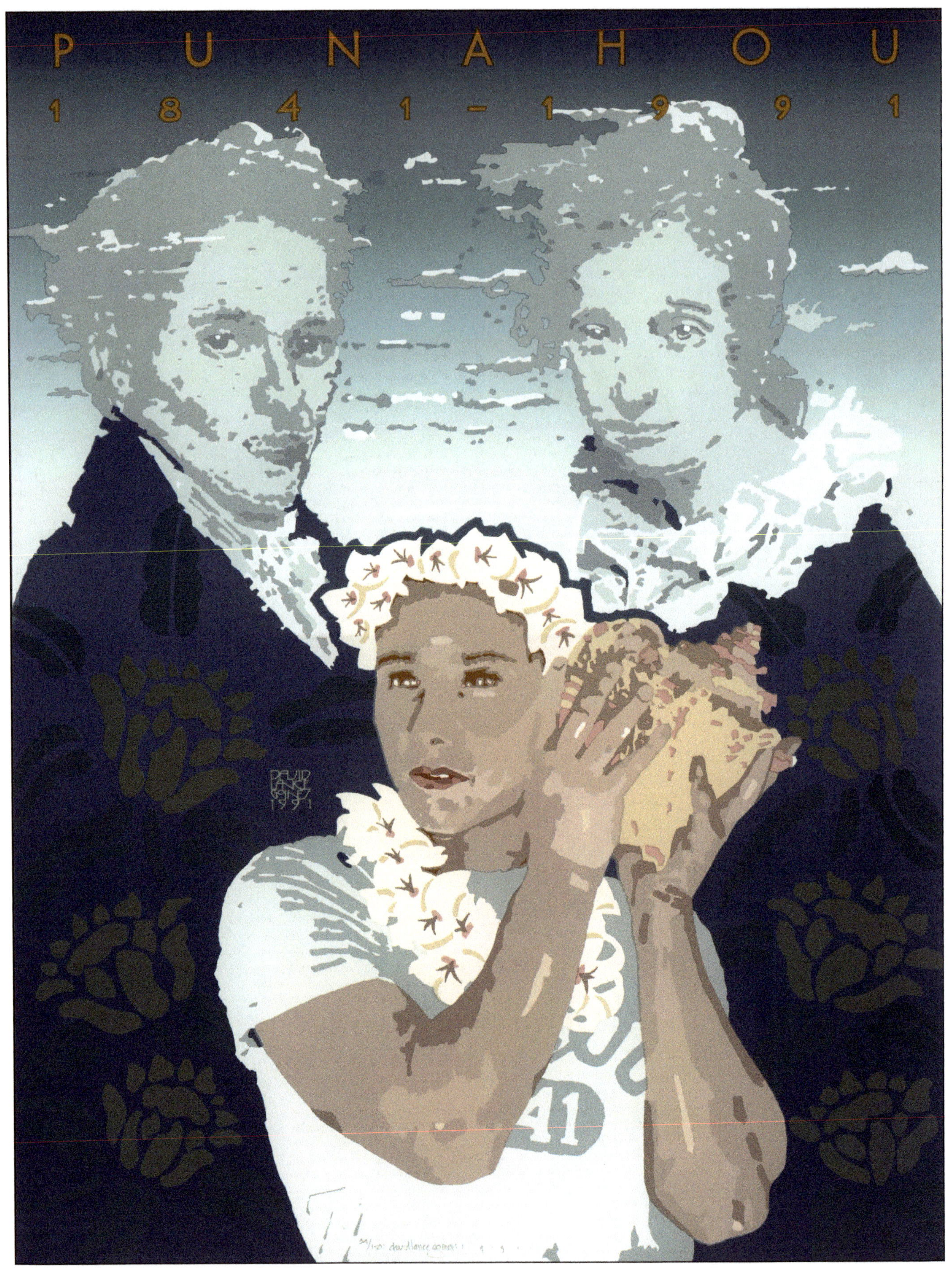

85. Punahou School, 1991, 17⅝" × 24"

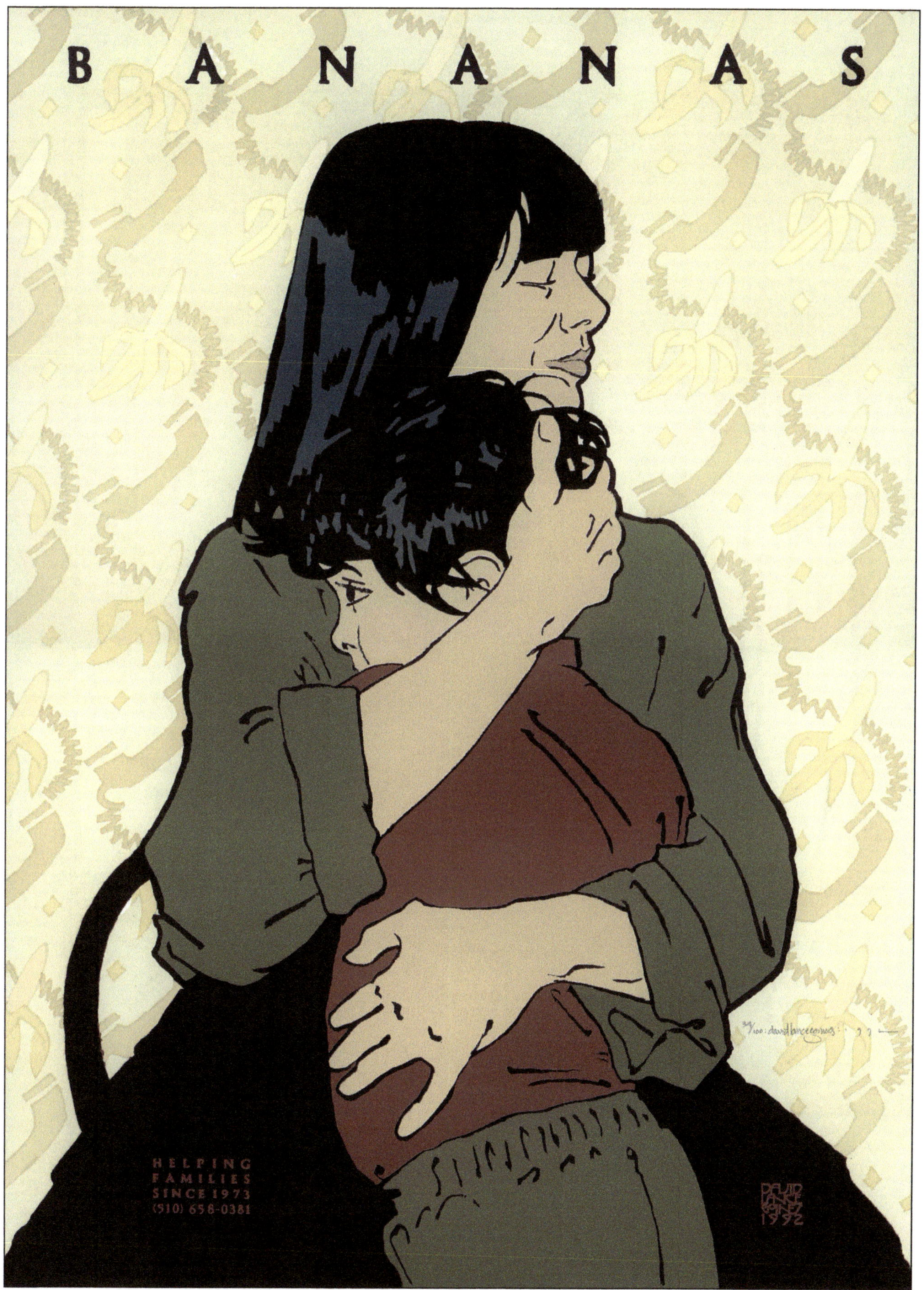

86. Bananas, 1992, 17" × 24"

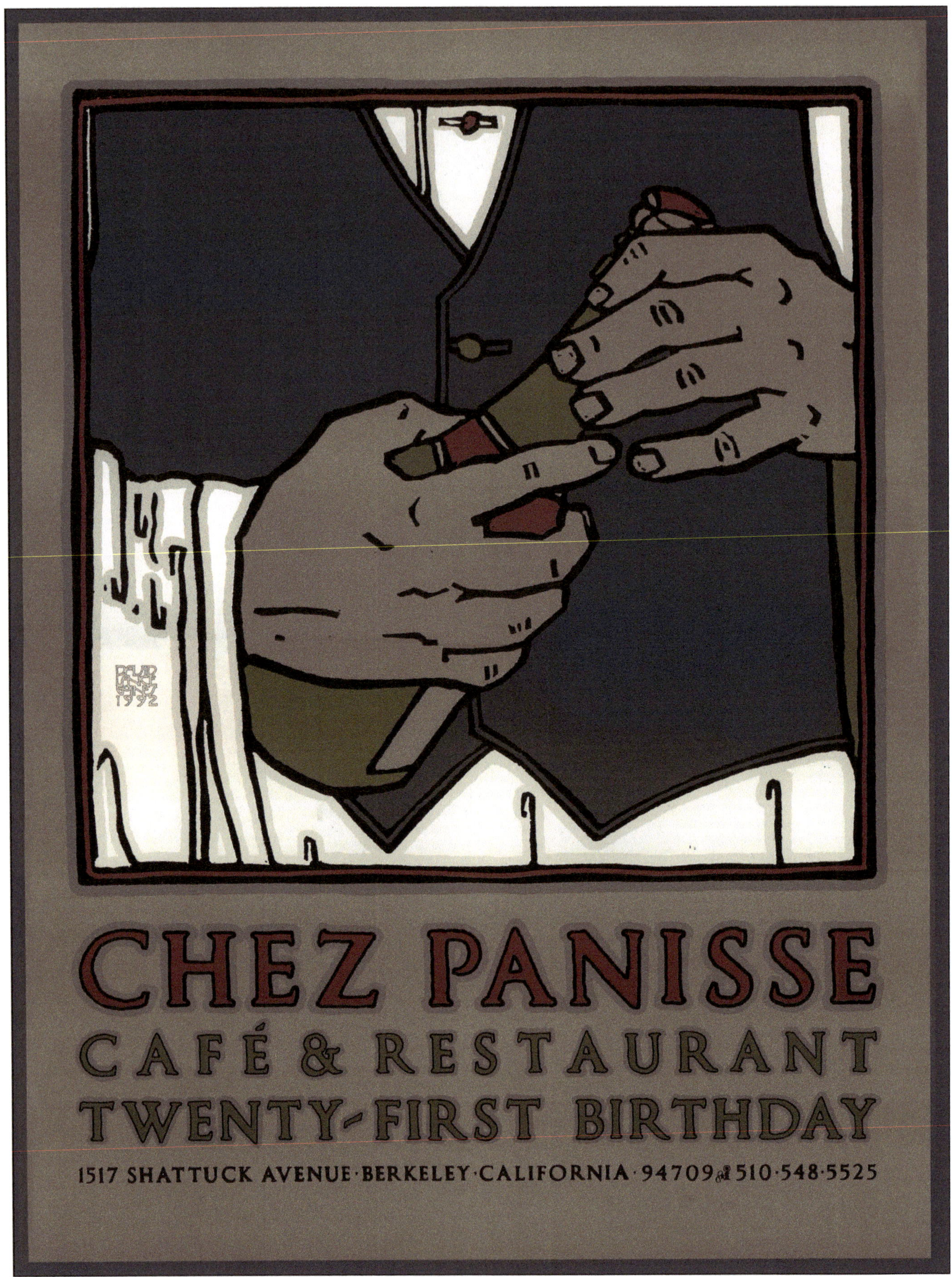

87. Chez Panisse Twenty-First Birthday, 1992, 17½" × 24"

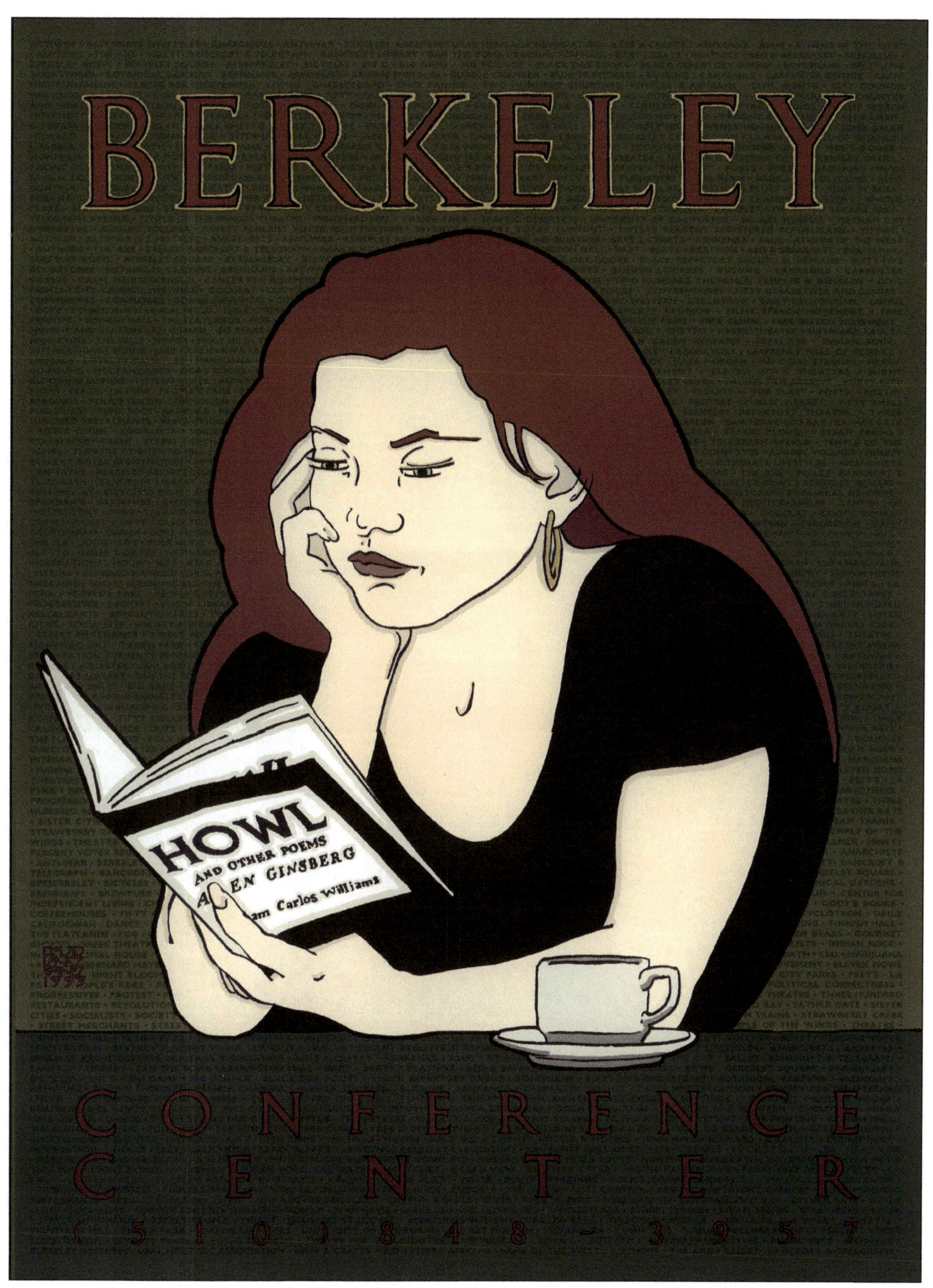

88. Berkeley Conference Center, 1993, 17⅜" × 24"

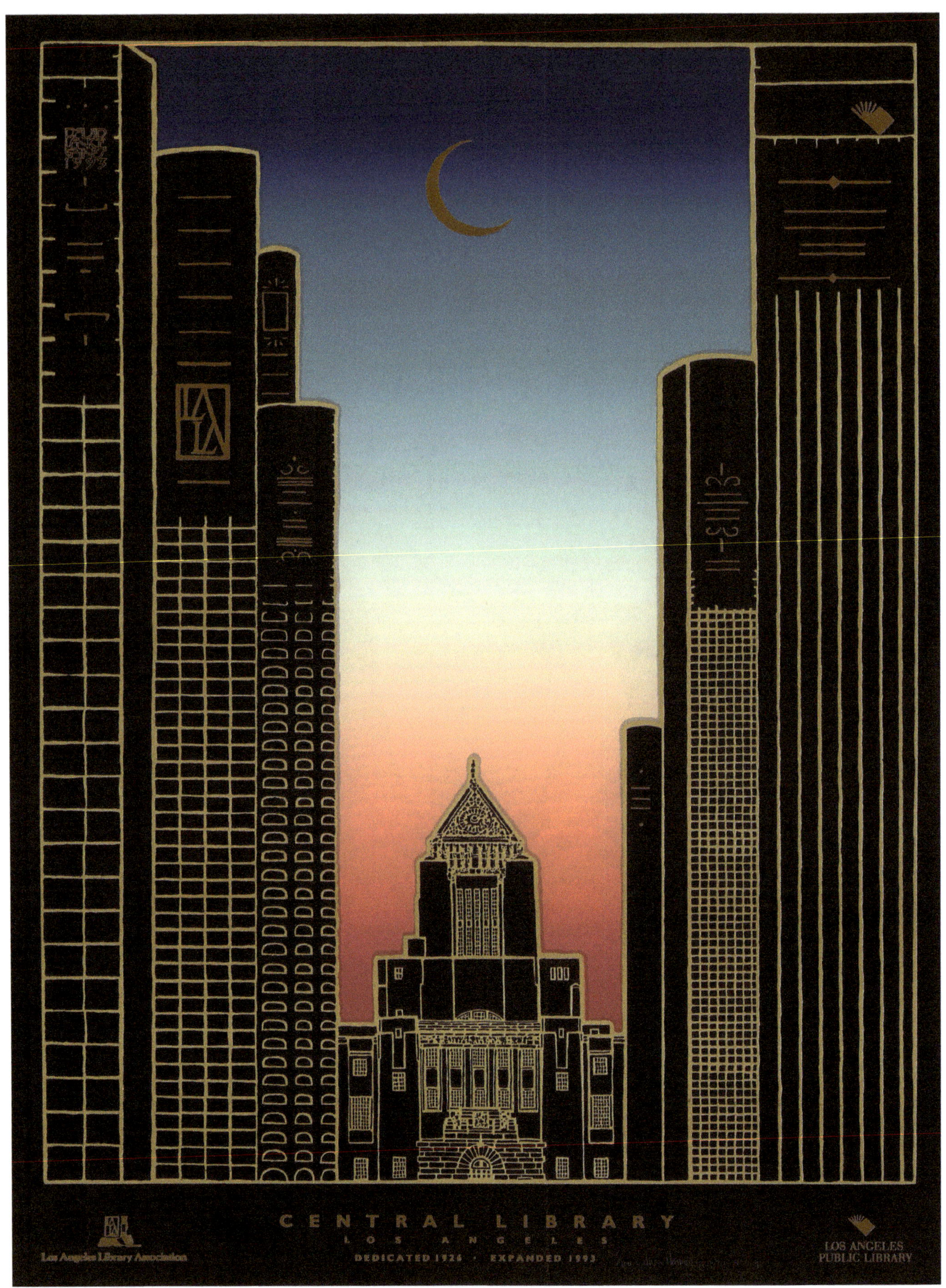

89. Central Library, Los Angeles, 1993, 17¼" × 24"

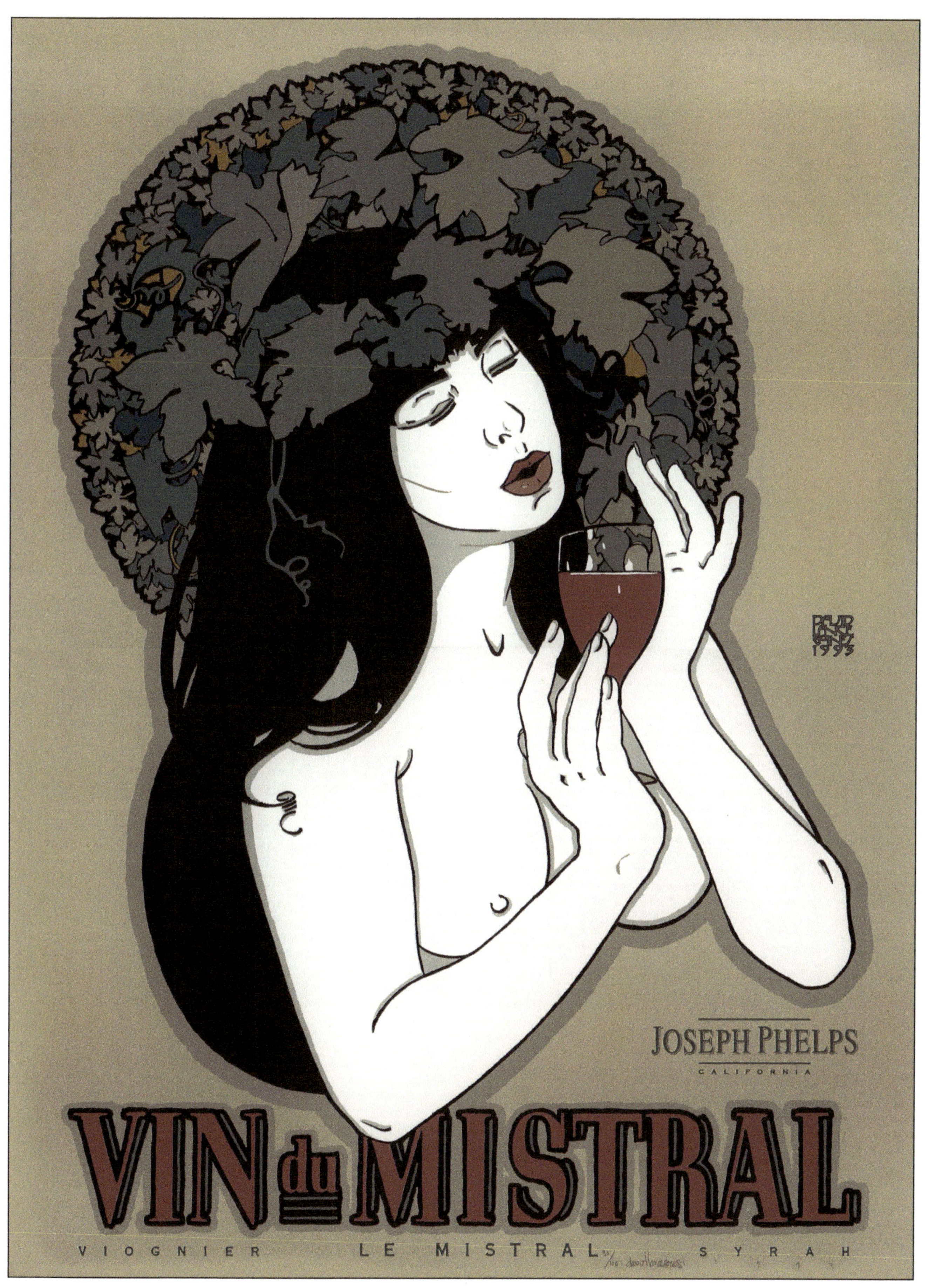

90. Vin du Mistral, 1993, 17½" × 24"

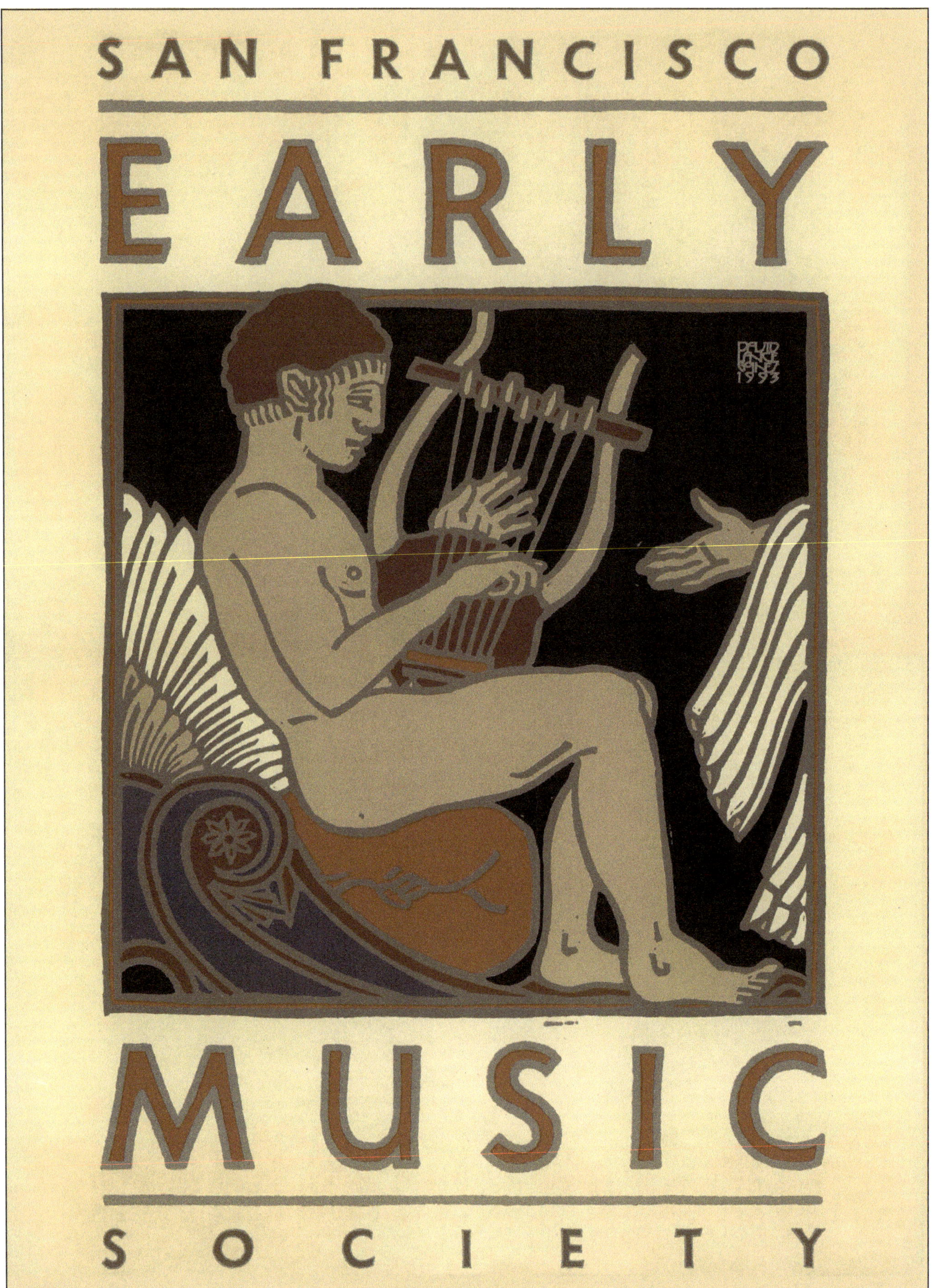

91. Early Music, 1993, 17⅛" × 24"

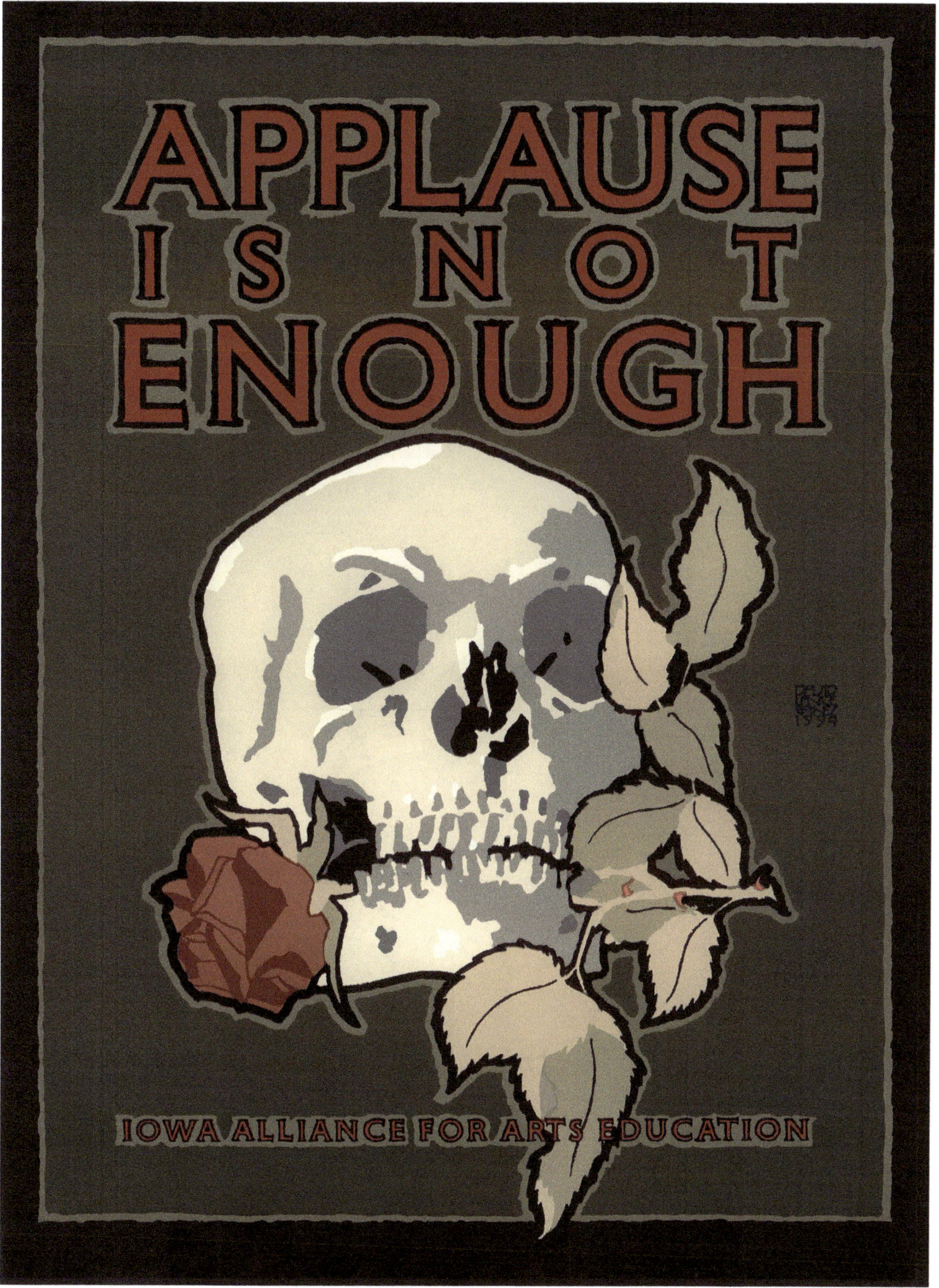

92. Applause Is Not Enough, 1994, 17⅜" × 24"

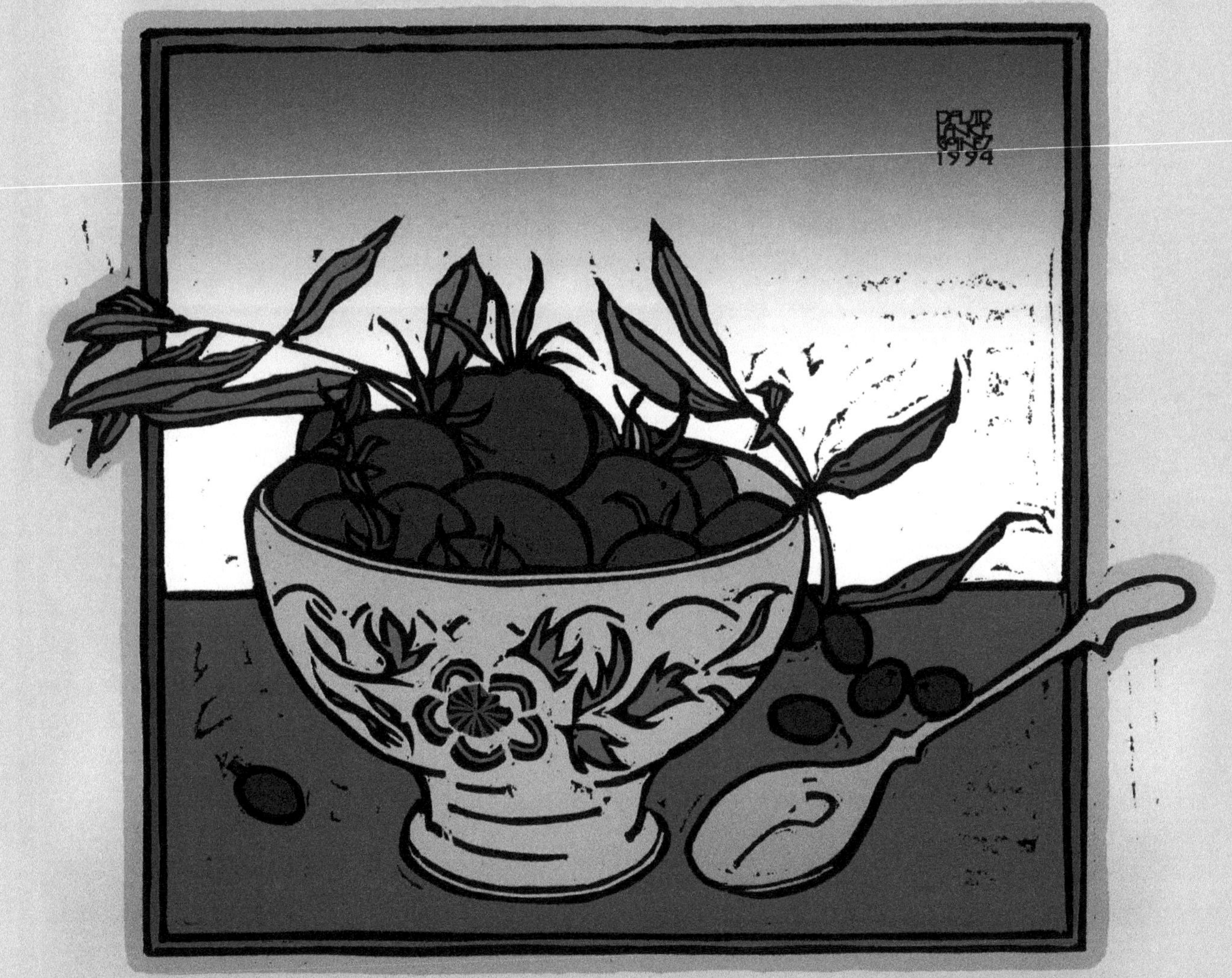

93. Chez Panisse Café Restaurant, 1994, 17⅛" × 24"

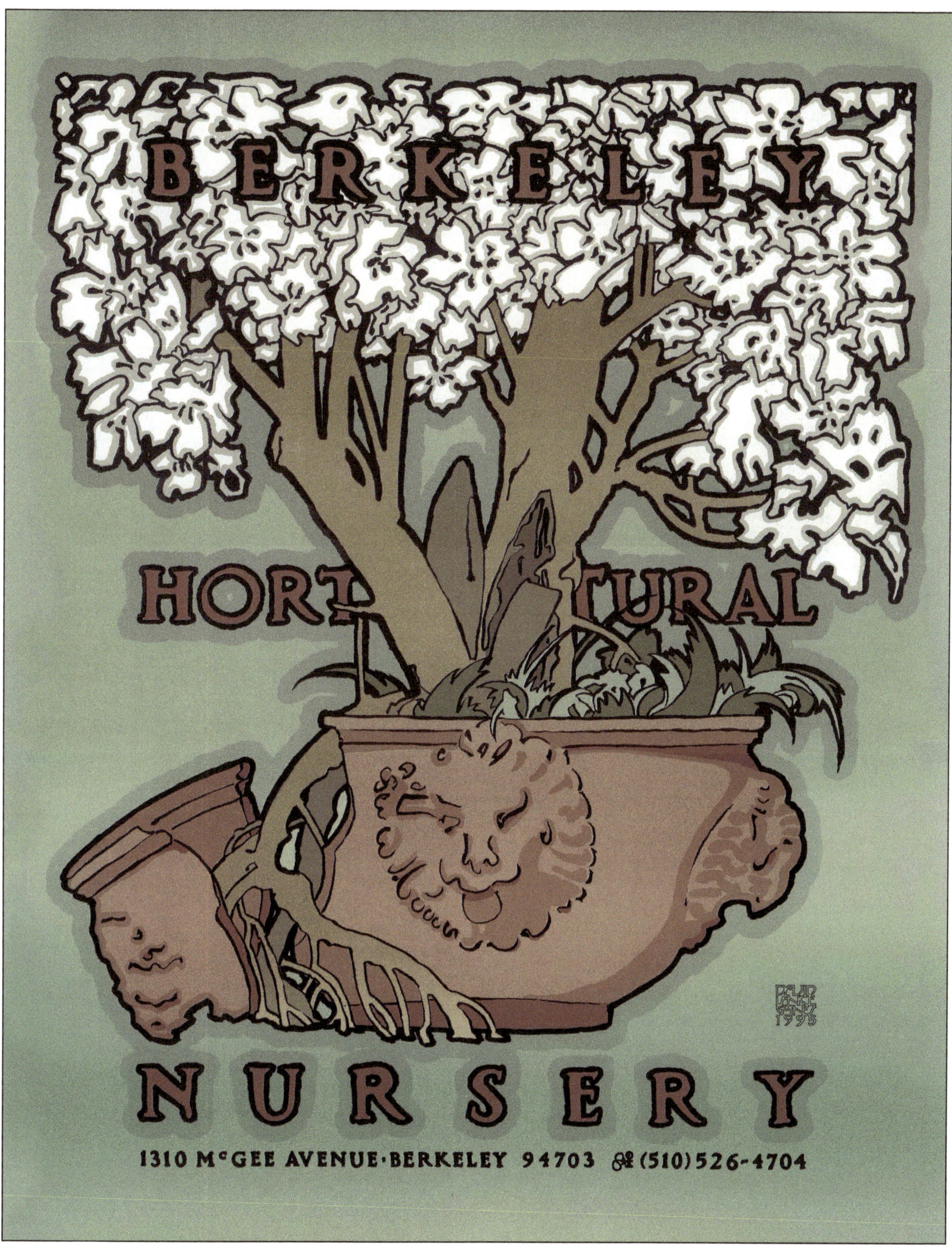

94. Berkeley Horticultural Nursery, 1995, 17⅛" × 24"

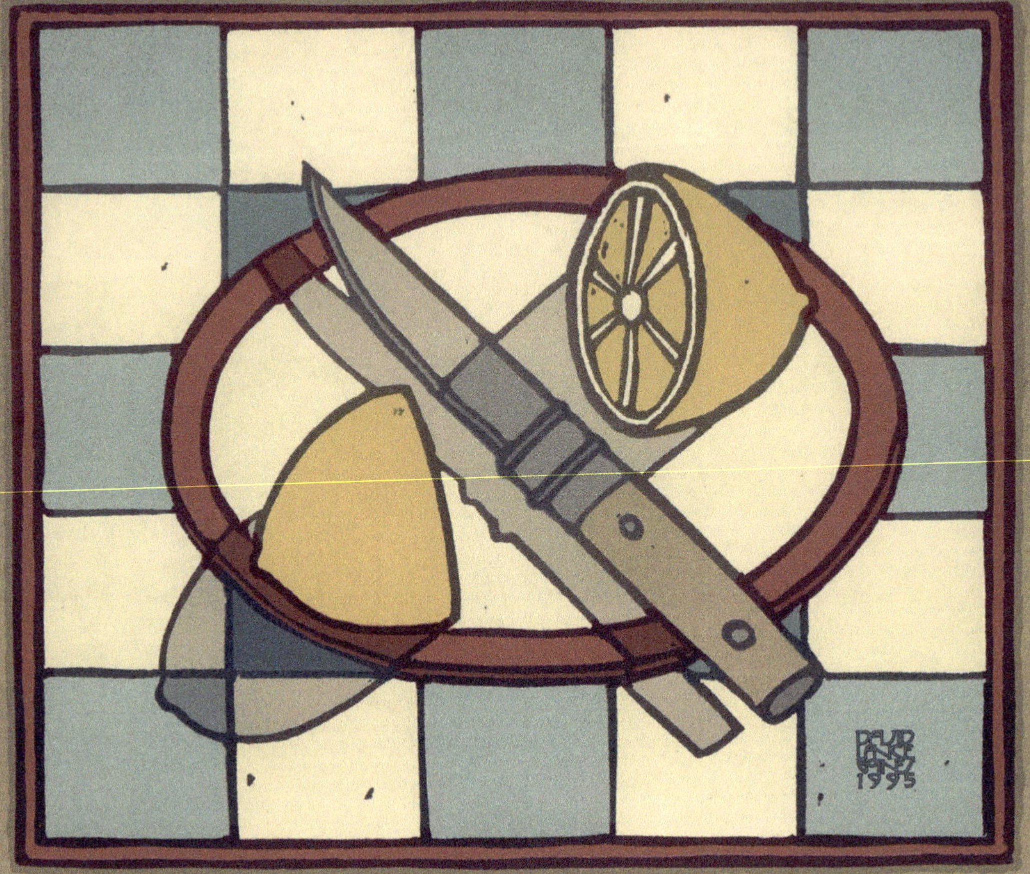

95. Chez Panisse Café Restaurant (Desserts), 1995, 17⅛" × 24"

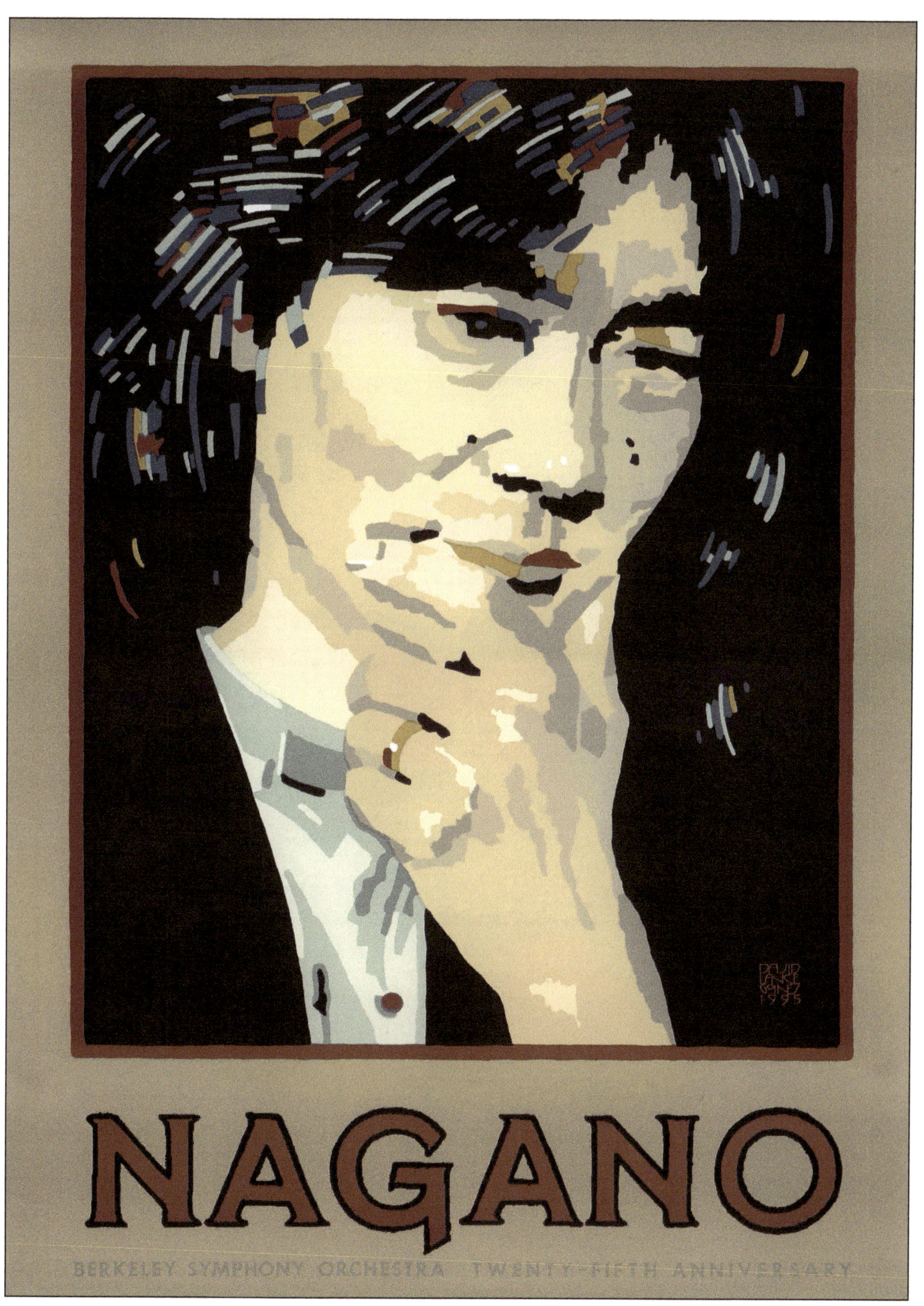

96. Nagano (Berkeley Symphony Orchestra Twenty-Fifth Anniversary), 1995, 16¾" × 24"

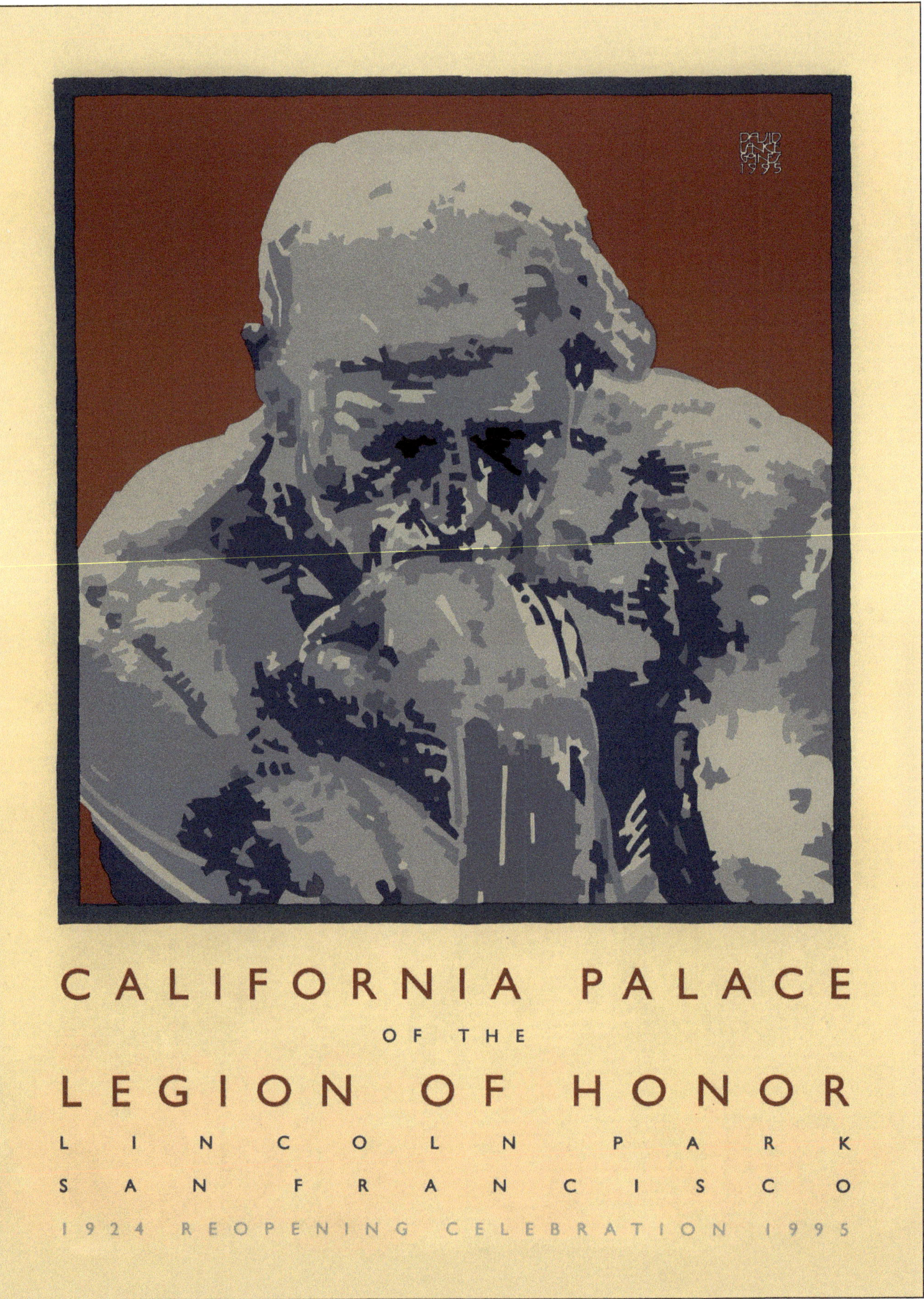

97. California Palace of the Legion of Honor, 1995, 17" × 24"

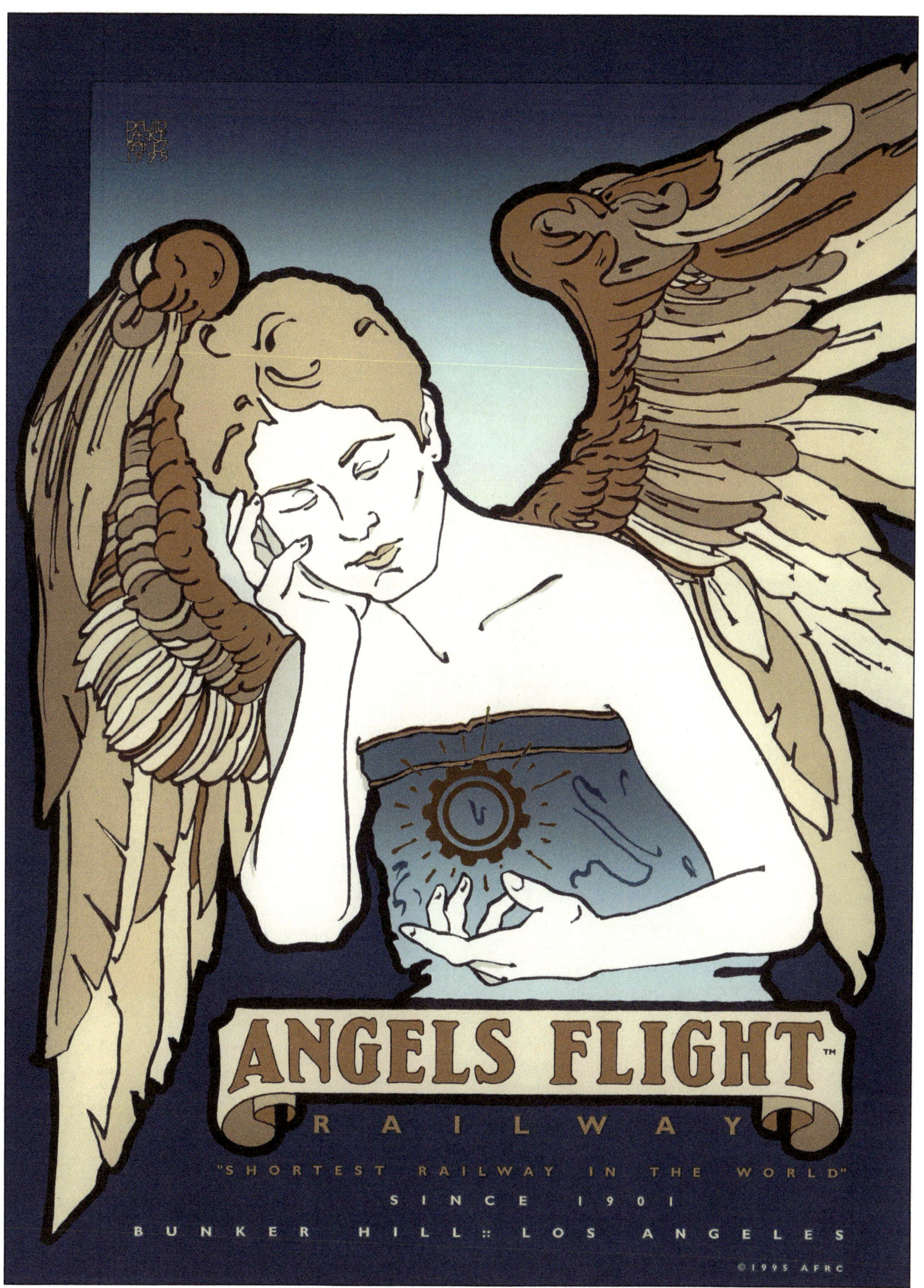

98. Angels Flight, 1996, 17" × 24"

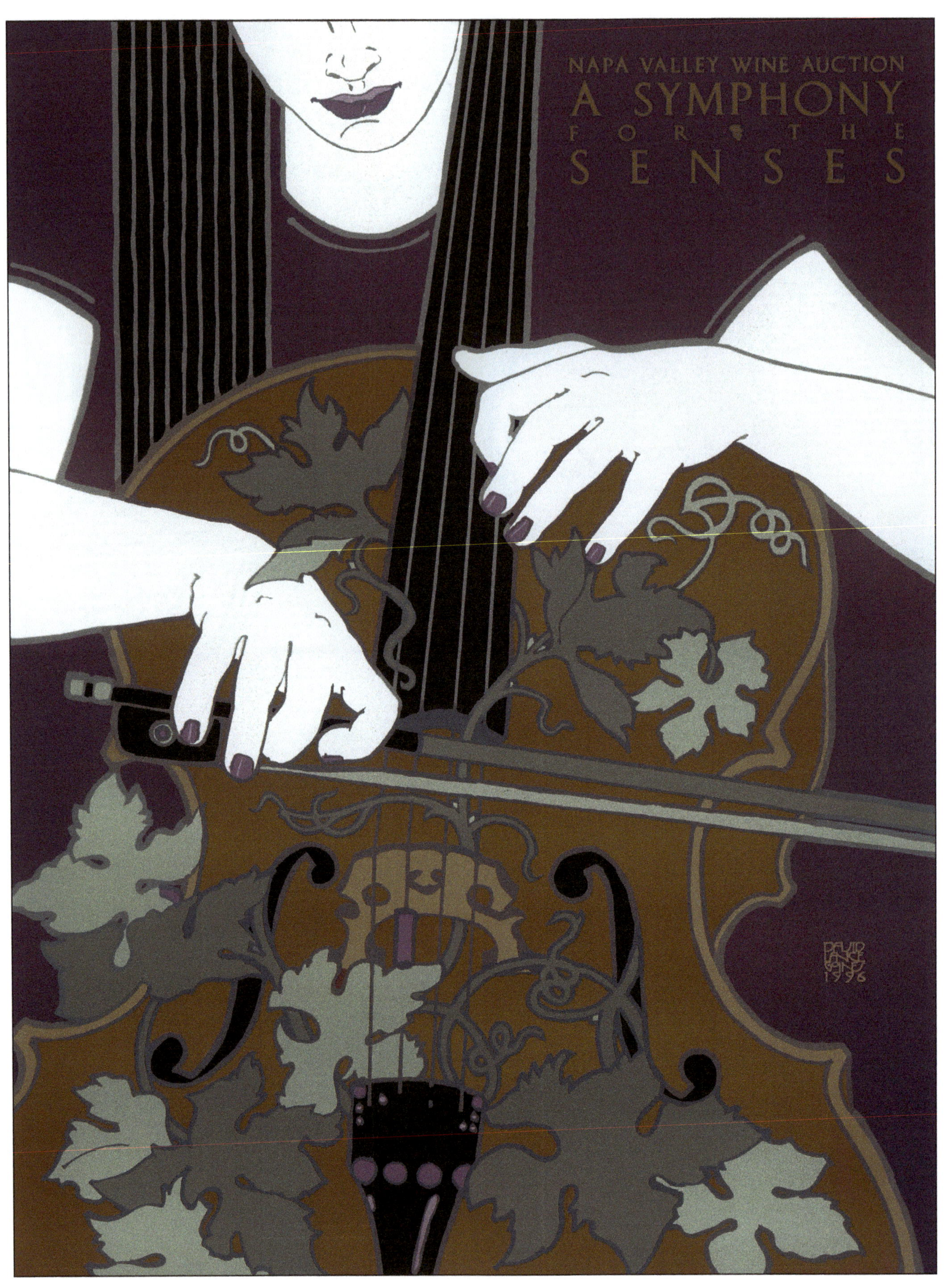

99. Napa Valley Wine Auction (A Symphony for the Senses), 1996, 17½" × 24"

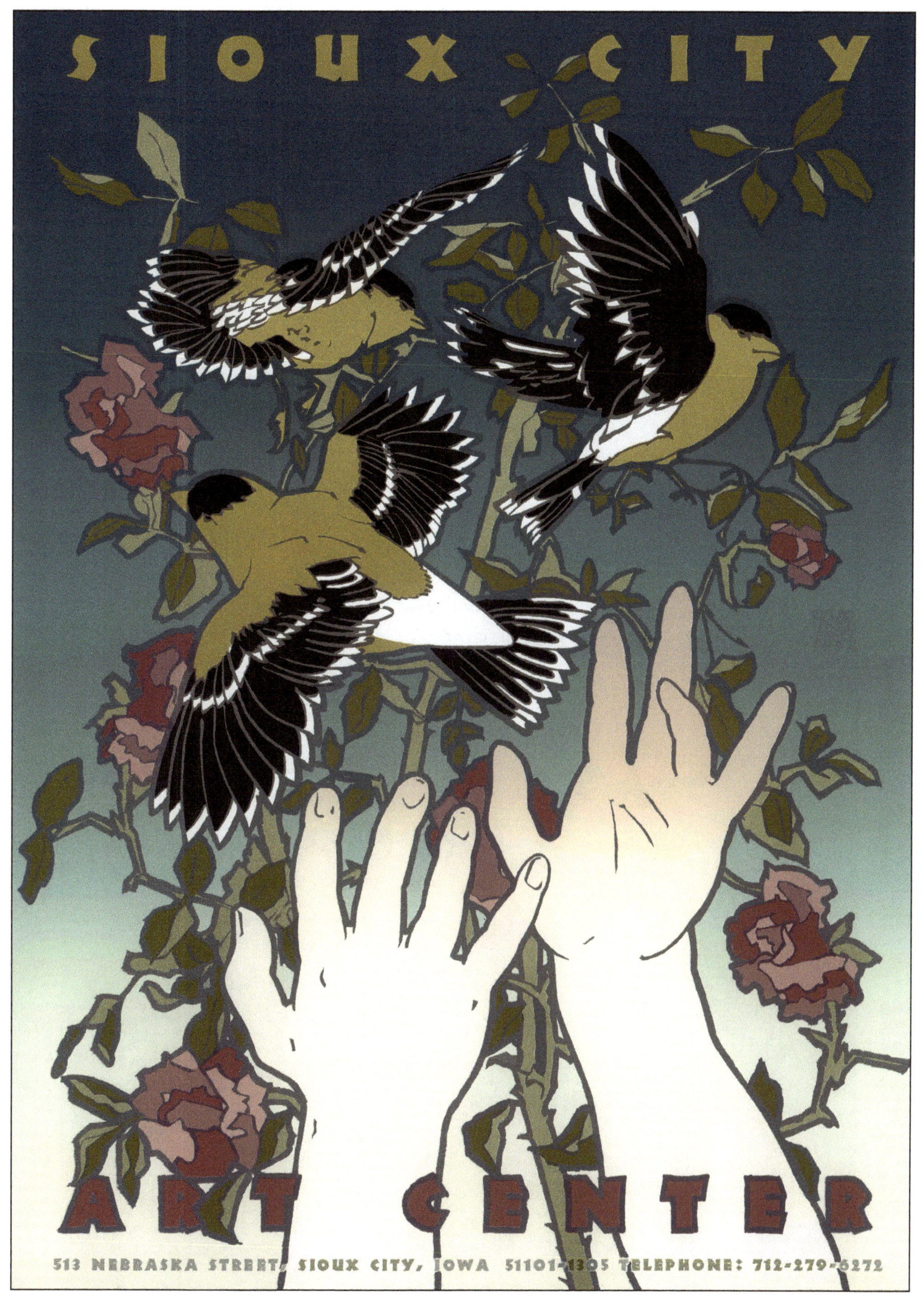

100. Sioux City Art Center, 1996, 16⅞" × 24"

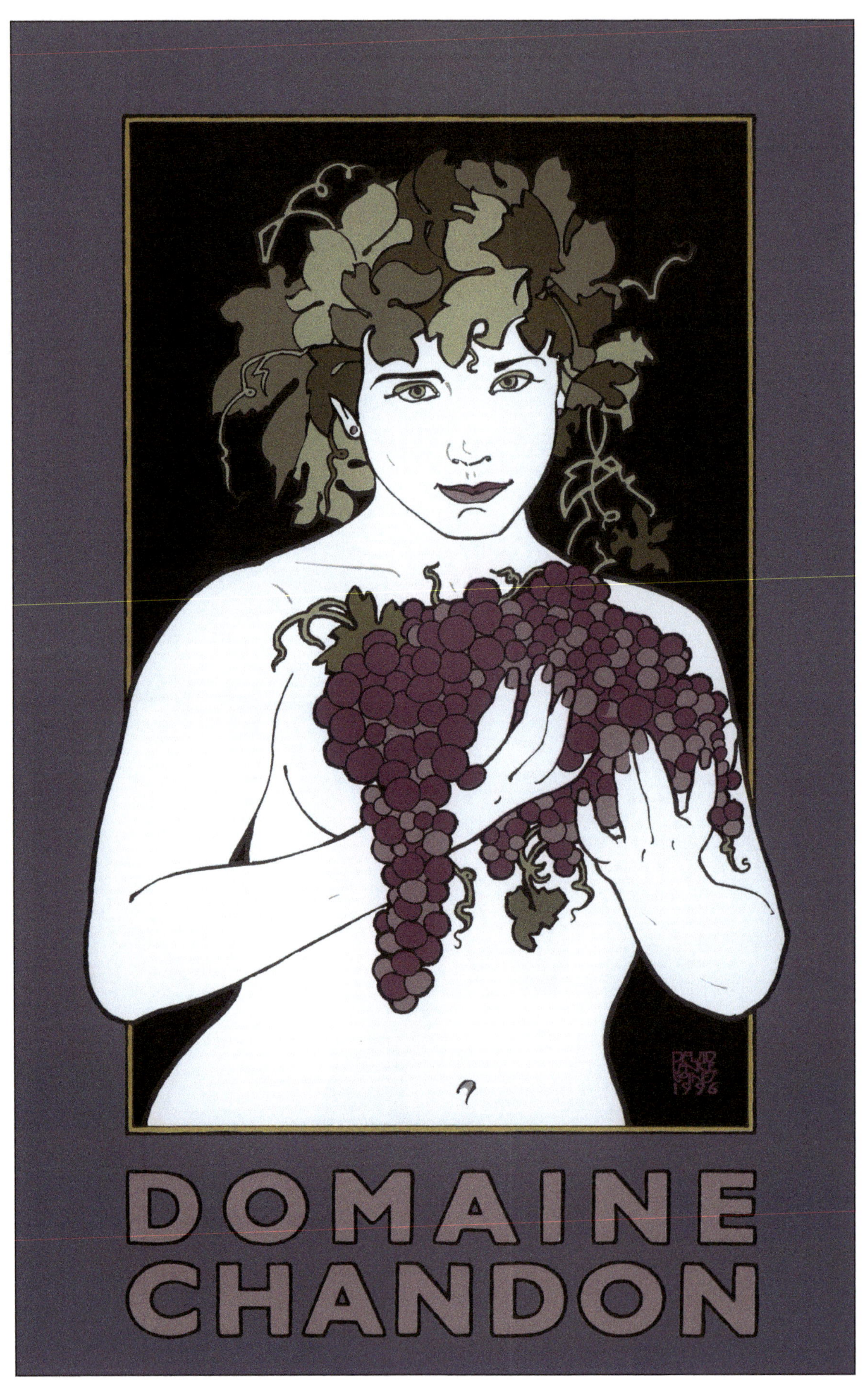

101. Domaine Chandon, 1996, 14⅞" × 24"

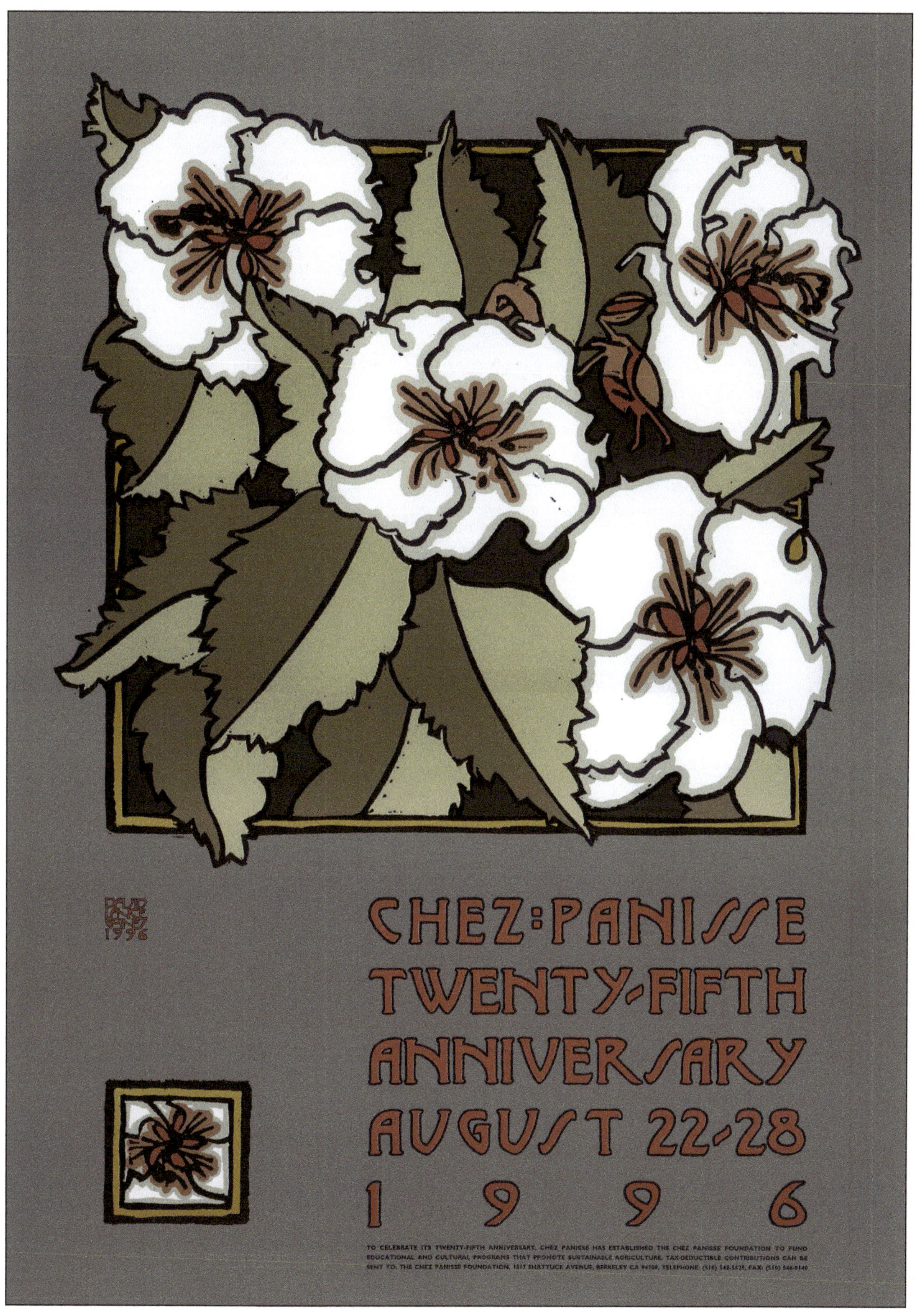

102. Chez Panisse Twenty-Fifth Anniversary, 1996, 16¾" × 24"

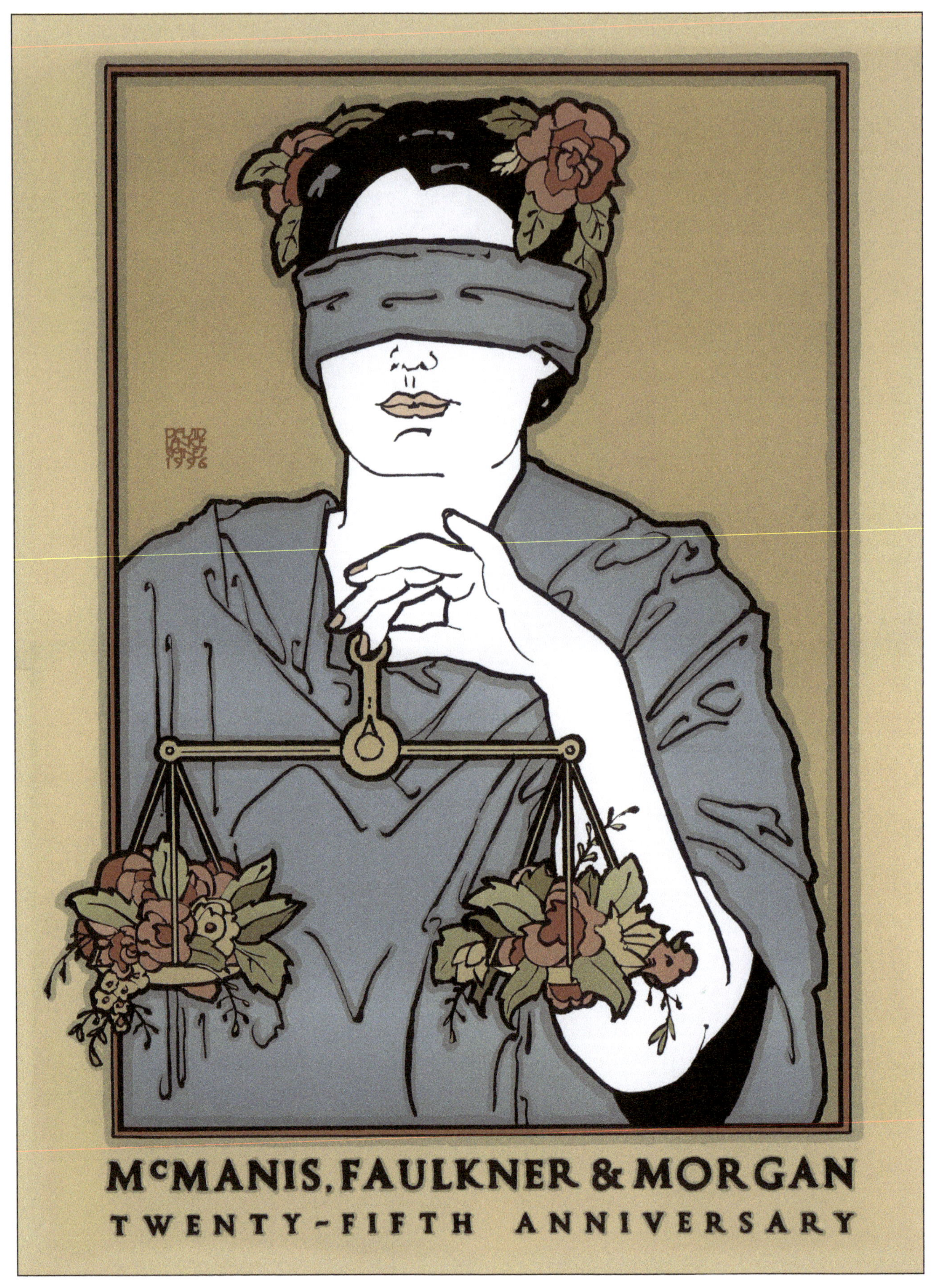

103. McManis, Faulkner & Morgan, 1996, 17⅜" × 24"

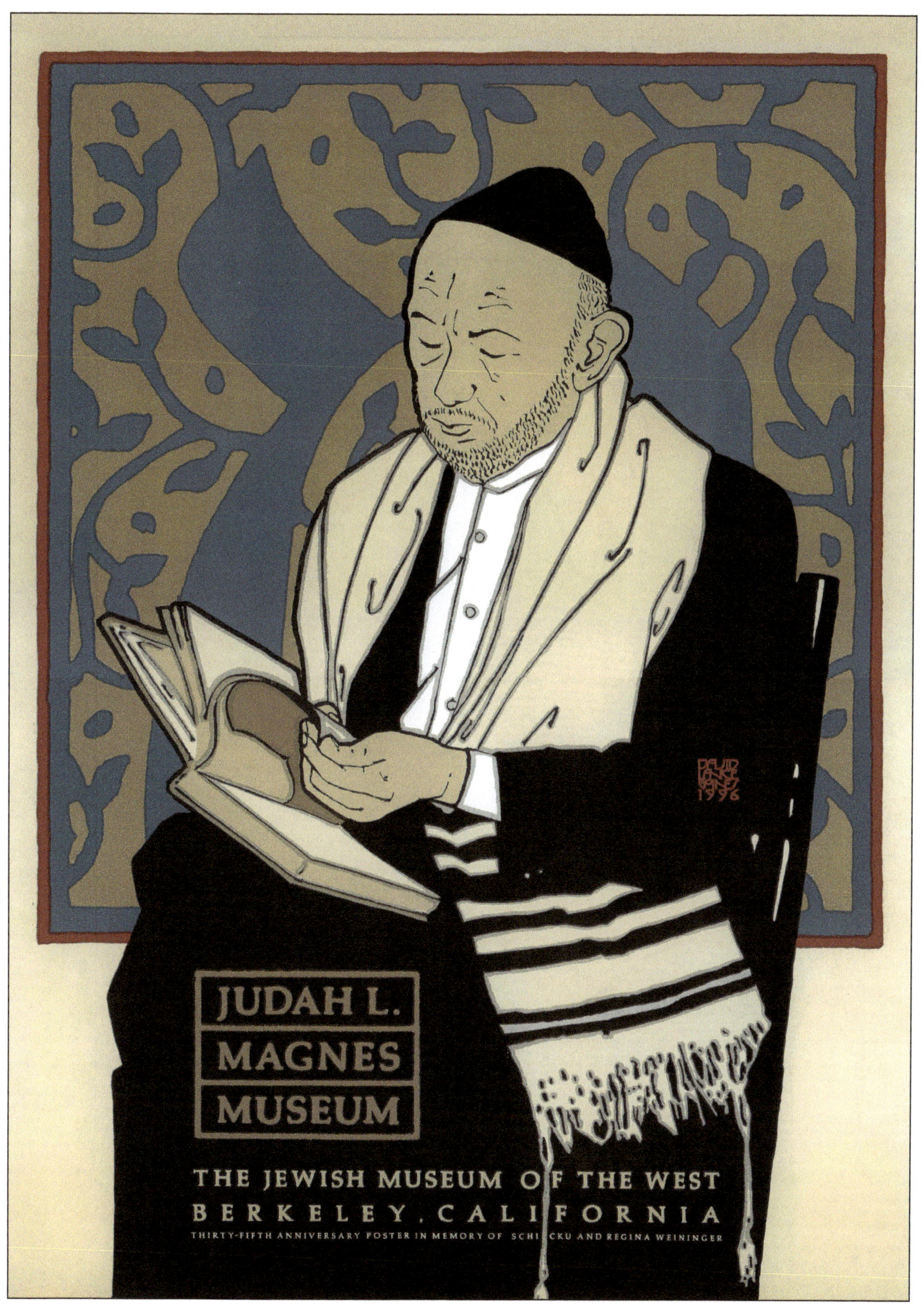

104. Judah L. Magnes Museum, 1997, 17⅛" × 24"

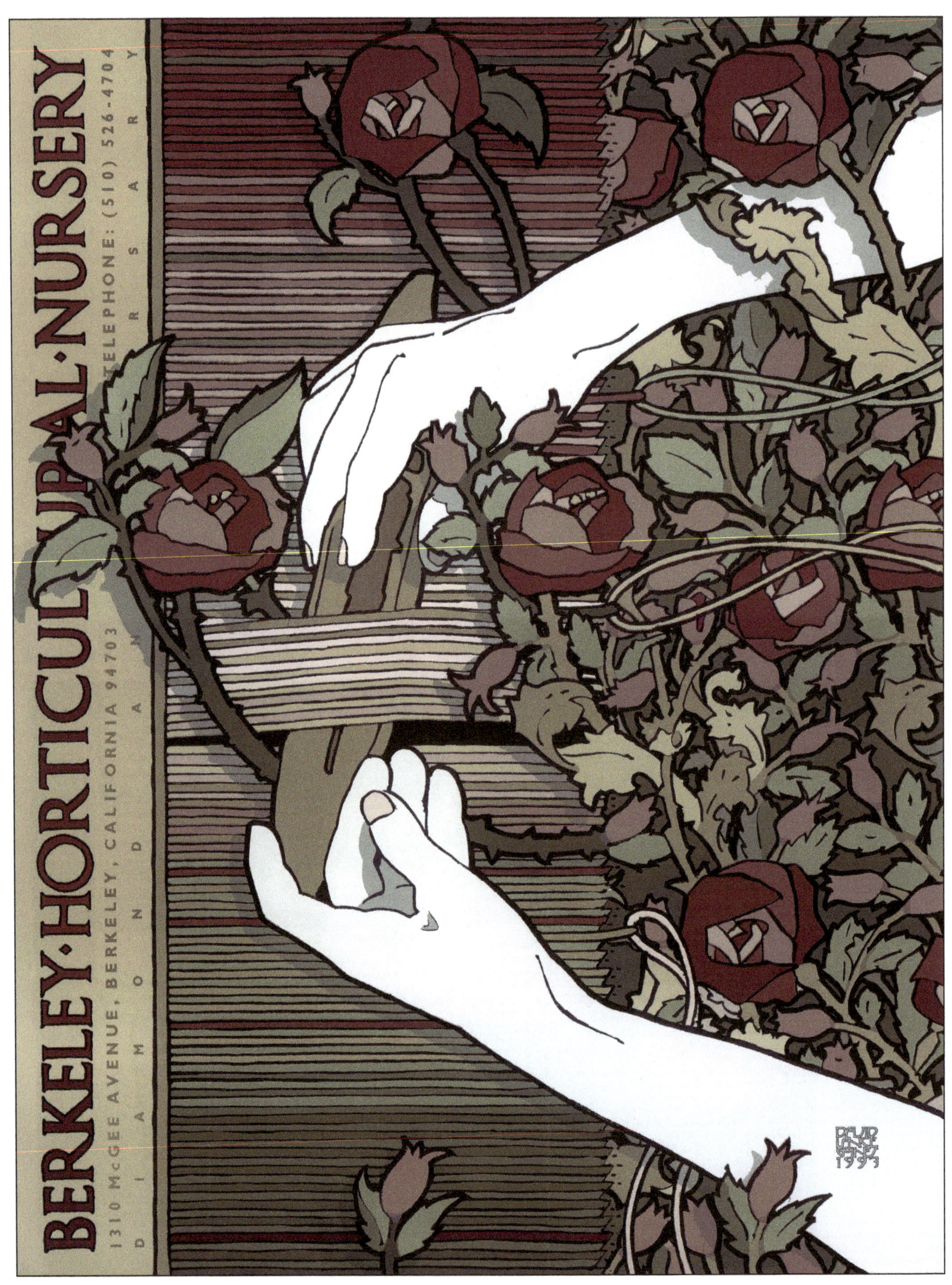

105. Berkeley Horticultural Nursery Diamond Anniversary, 1997, 17½" × 24"

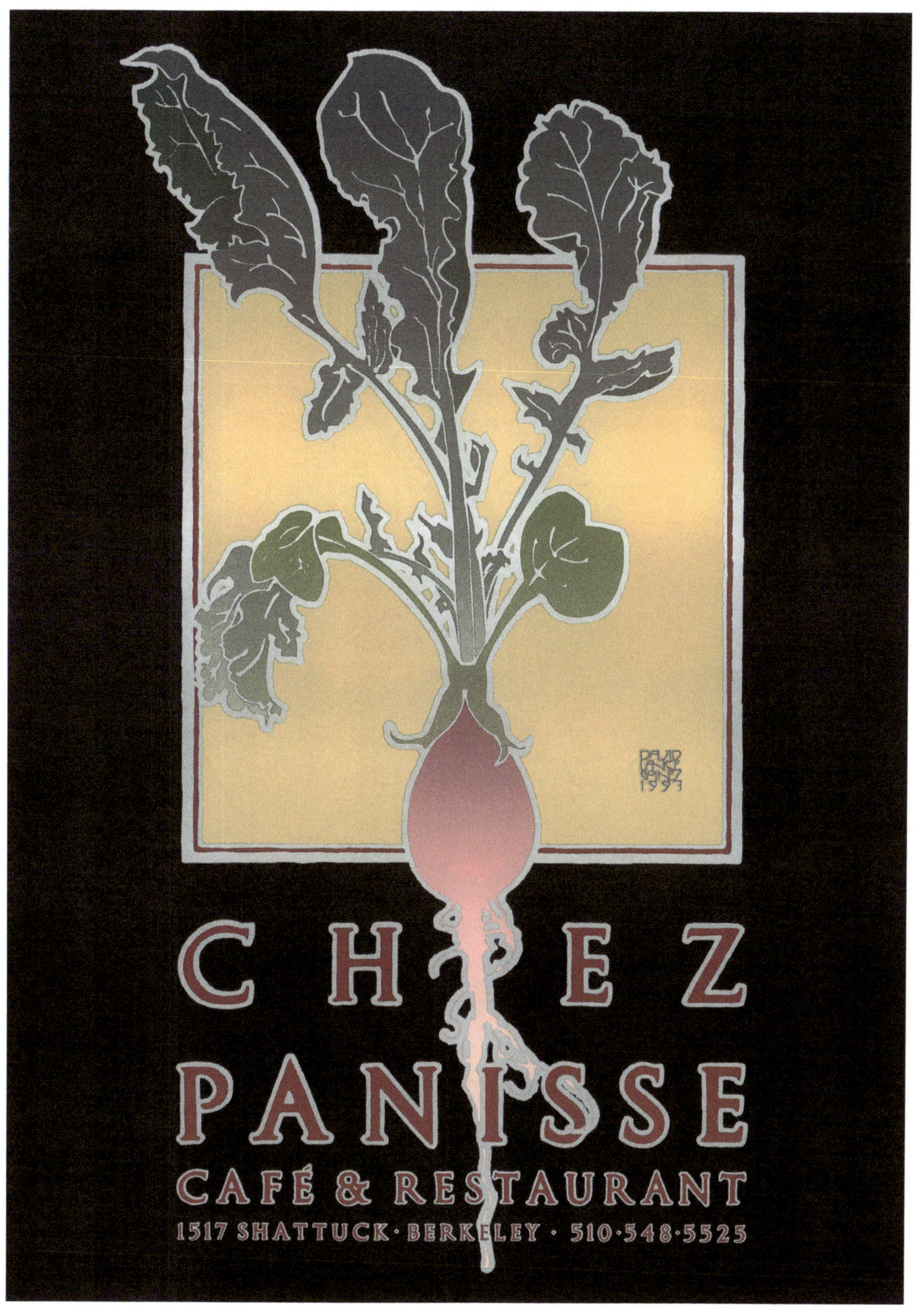

106. Chez Panisse Twenty-Sixth Anniversary, 1997, 16¾" × 24"

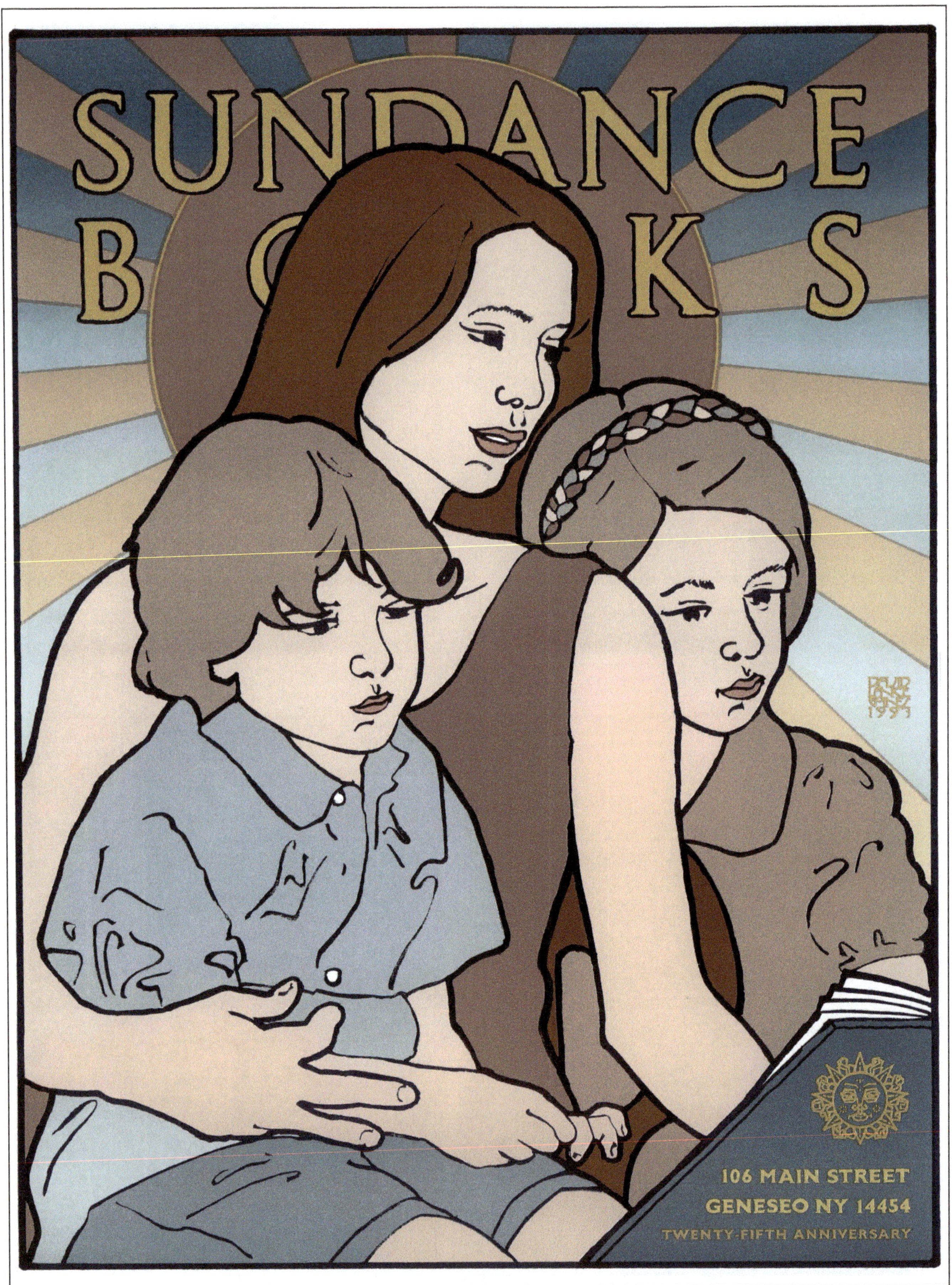

107. Sundance Books, 1997, 18" × 24"

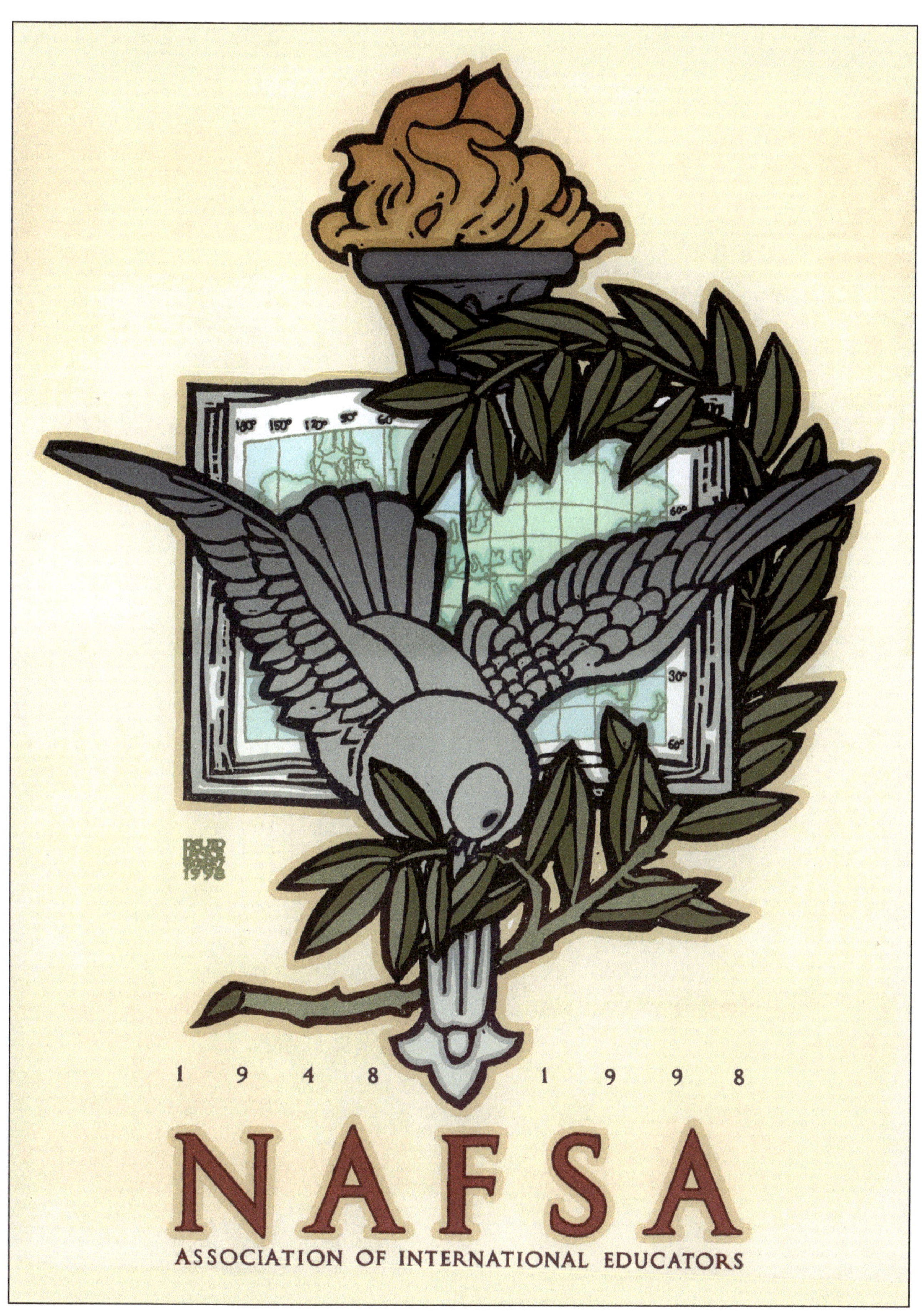

108. NAFSA (Association of International Educators), Fiftieth Anniversary, 1998, 17" × 24"

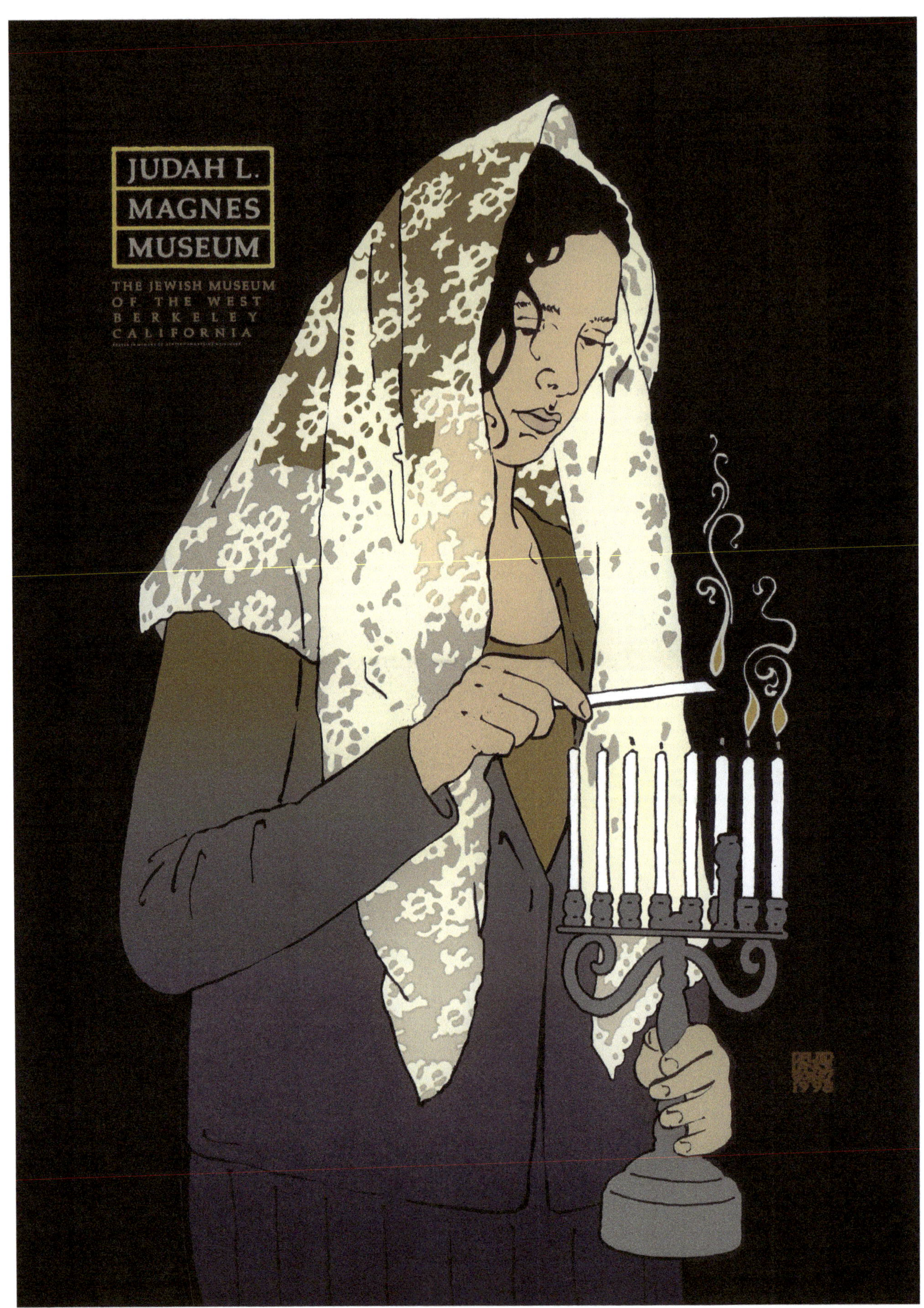

109. Judah L. Magnes Museum, 1998, 17½" × 24"

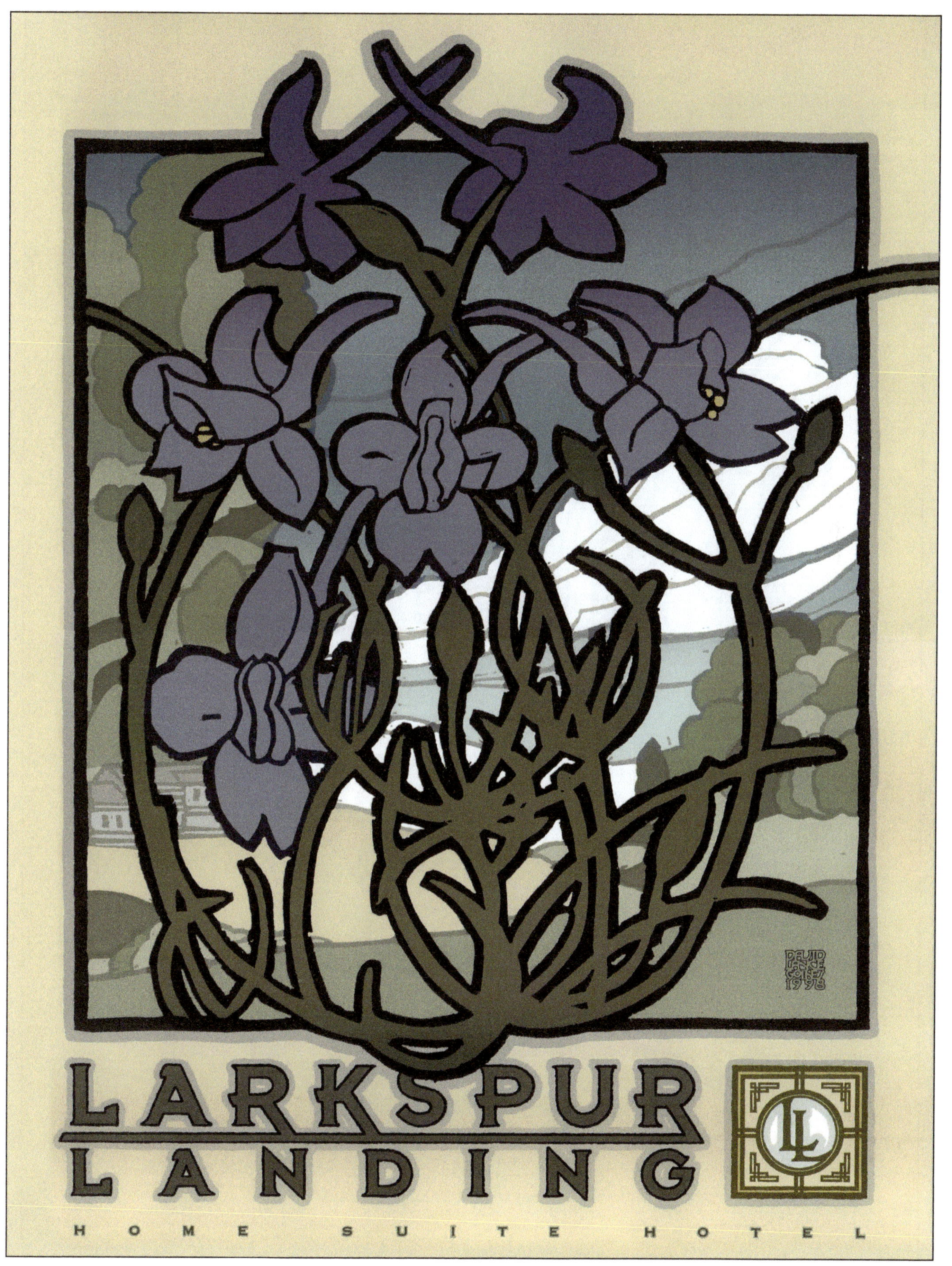

110. Larkspur Landing, 1998, 17½" × 24"

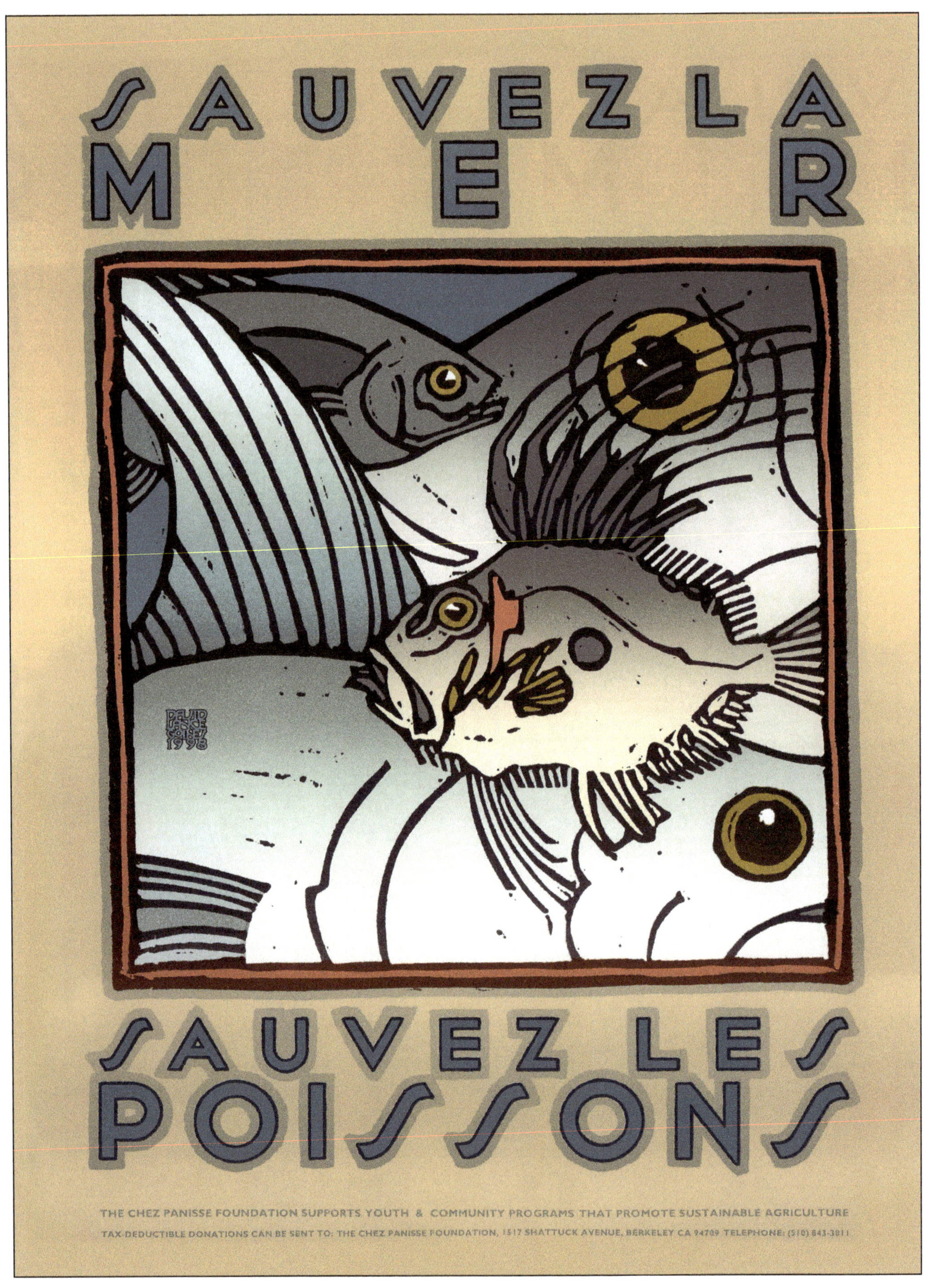

111. Chez Panisse Twenty-Seventh (Sauvez la Mer), 1998, 17½" × 24"

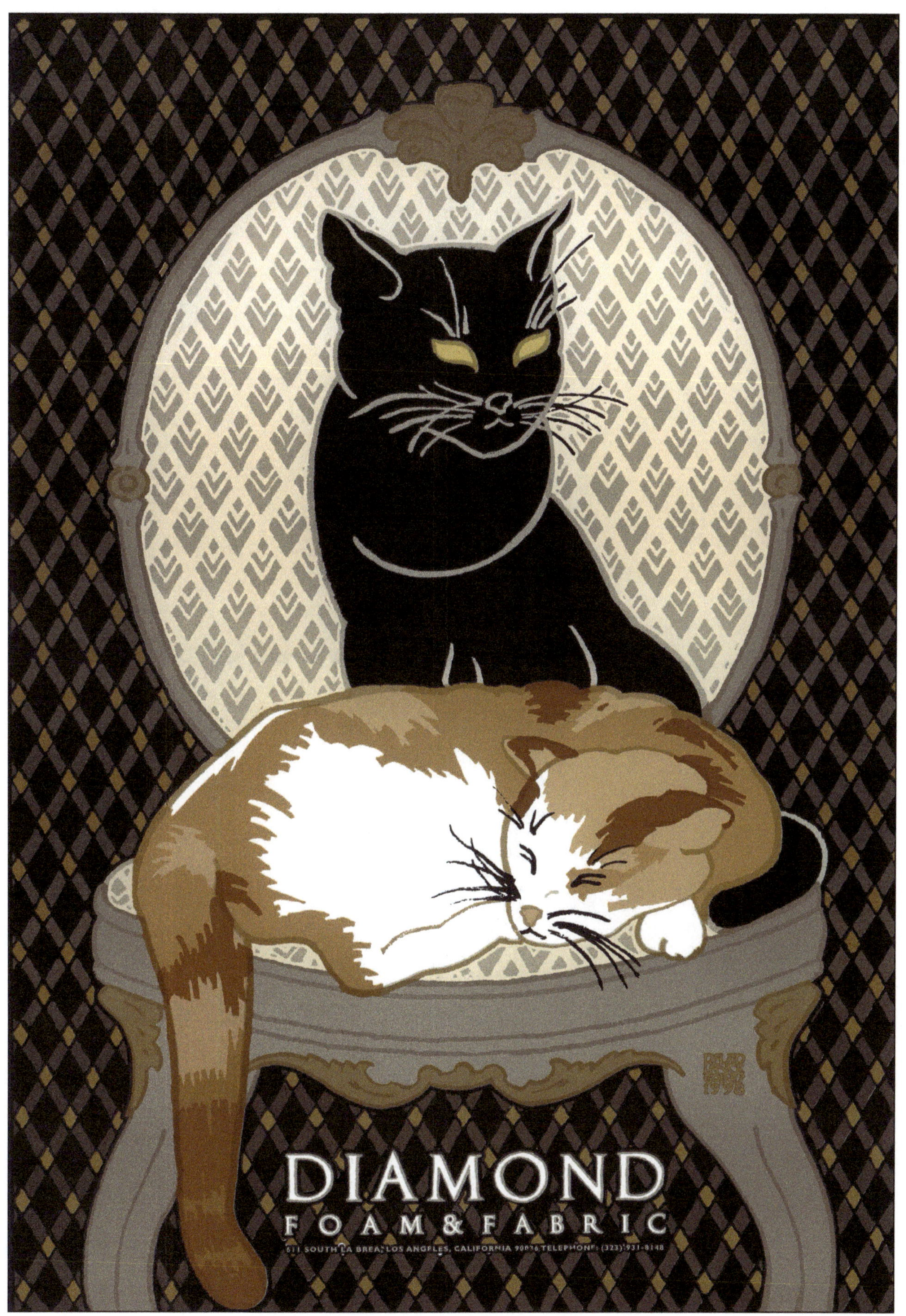

112. Diamond Foam and Fabric, 1998, 16⅜" × 24"

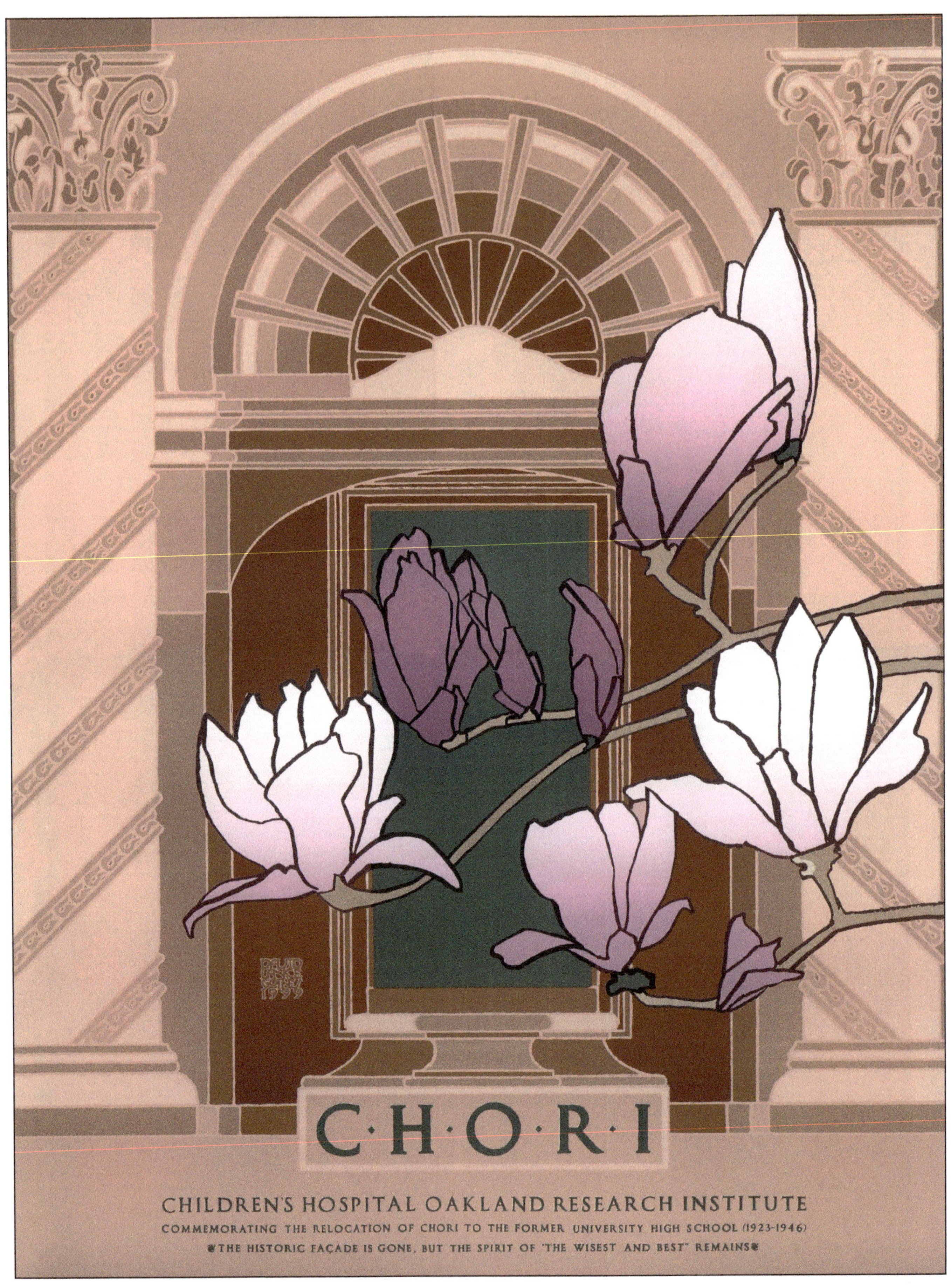

113. CHORI (Children's Hospital Oakland Research Institute), 1999, 17½" × 24"

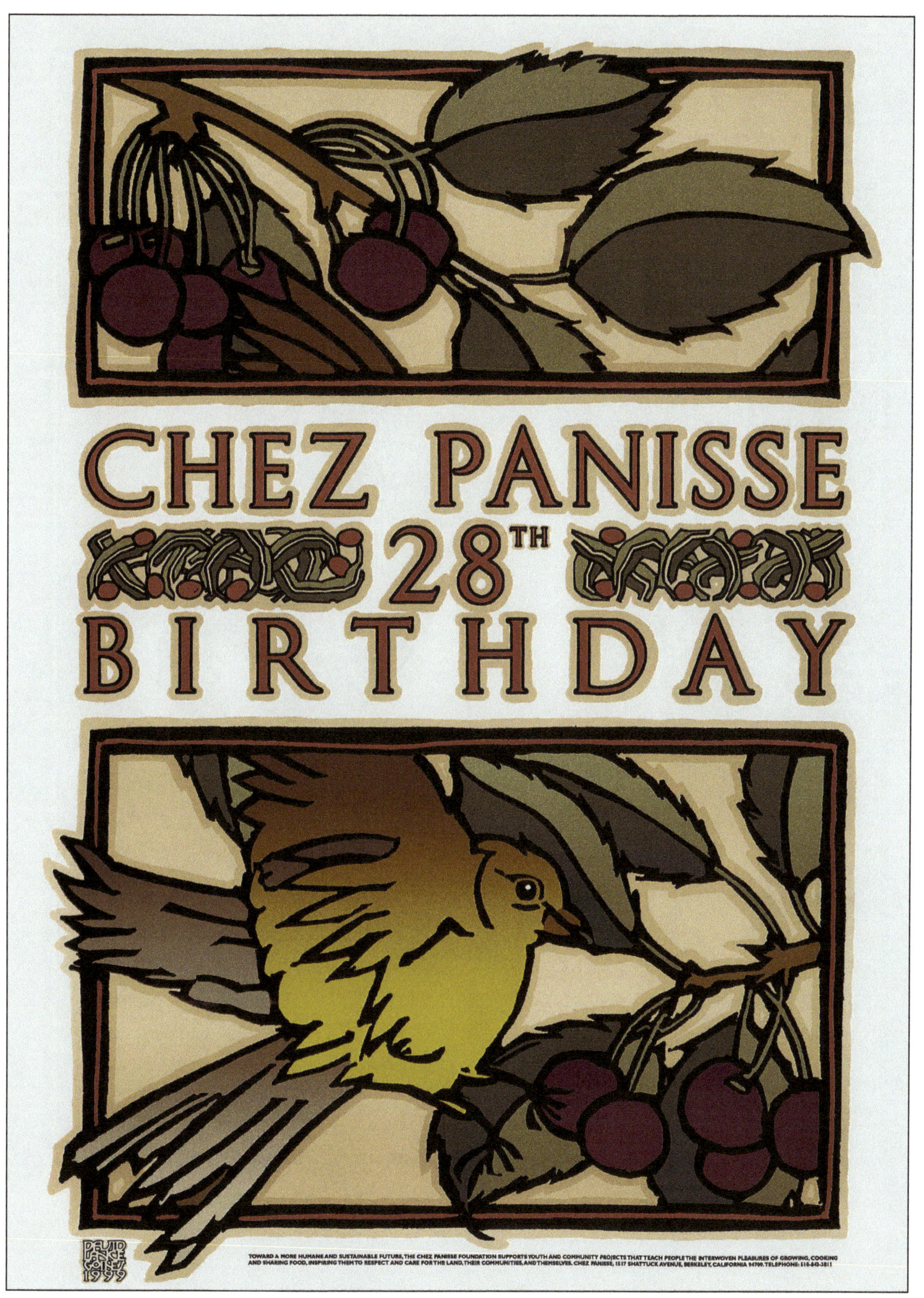

114. Chez Panisse Twenty-Eighth Birthday, 1999, 16⅞" × 24"

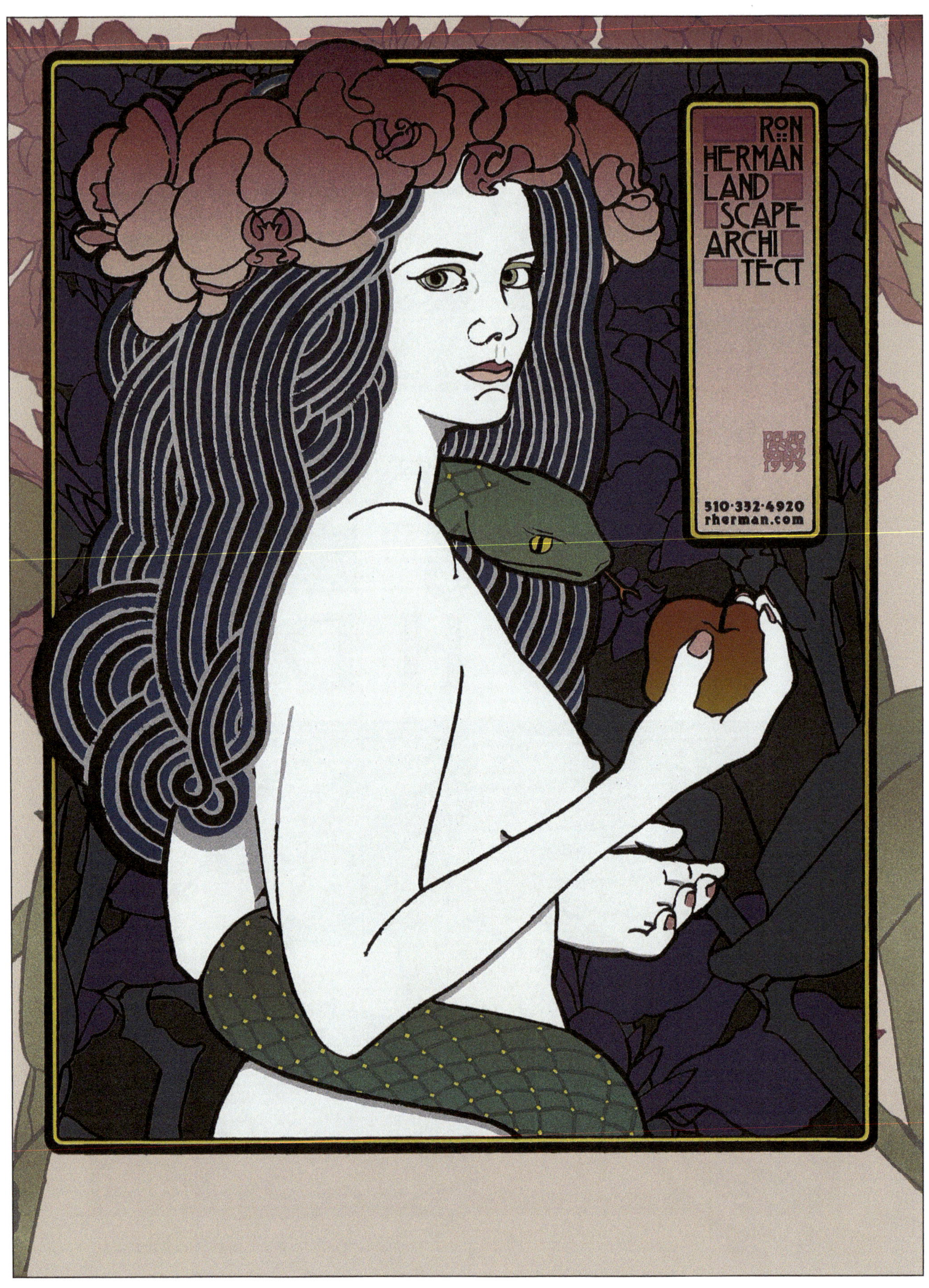

115. Ron Herman Landscape Architect, 1999, 17" × 24"

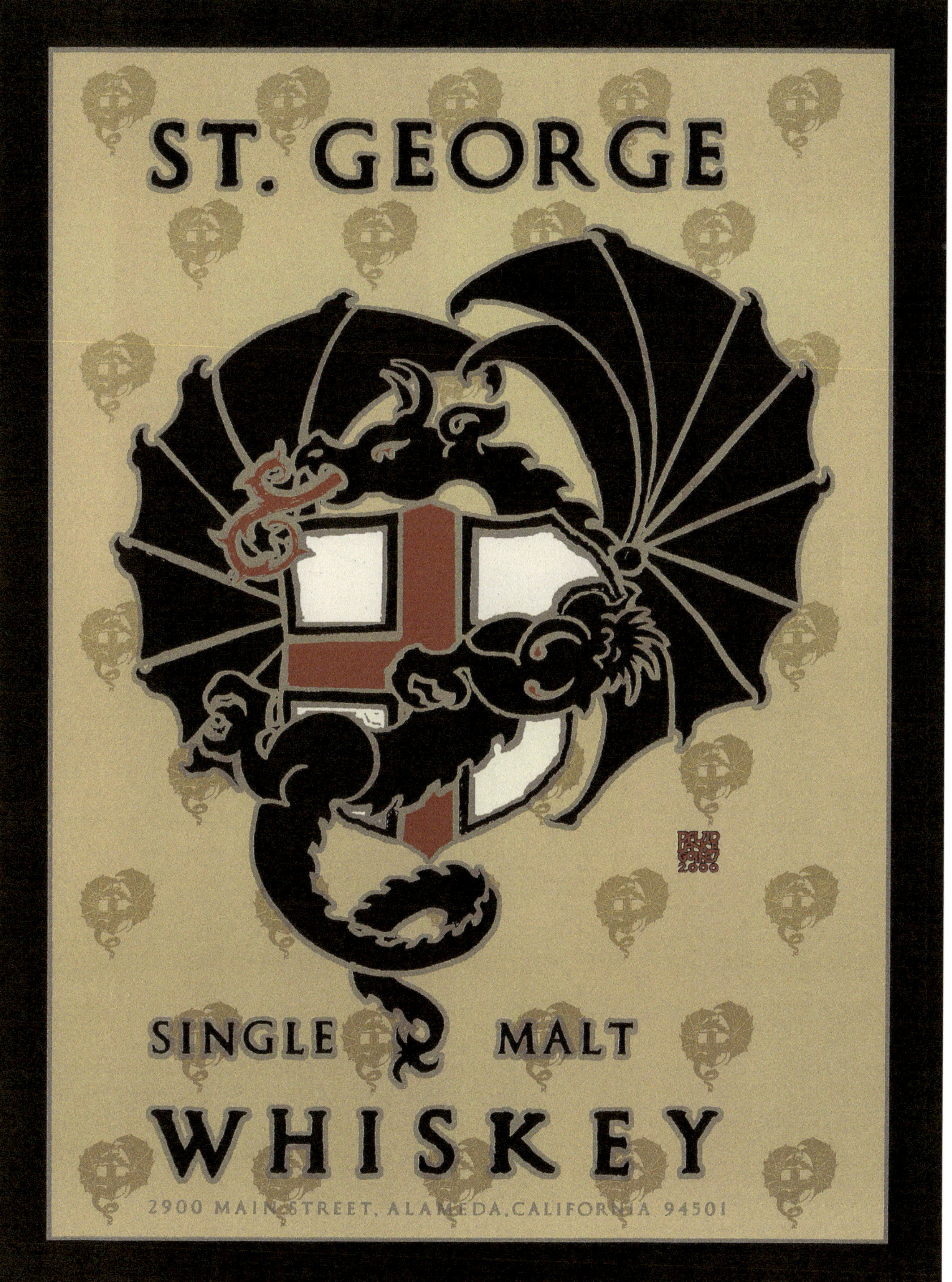

116. St. George Single Malt Whiskey, 2000, 17¼" × 24"

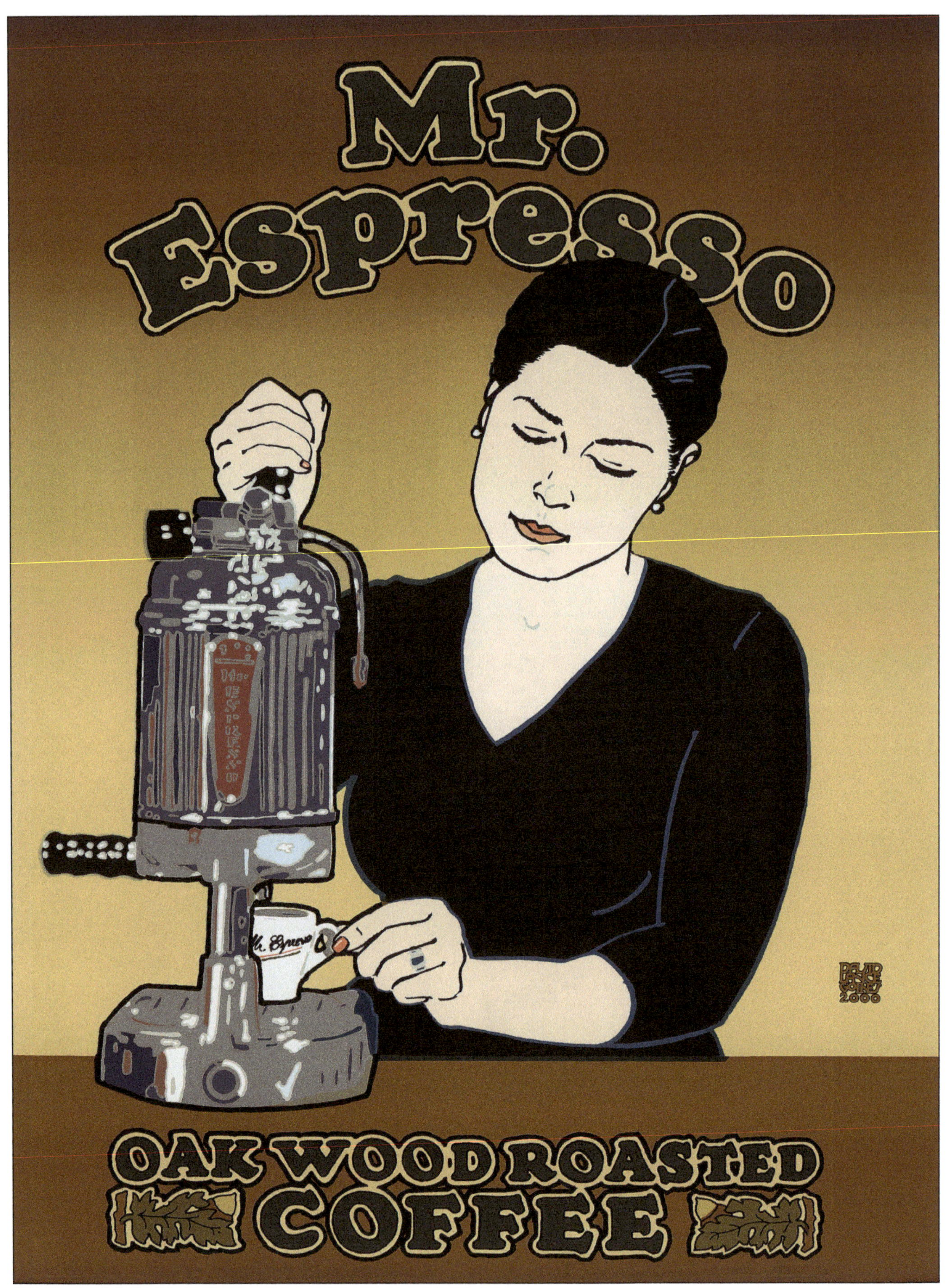

117. Mr. Espresso, 2000, 17⅜" × 24"

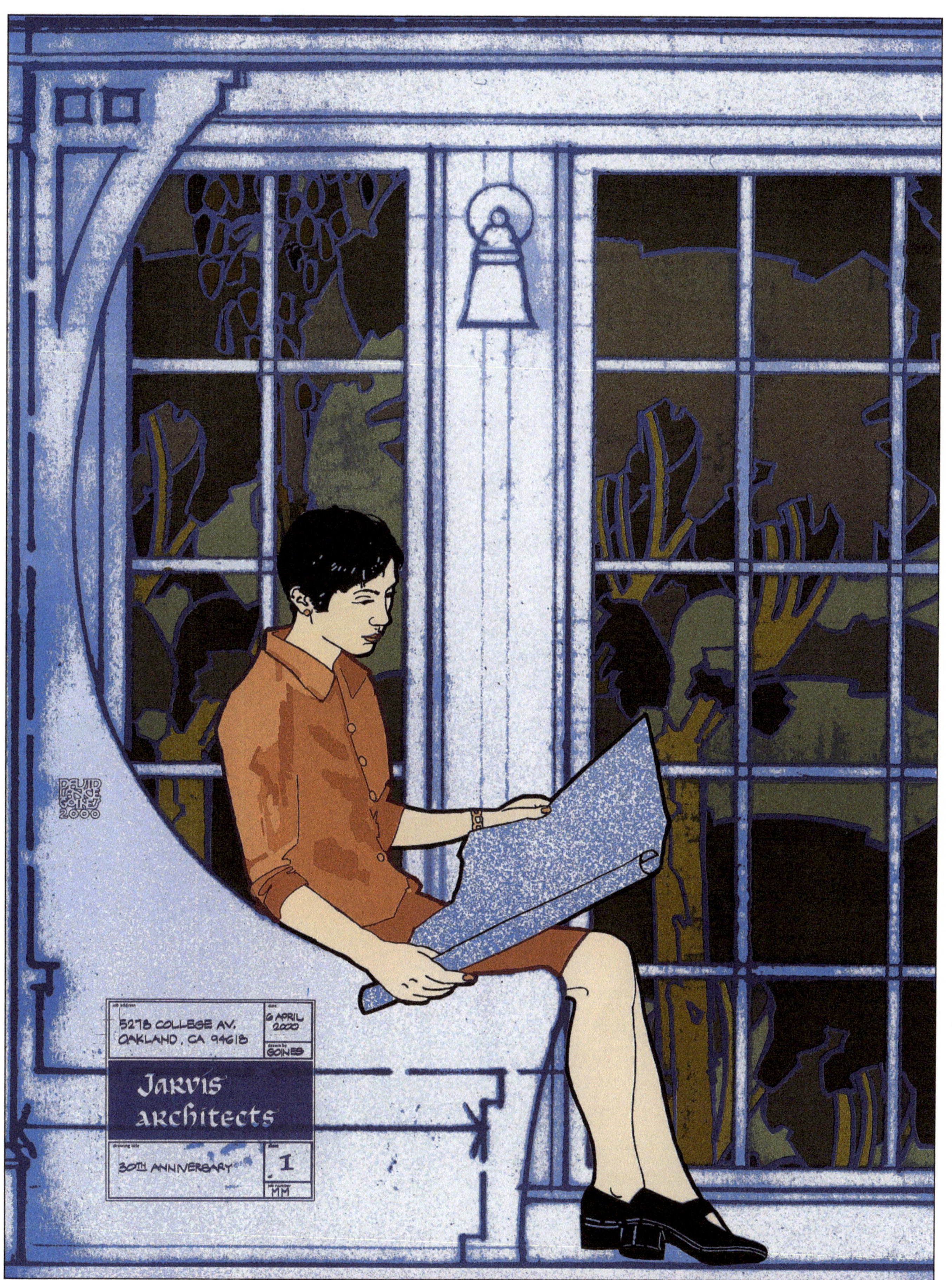

118. Jarvis Architects, 2000, 17½" × 24"

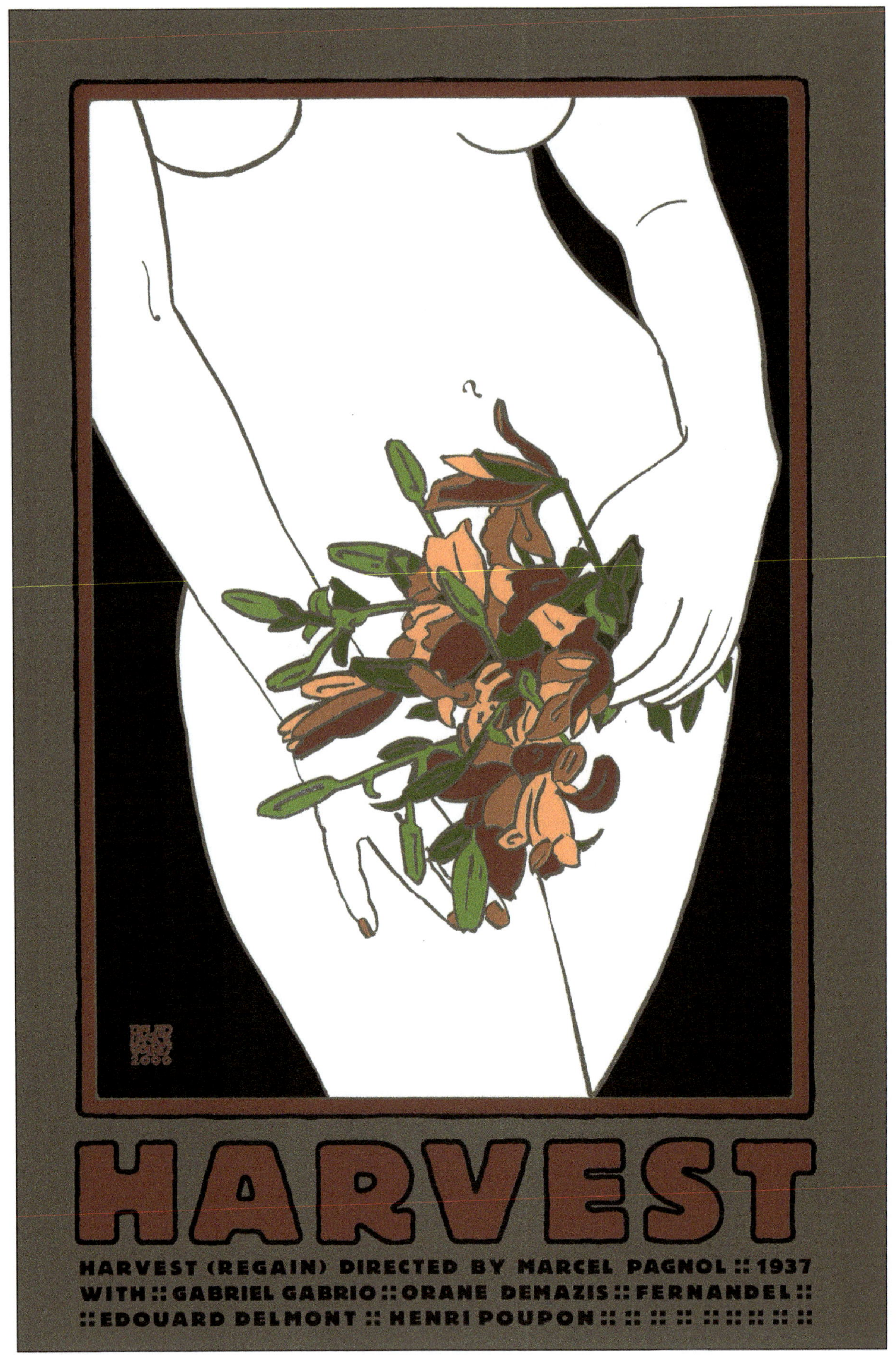

119. Harvest, 2000, 16½" × 24"

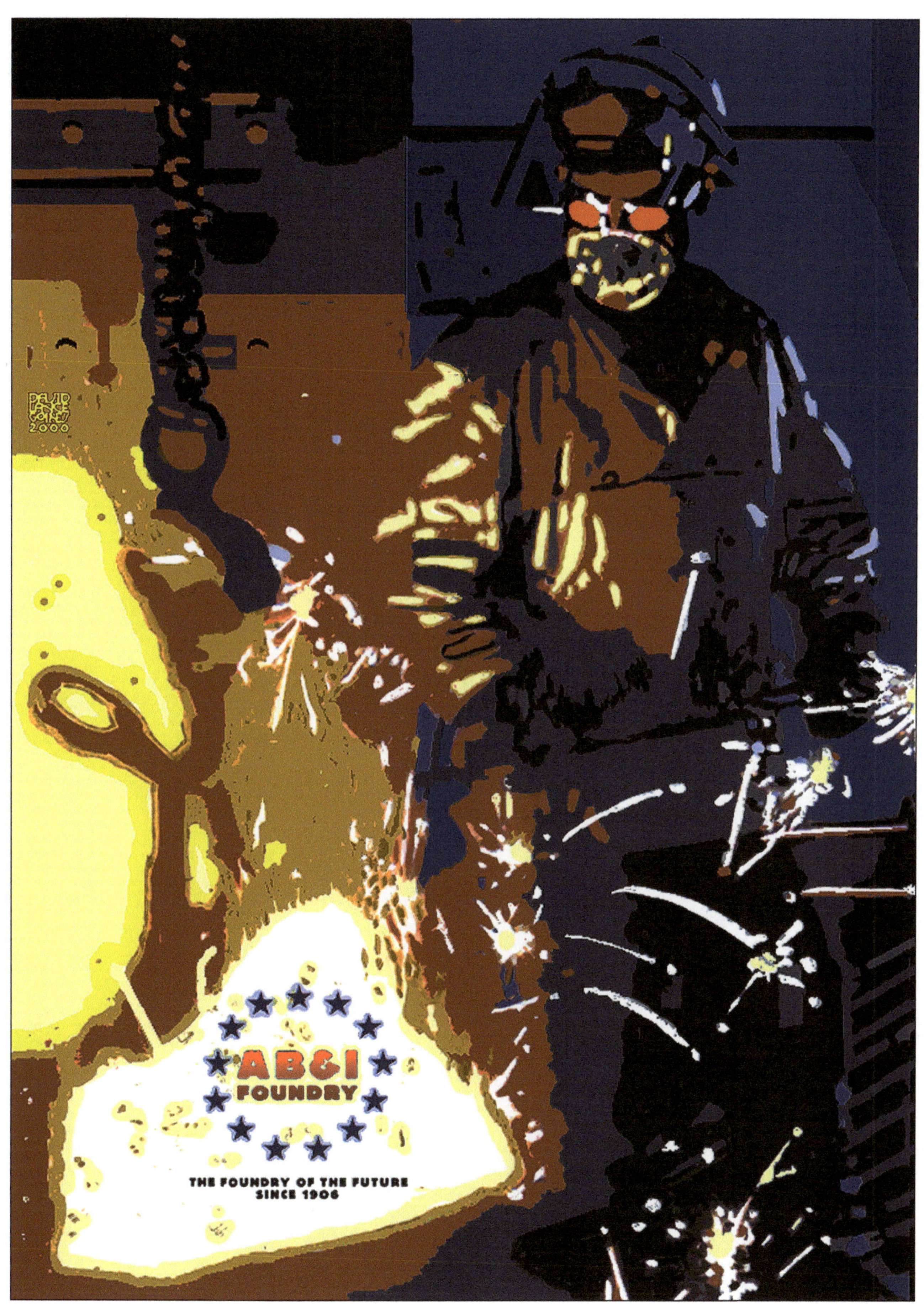

120. American Brass & Iron, 2000, 16⅞" × 24"

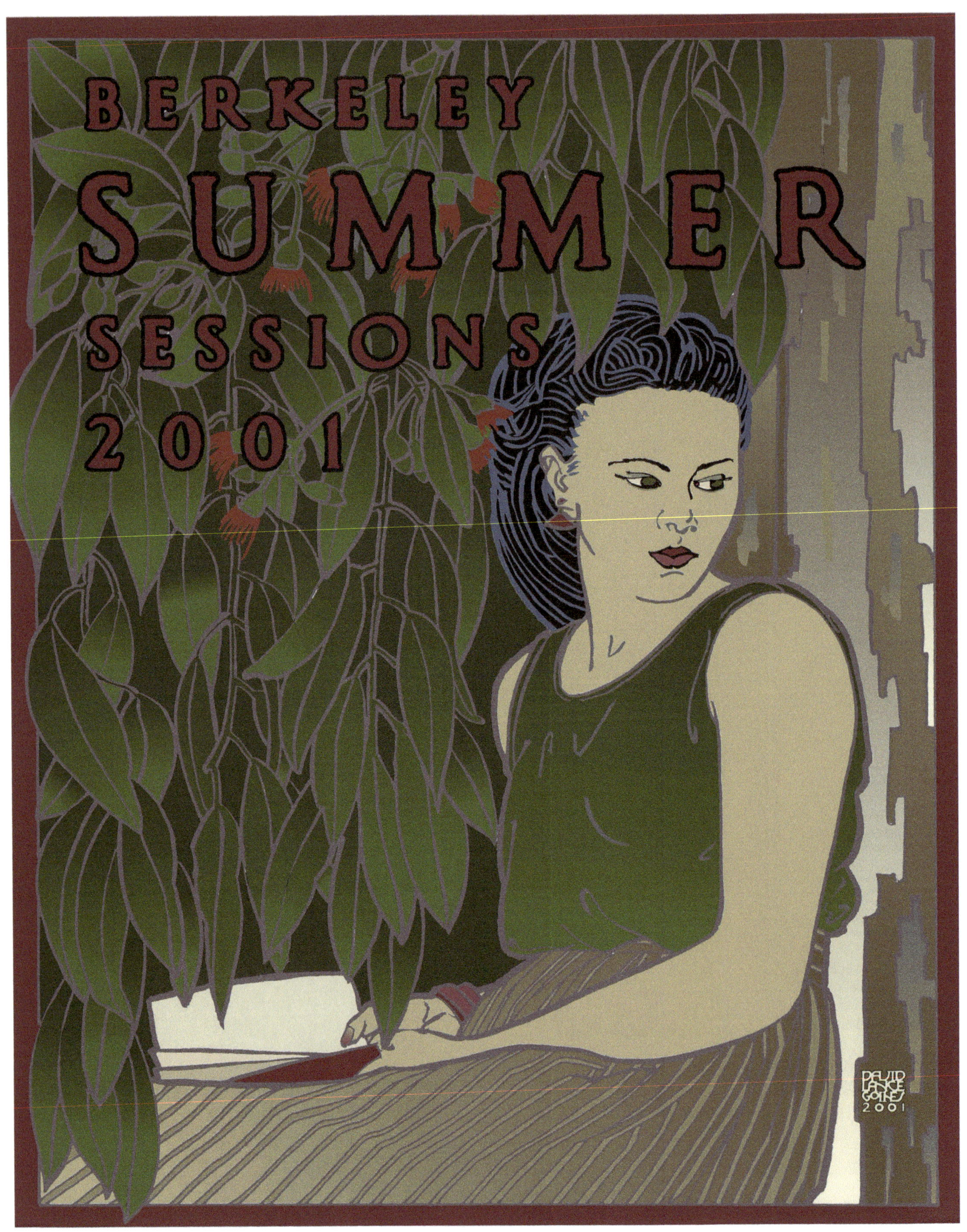

121. Berkeley Summer Sessions, 2001, 18¾" × 23⅞"

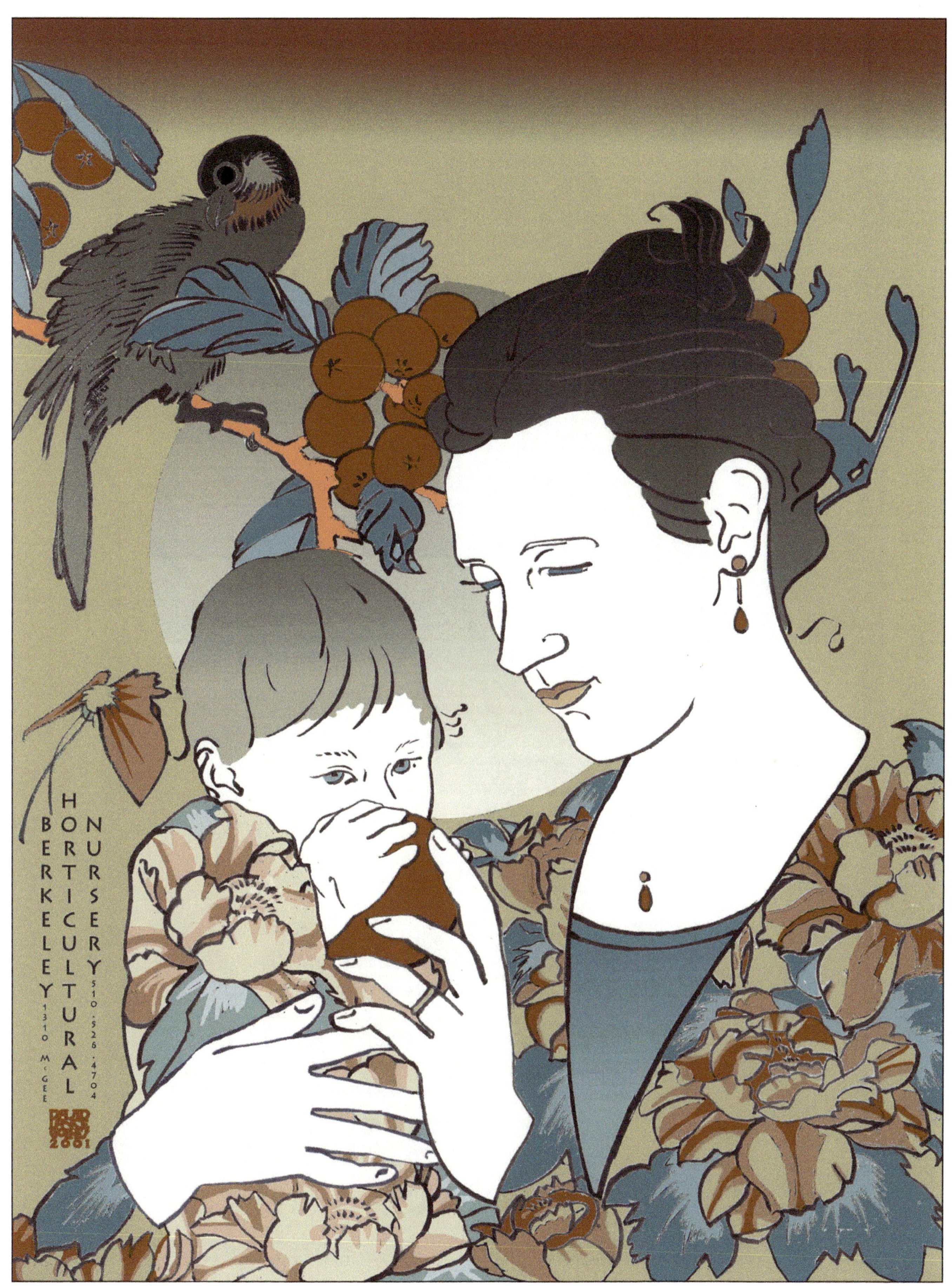

122. Berkeley Horticultural Nursery, 2001, 17½" × 24"

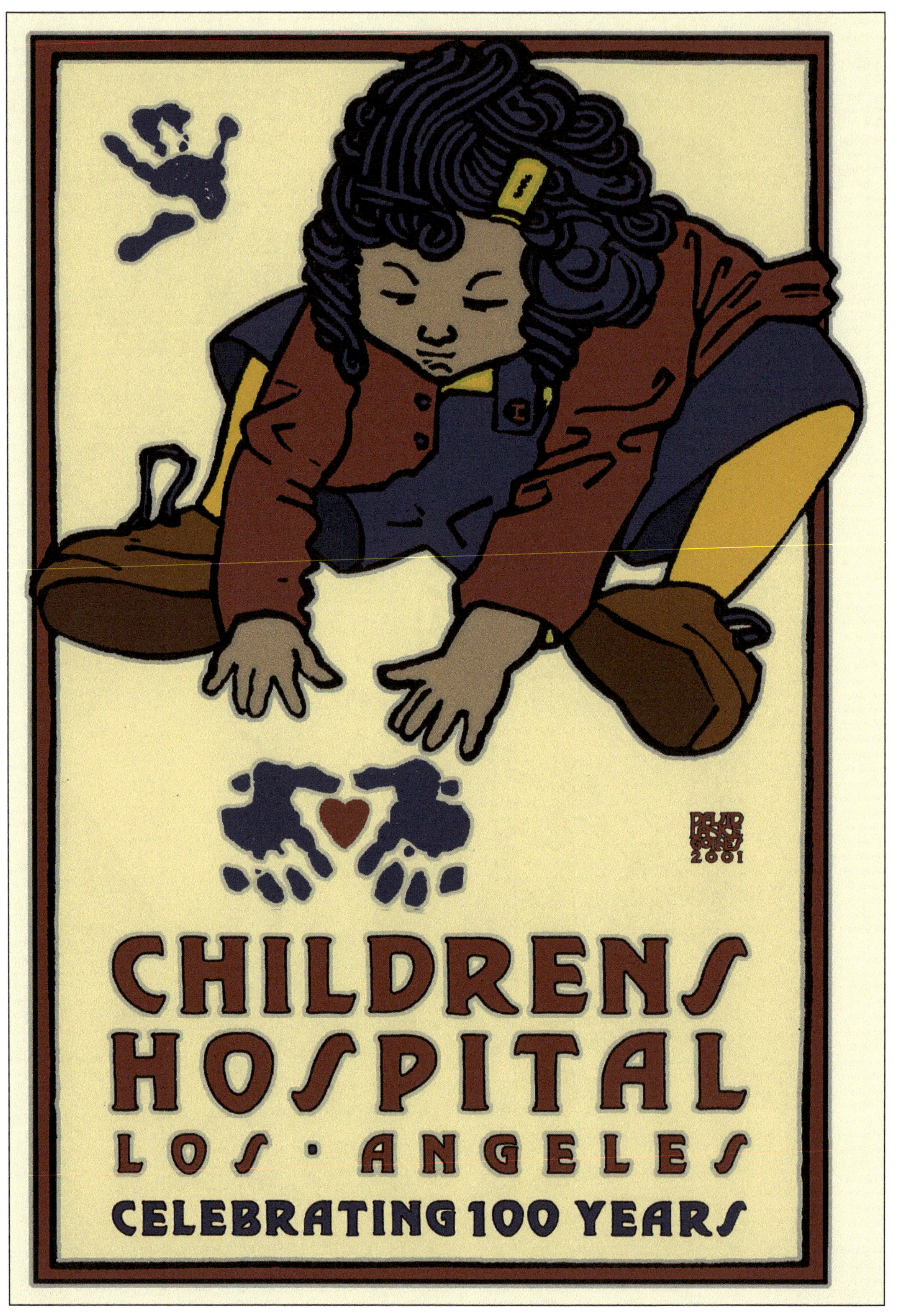

123. Centennial of Children's Hospital, Los Angeles, 2001, 16⅜" × 24"

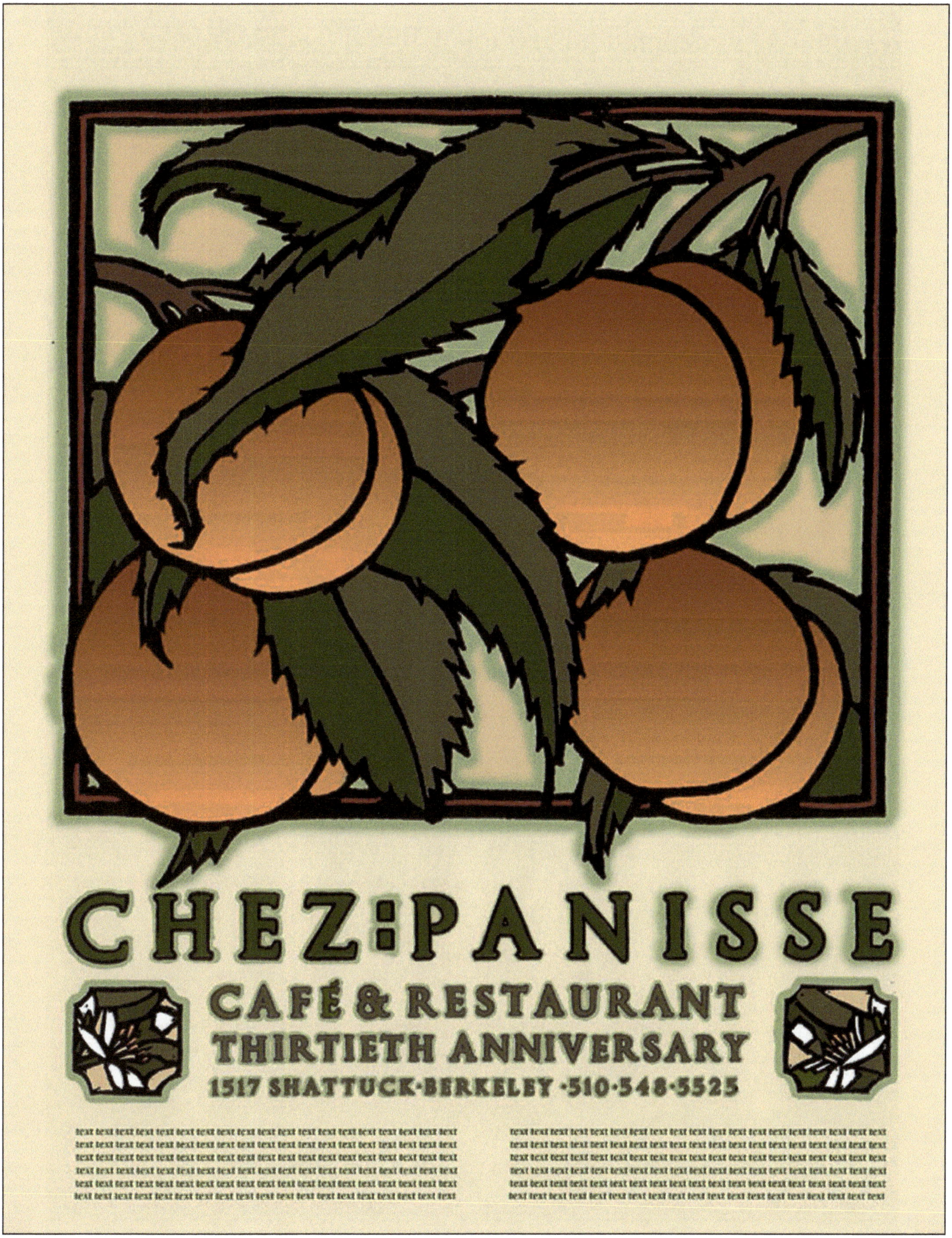

CHEZ:PANISSE

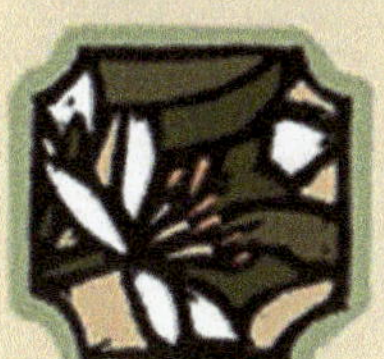

CAFÉ & RESTAURANT
THIRTIETH ANNIVERSARY
1517 SHATTUCK·BERKELEY ·510·548·5525

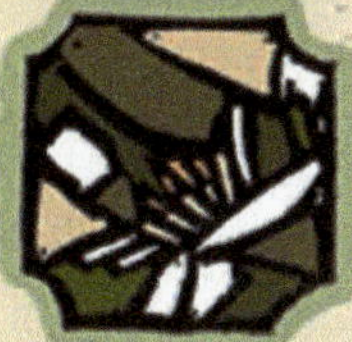

124. Chez Panisse Thirtieth Anniversary, 2001, 17½" × 24"

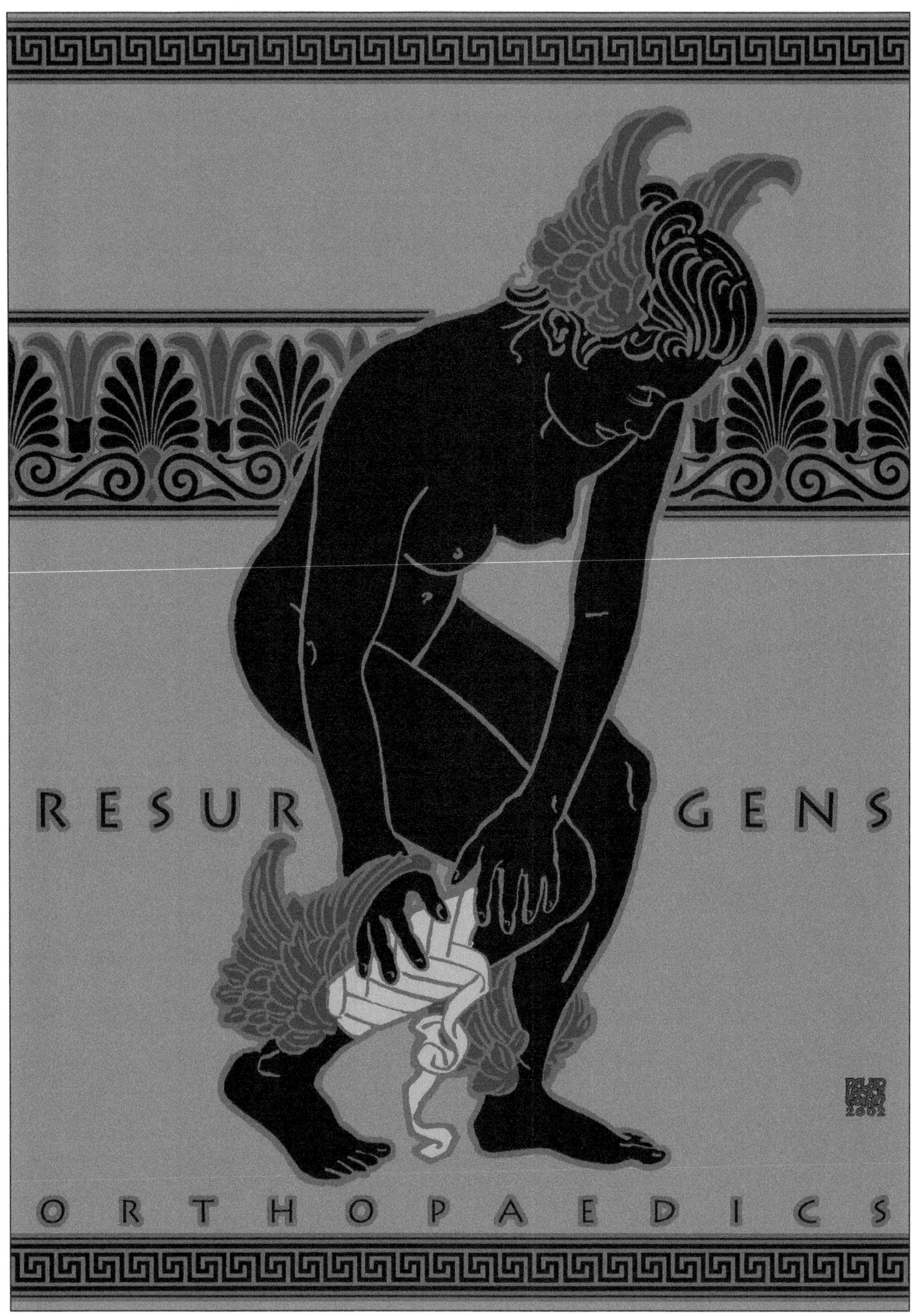

125. Resurgens Orthopaedics, 2002, 16⅜" × 24"

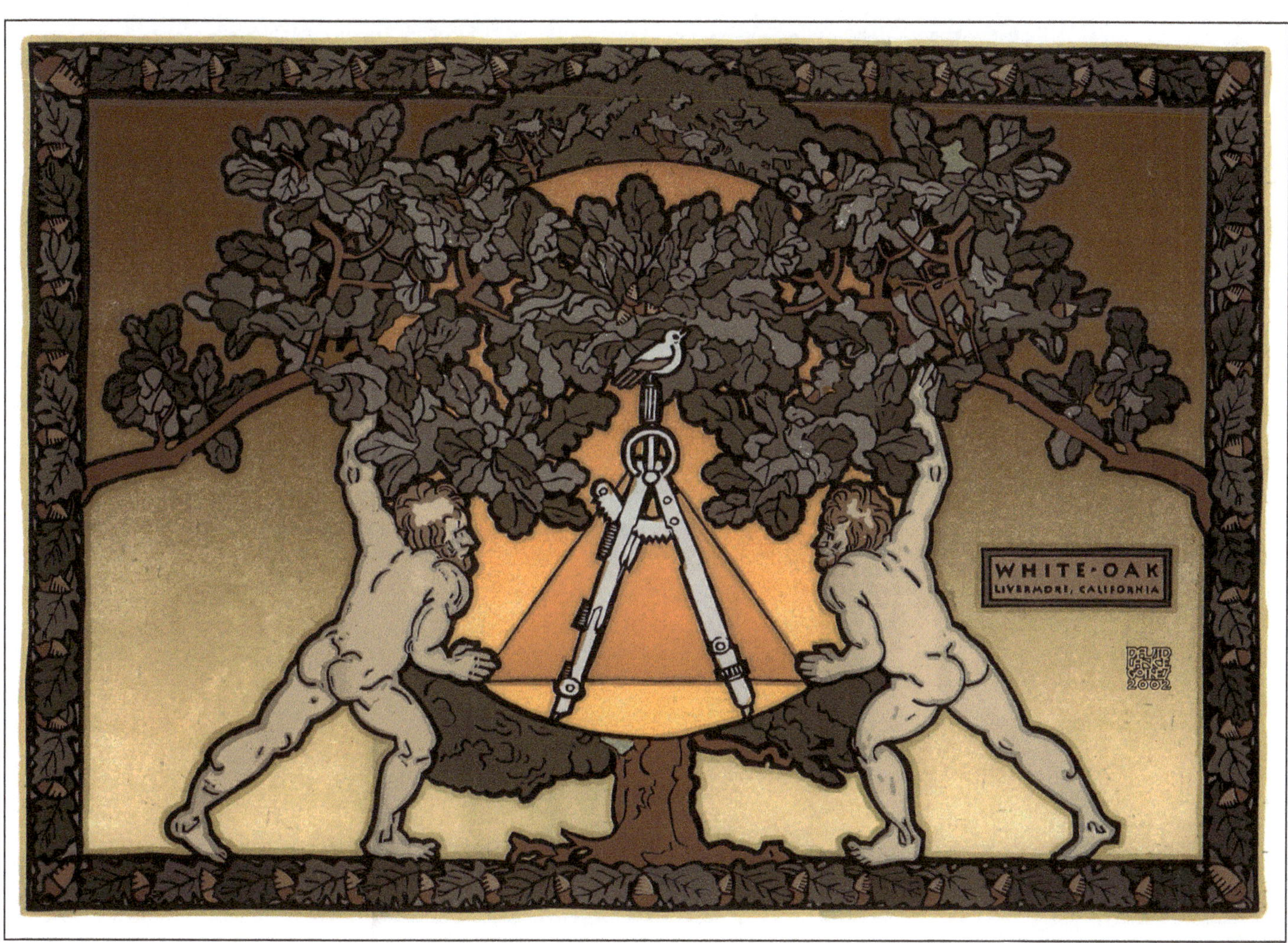

126. White Oak, 2002, 24" × 18"

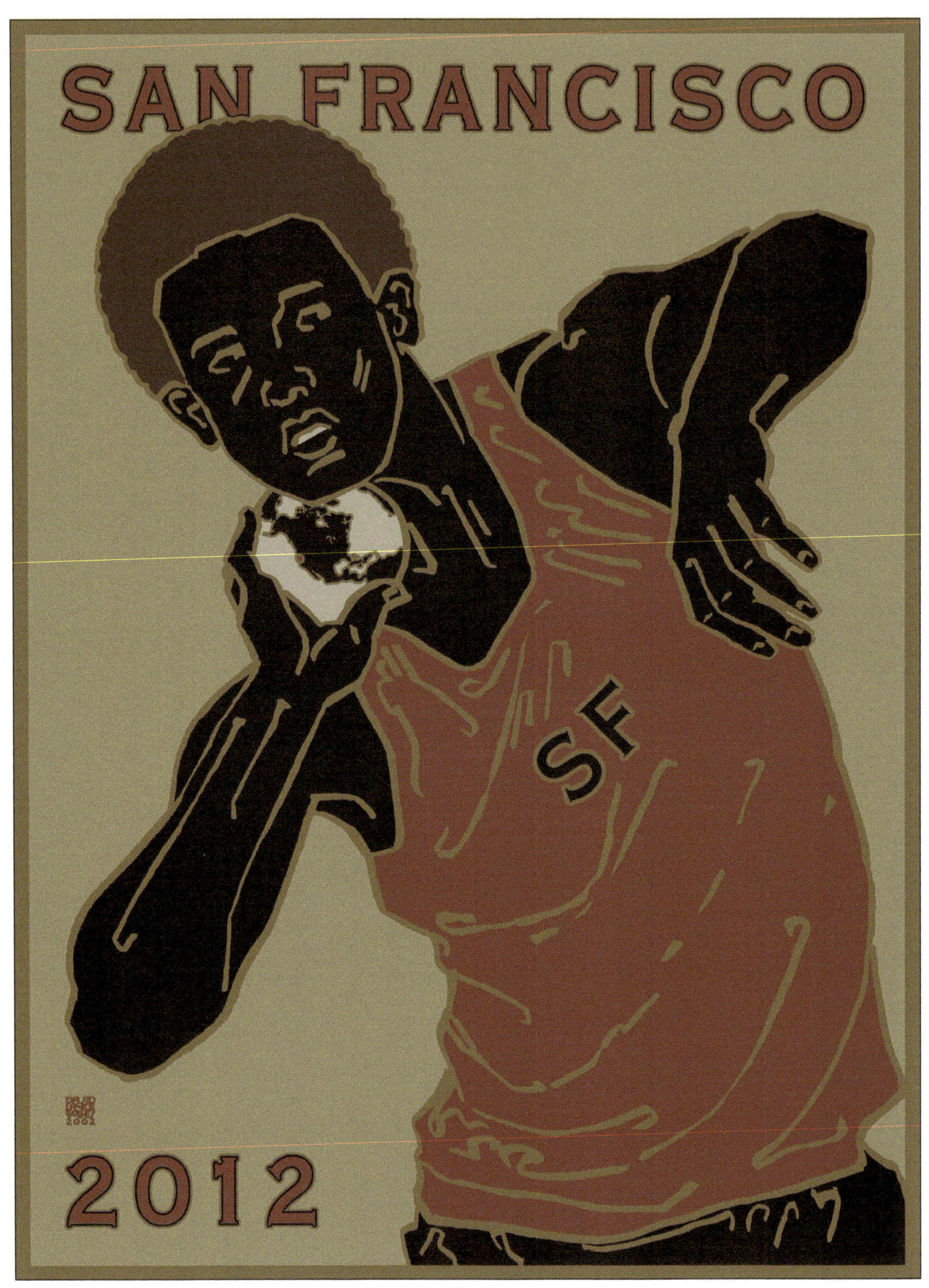

127. San Francisco 2012 Olympic Bid, 2002, 23" × 35" and 18" × 27" formats

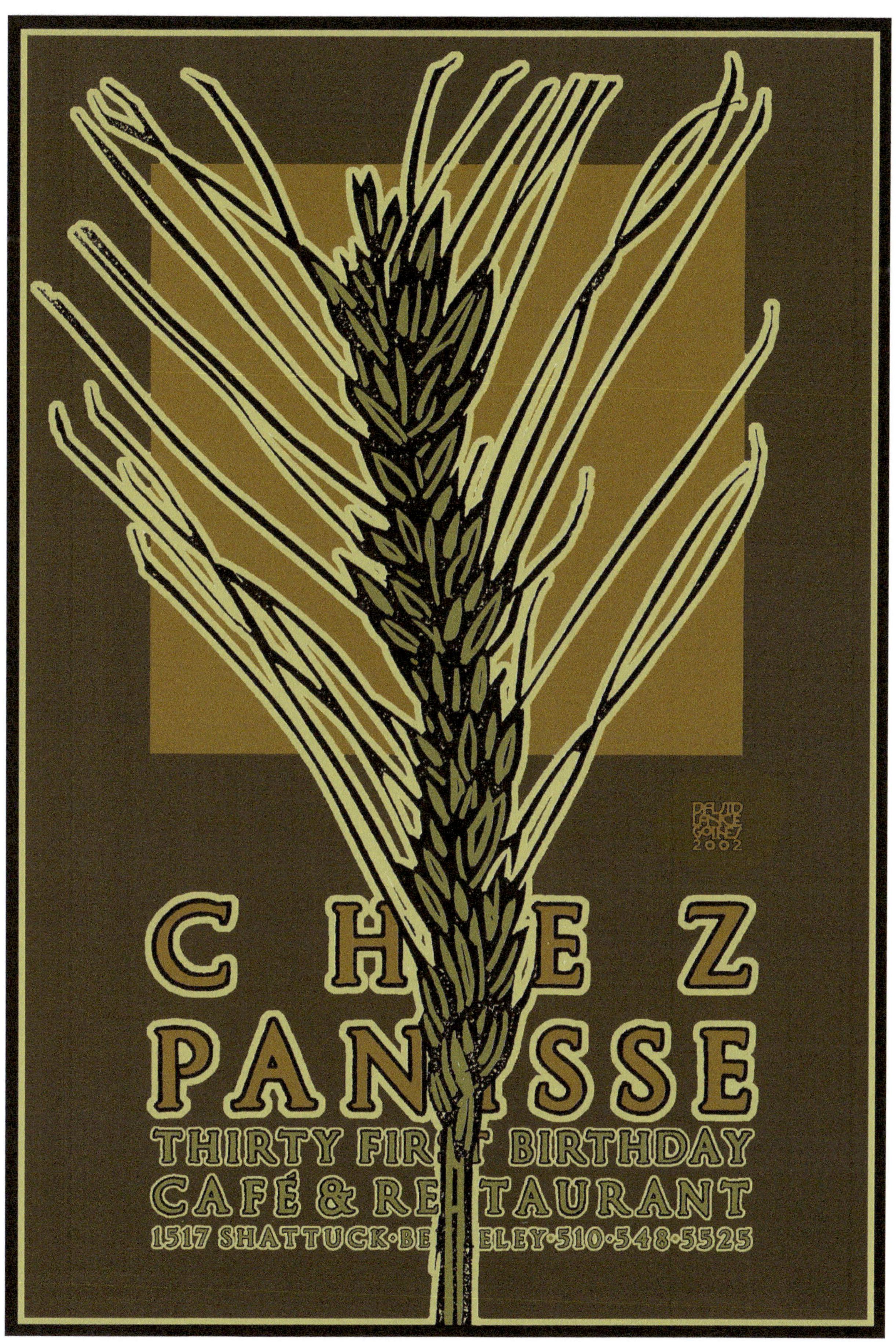

128. Chez Panisse Thirty-First Birthday, 2002, 16¼" × 24"

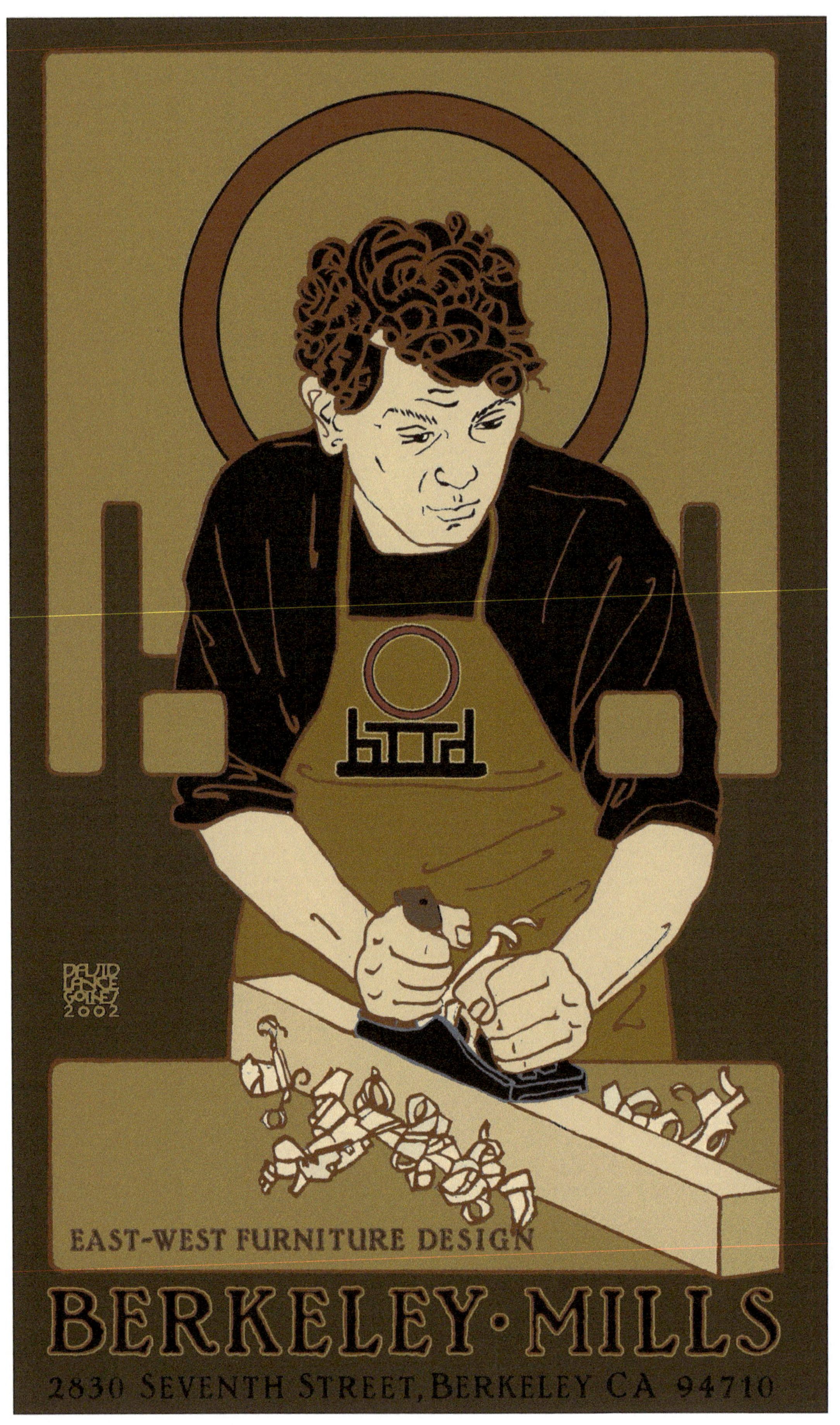

129. BERKELEY MILLS, 2003, 15⅞" × 24"

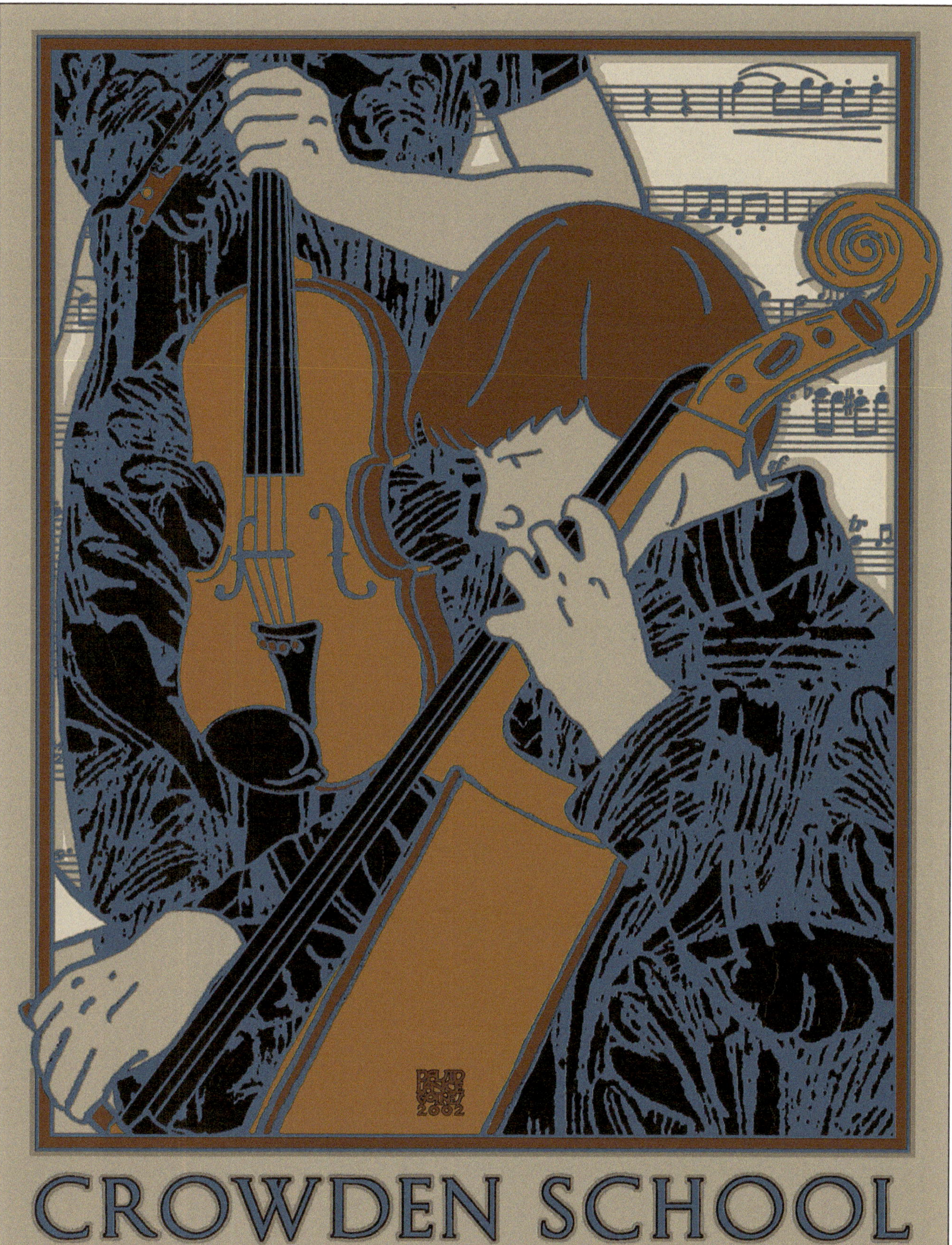

130. Crowden School, 2003, 17⅜" × 24"

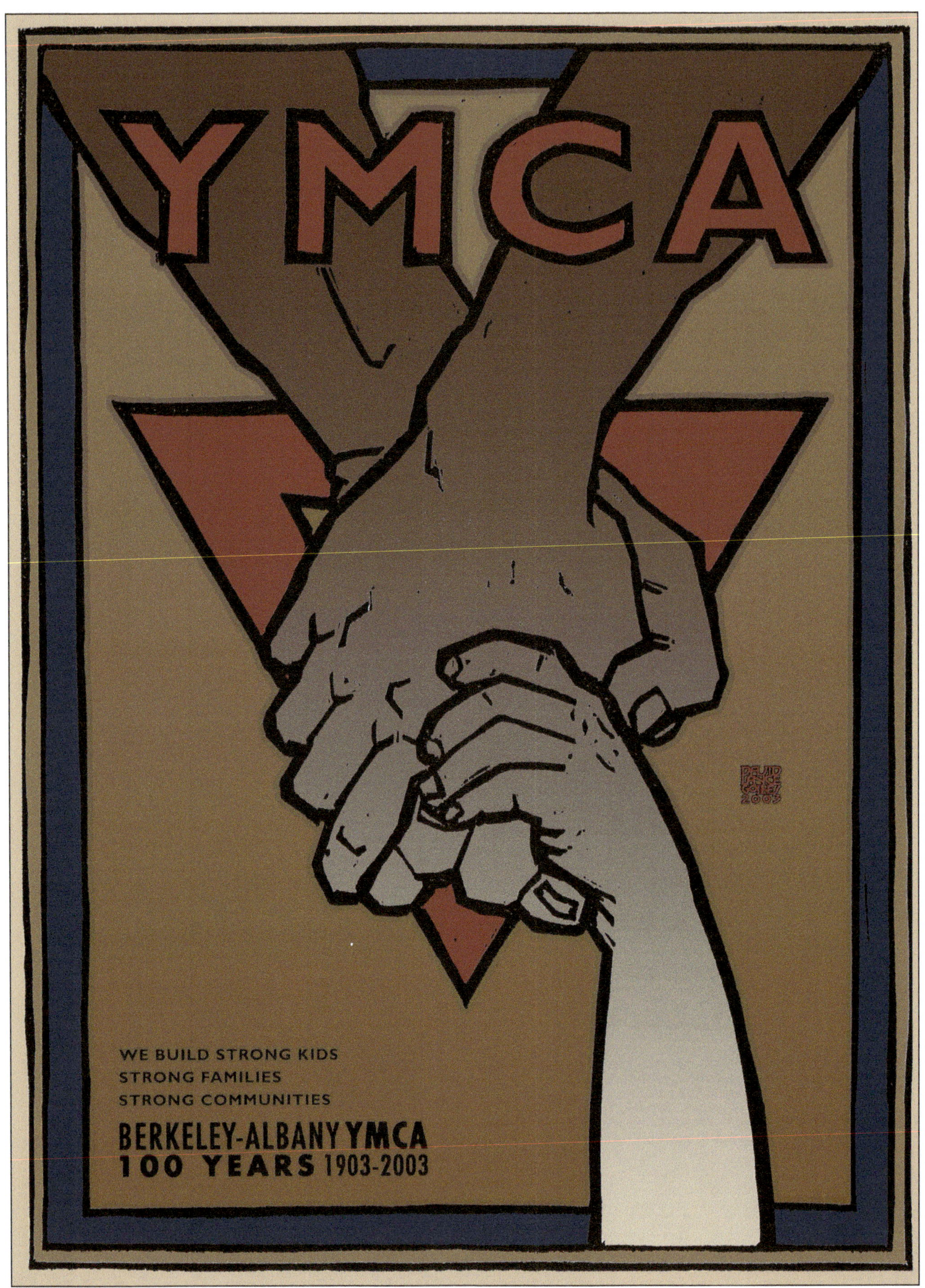

131. YMCA, 2003, 17 3/16" × 24"

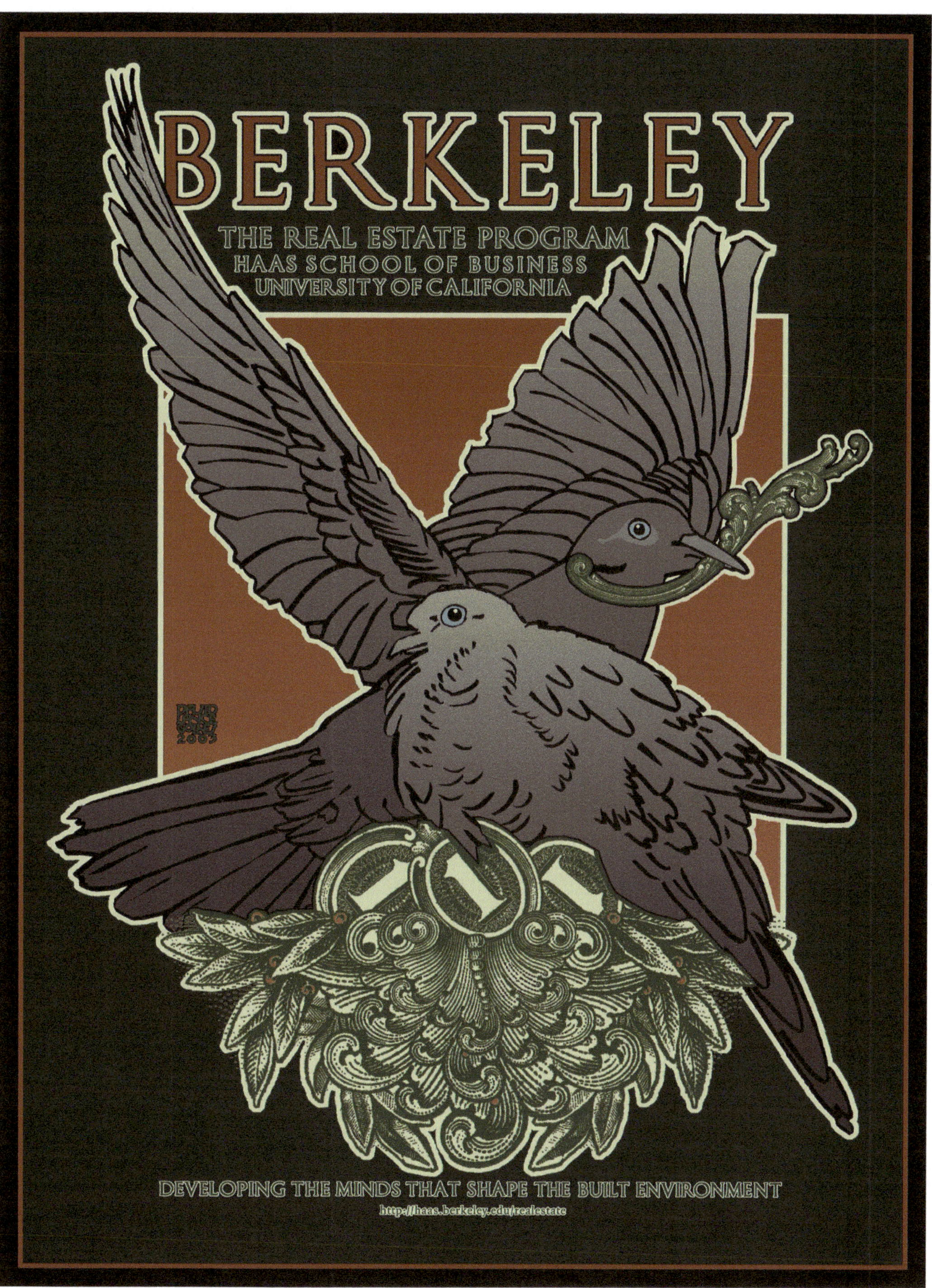

132. UC Berkeley Real Estate Program, Haas School of Business, 2003, 17⅜" × 24"

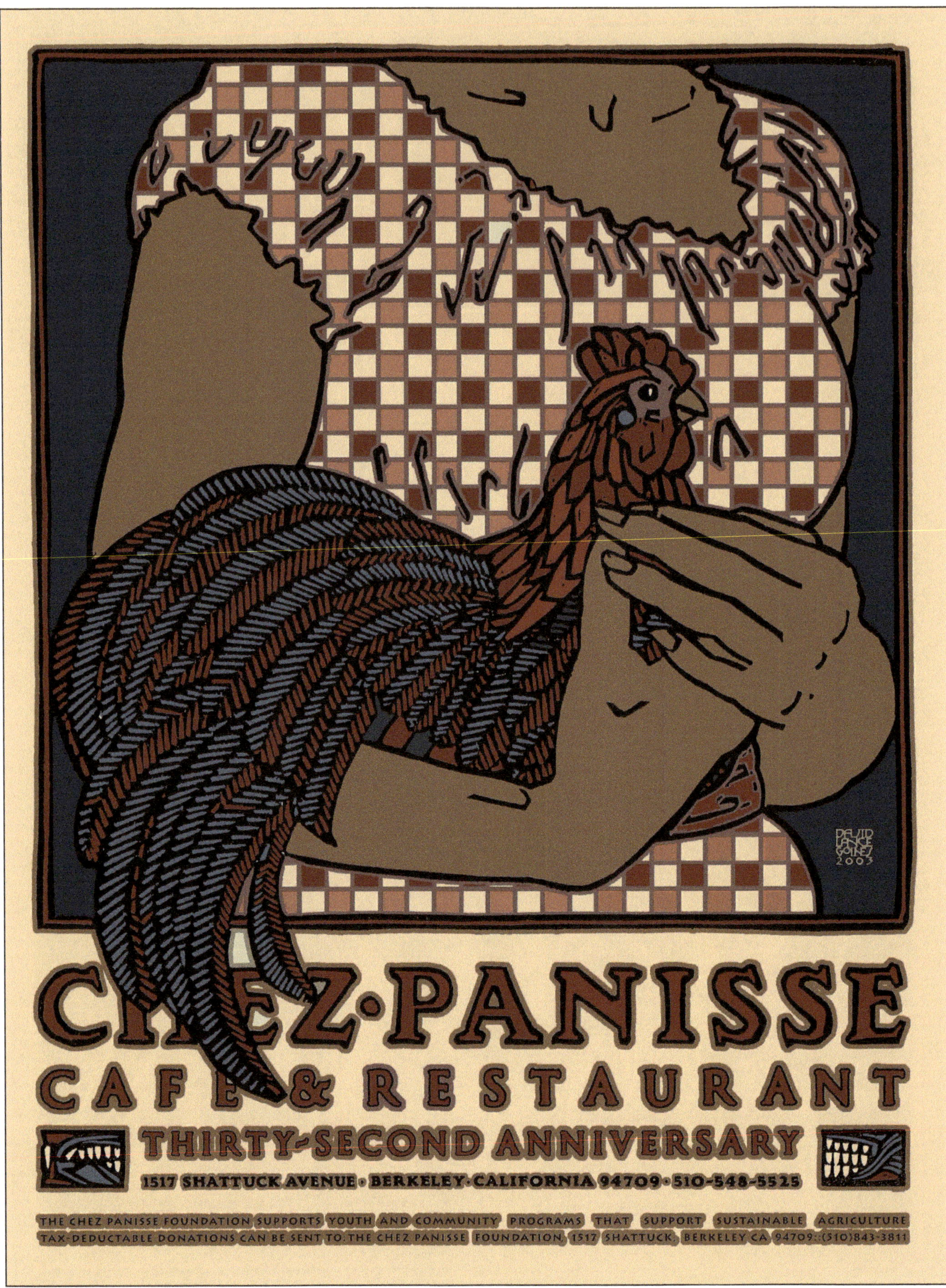

133. Chez Panisse Thirty-Second Birthday, 2003, 17½" × 24"

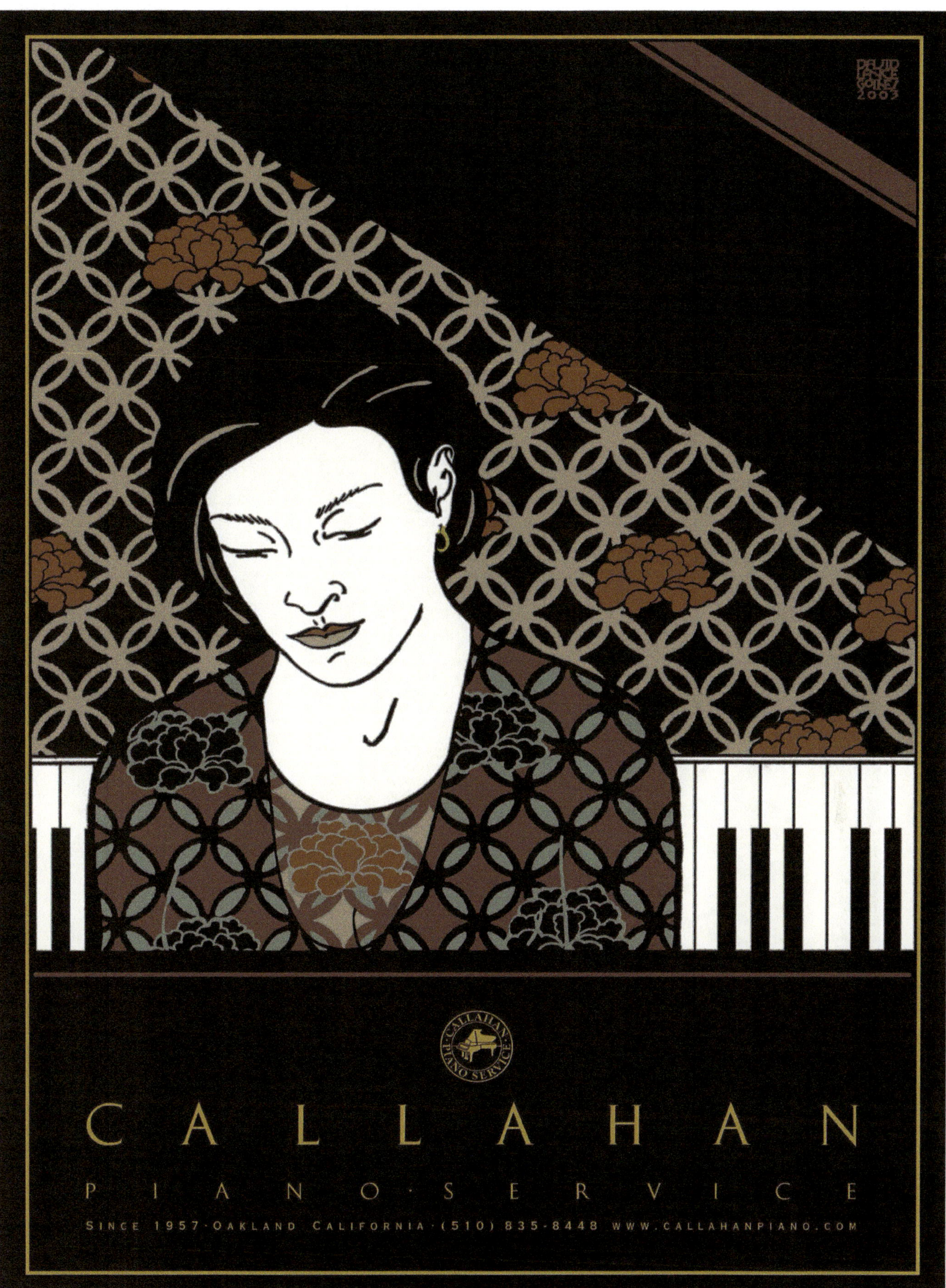

134. Callahan Piano Service, 2003, 17½" × 24"

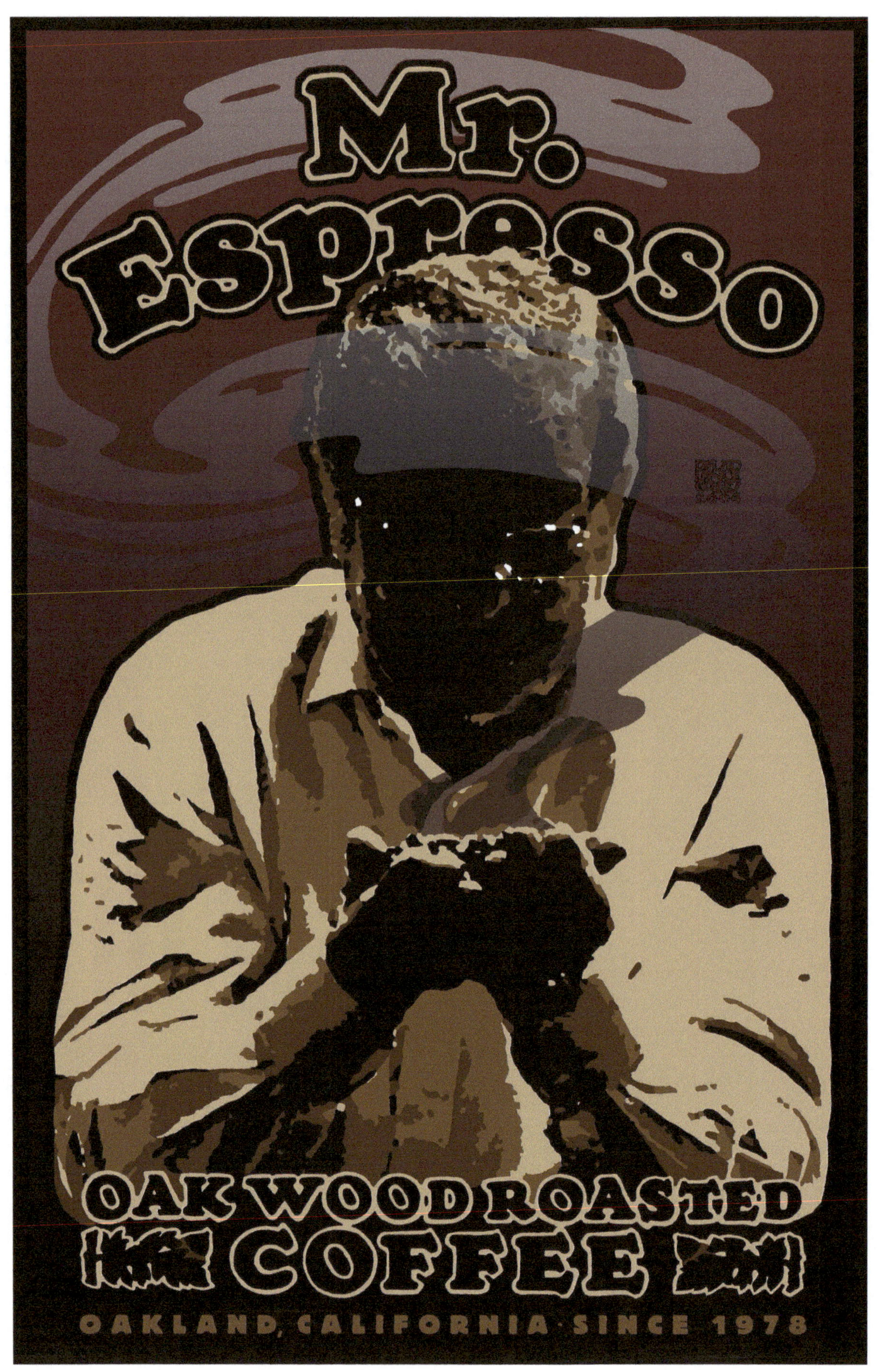

135. Mr. Espresso, 2004, 15⅛" × 24"

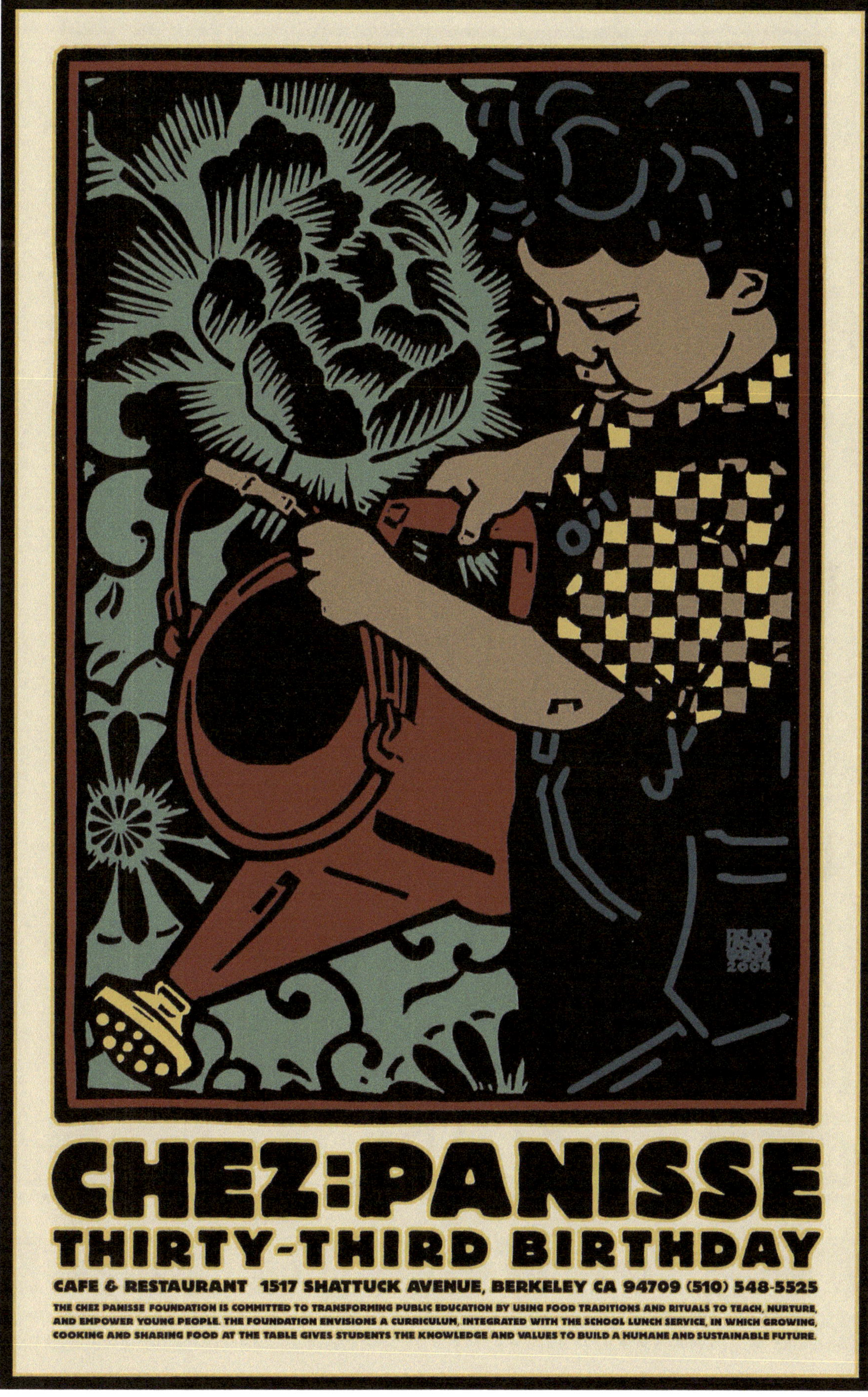

136. Chez Panisse Thirty-Third Birthday, 2004, 15" × 24"

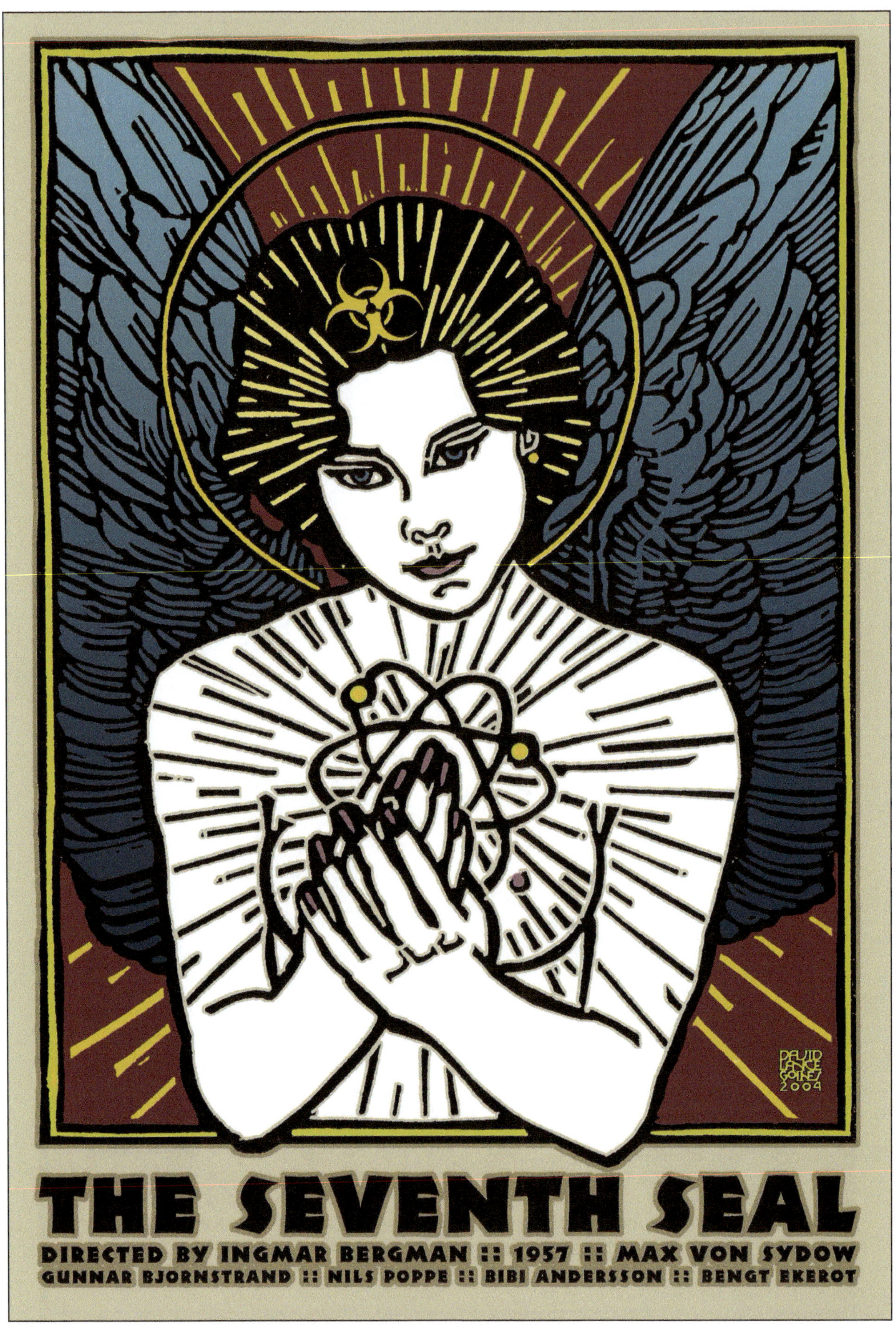

137. The Seventh Seal, 2004, 17⅝" × 24"

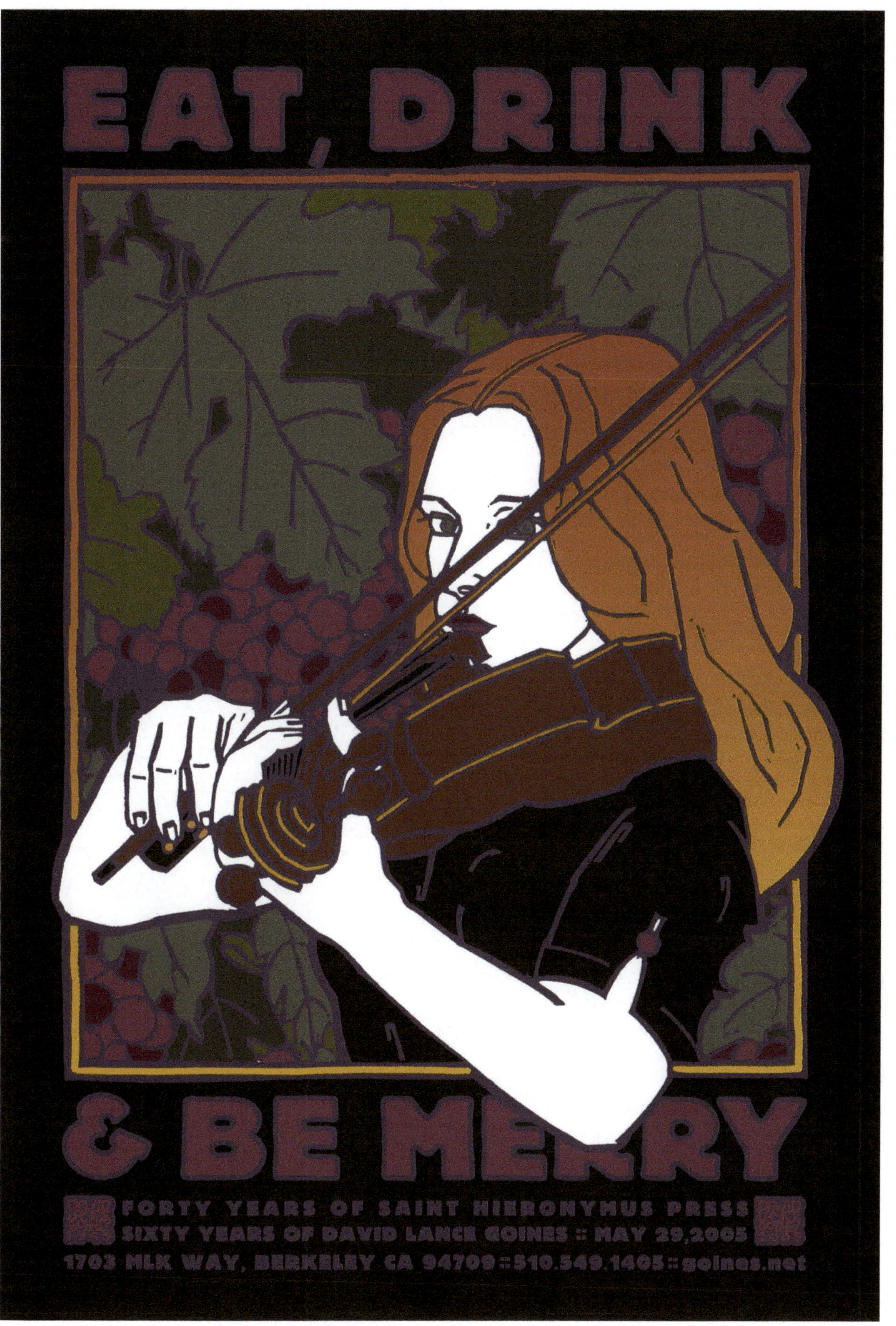

138. Eat, Drink & Be Merry, 2005, 16³⁄₁₆" × 24"

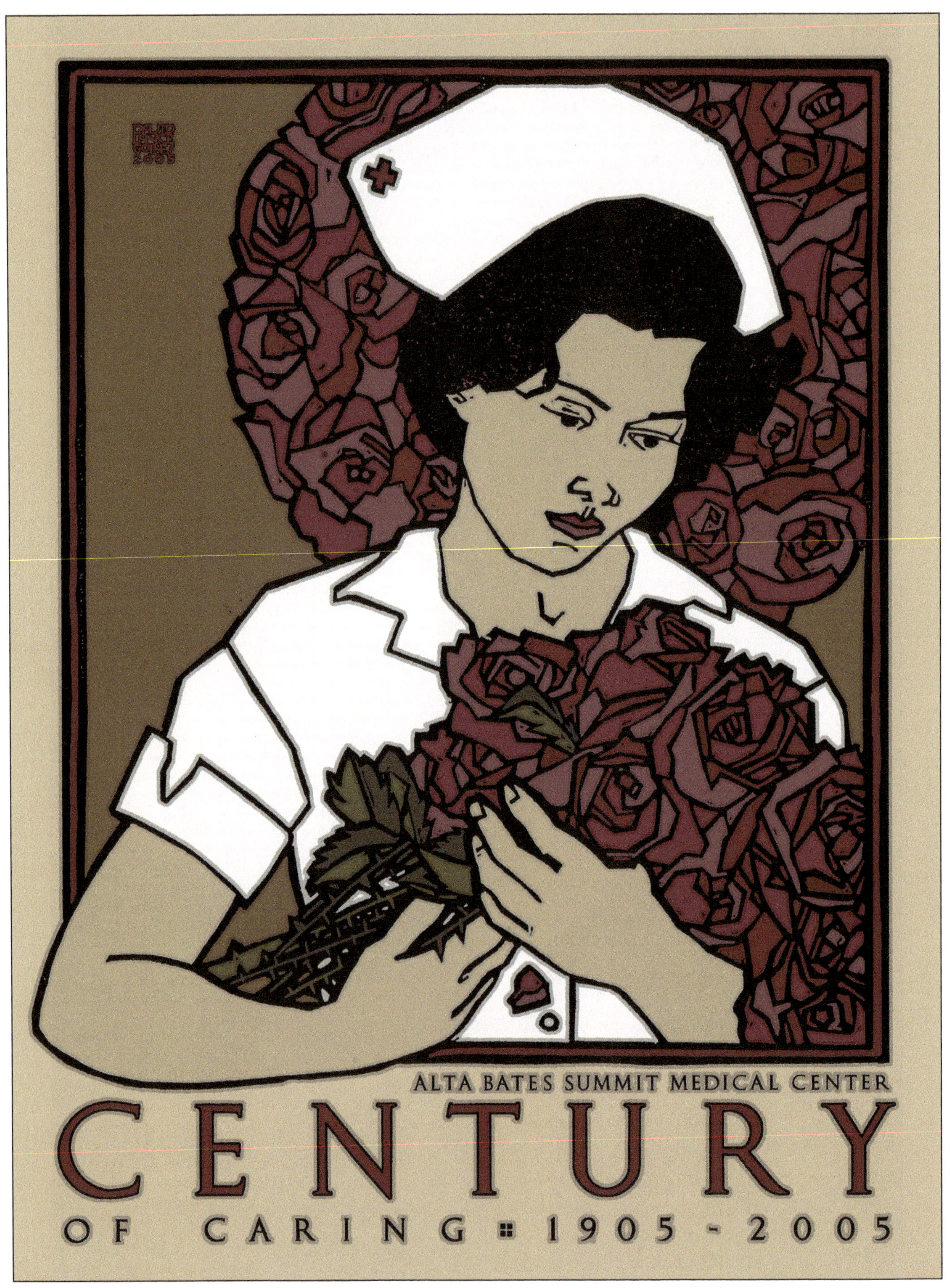

139. Alta Bates Summit Medical Center Centennial, 2005, 17⅜" × 24"

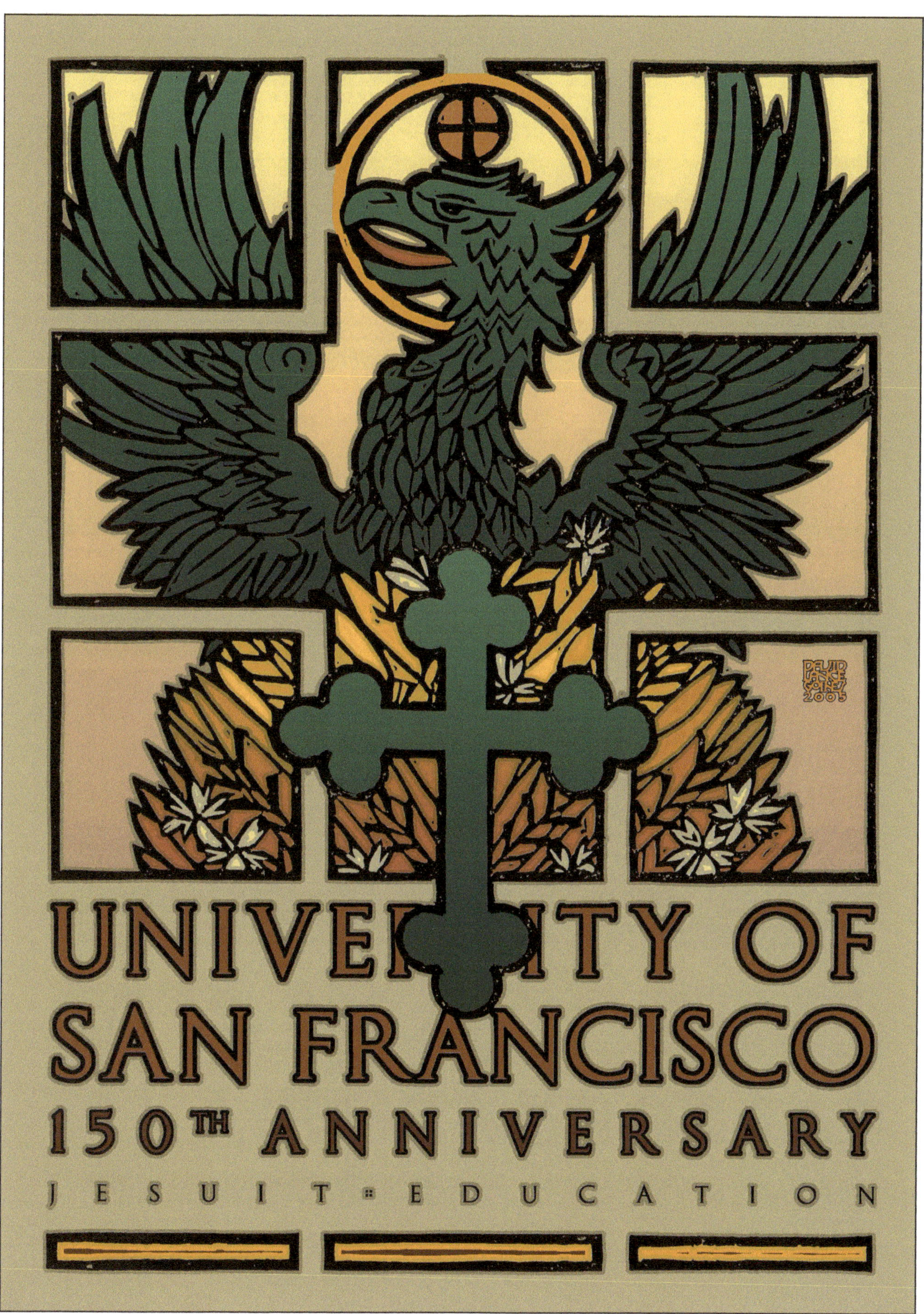

140. University of San Francisco, 150th Anniversary, 2005, 16⅞" × 24"

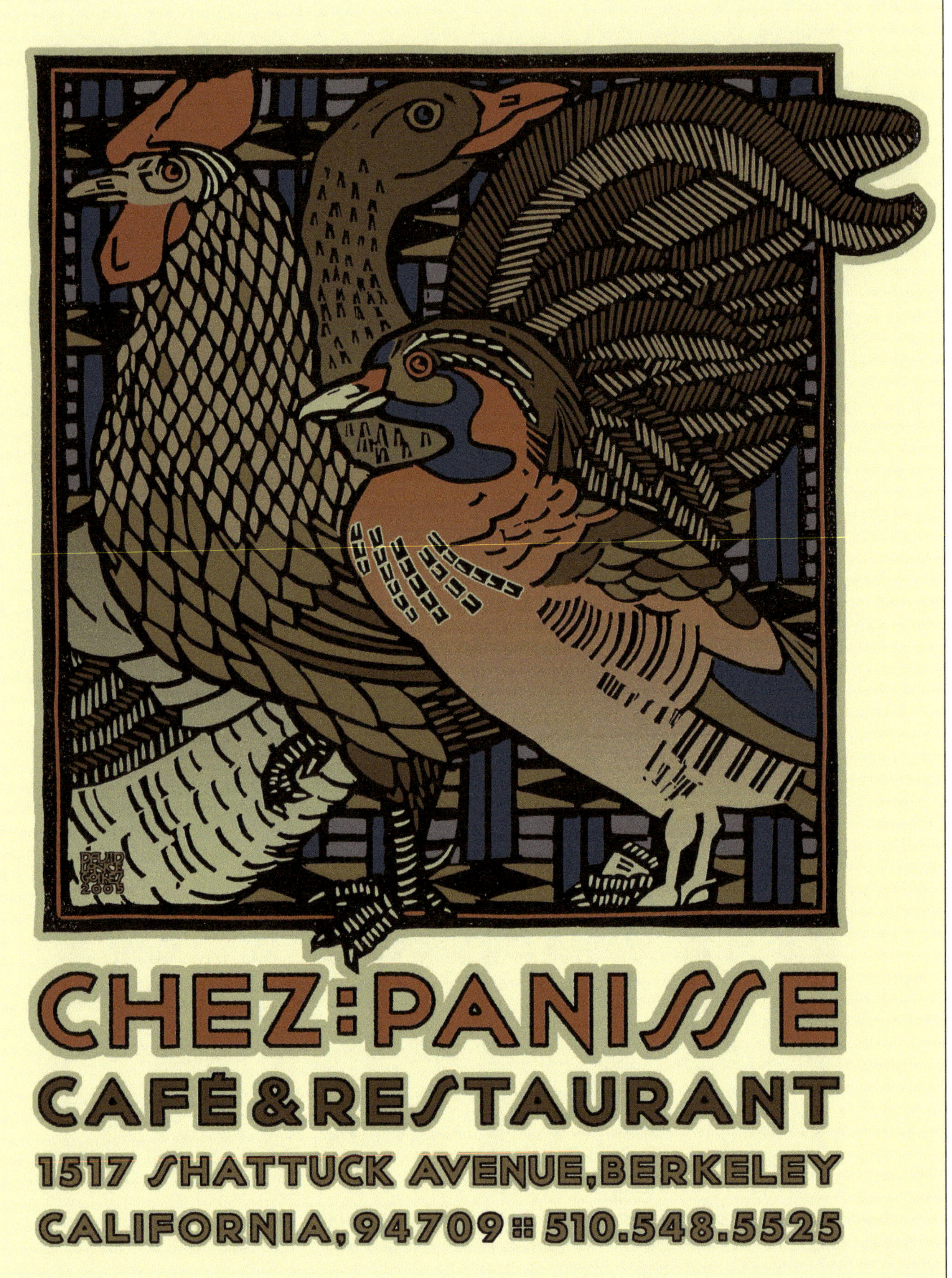

141. Chez Panisse Café & Restaurant, 2005, 17¾" × 24"

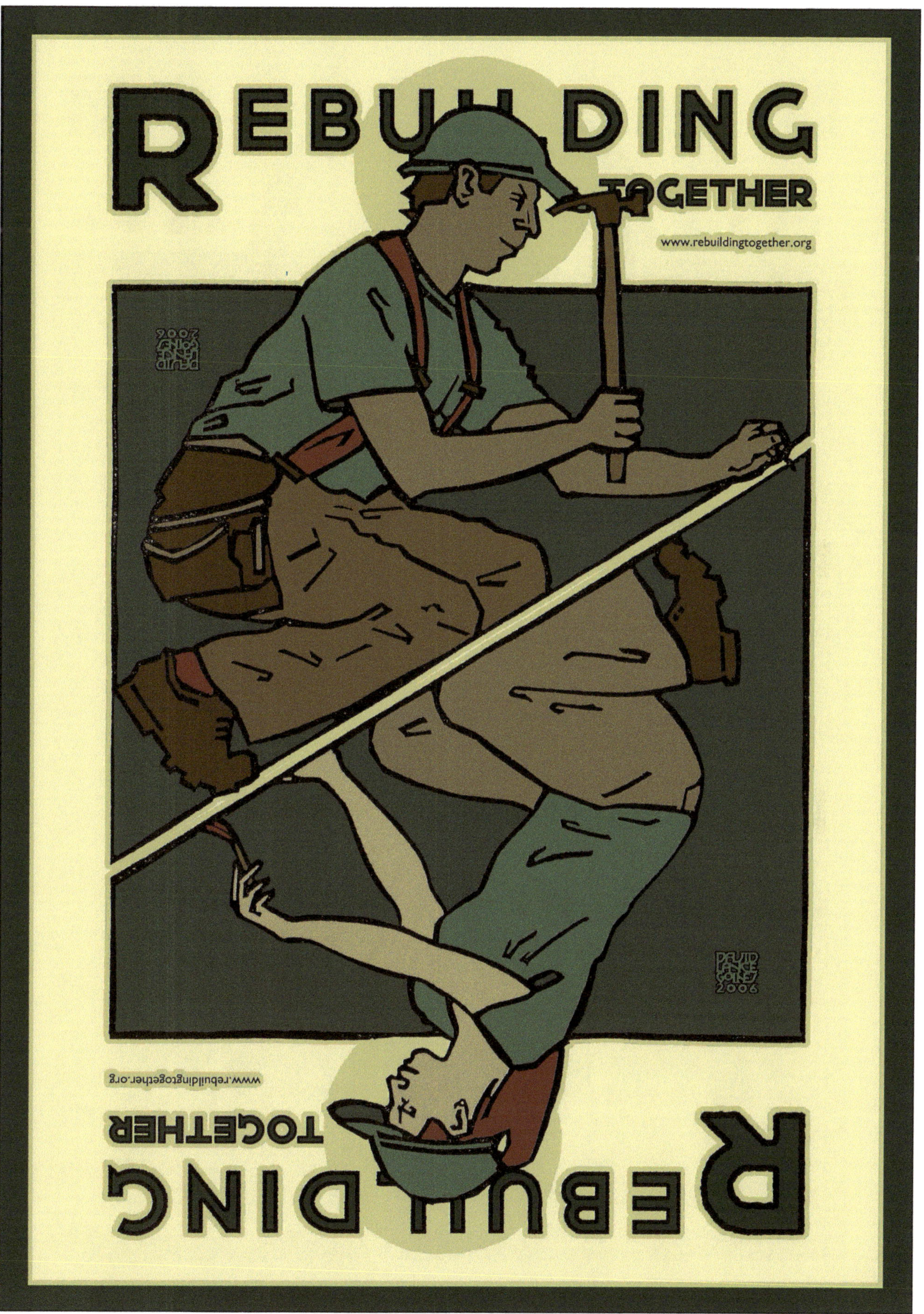

142. Rebuilding Together, 2006, 16⅝" × 24"

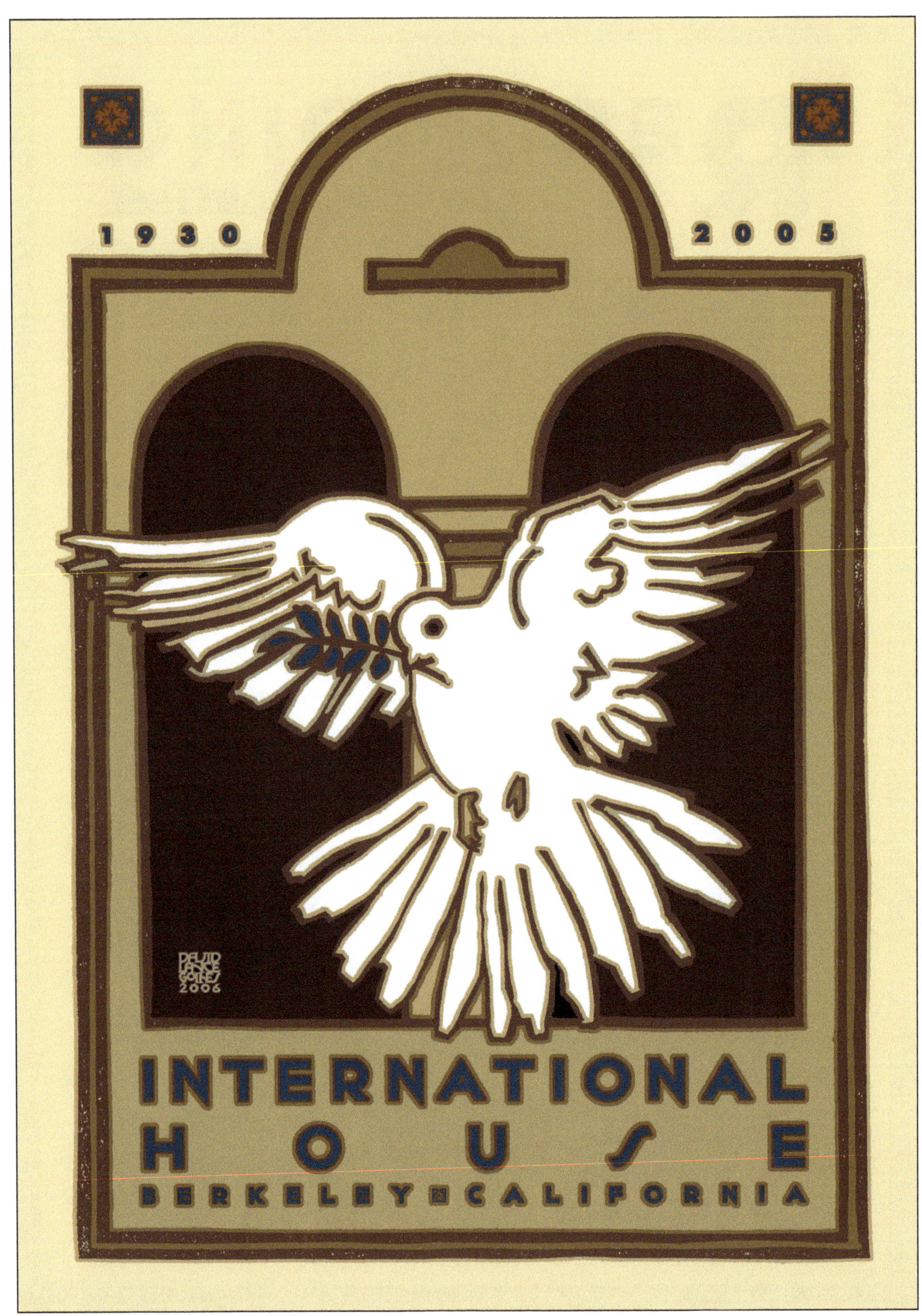

143. International House, 2006, 17¾" × 24"

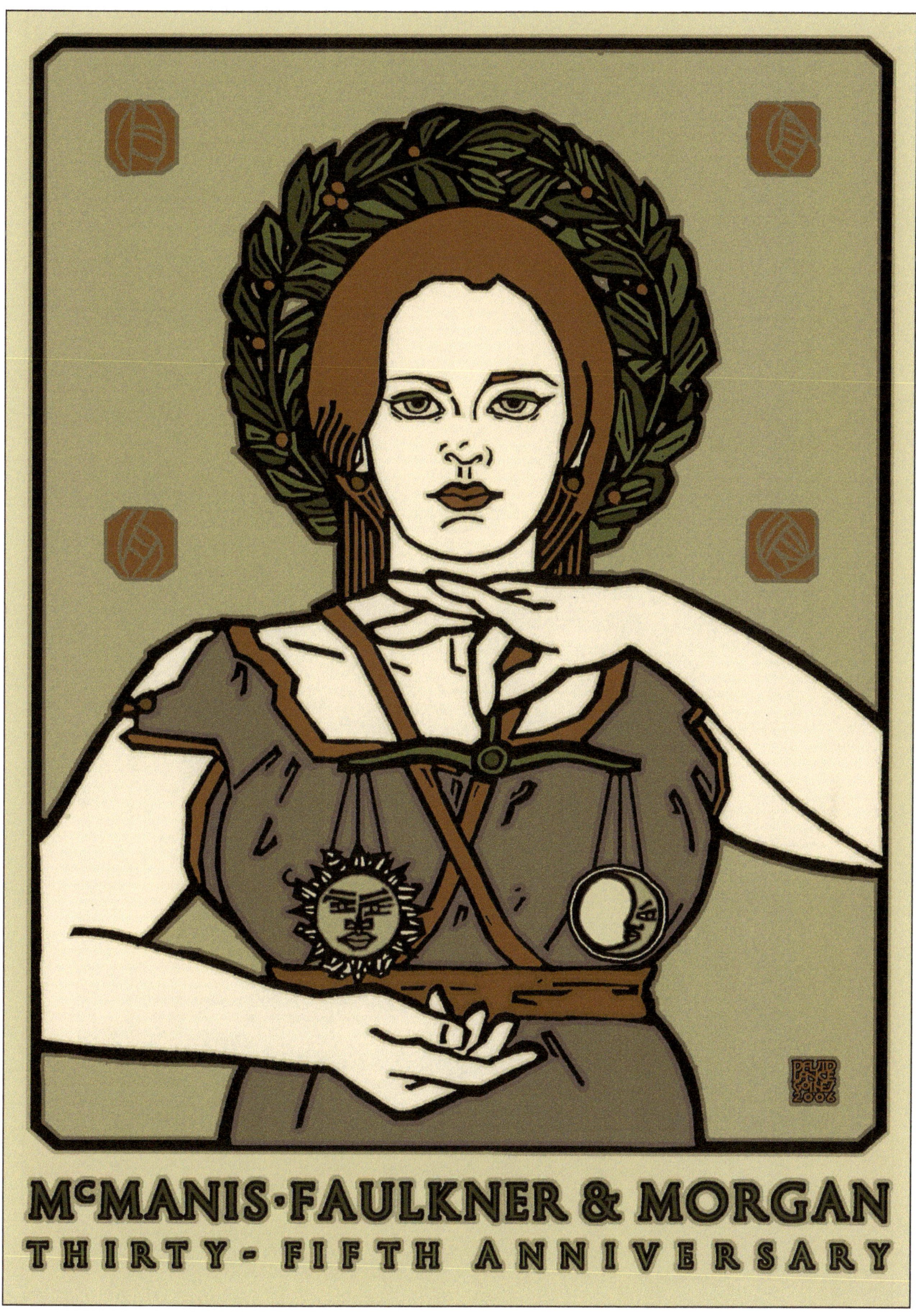

144. McManis, Faulkner & Morgan, 2006, 17" × 24"

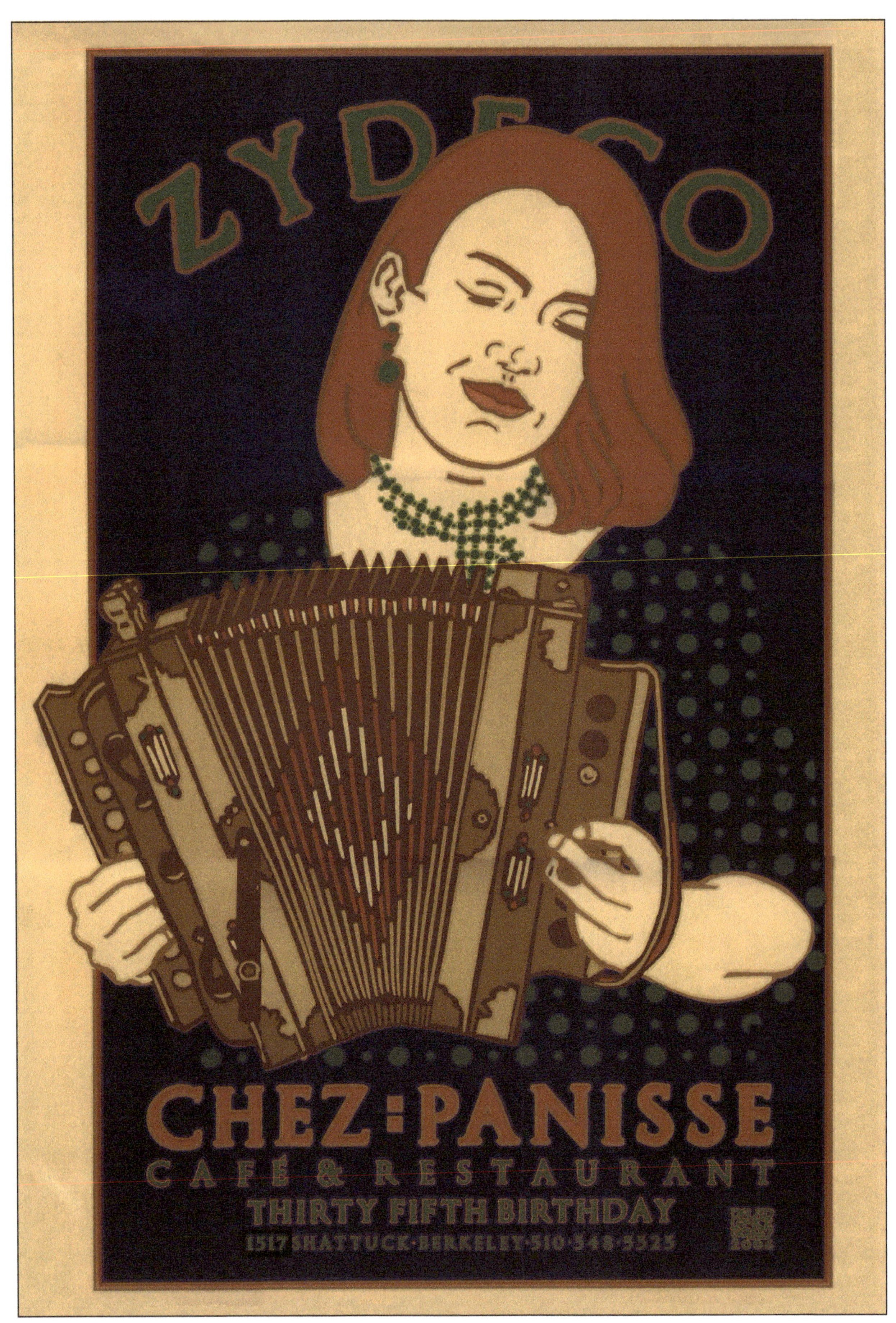

145. Chez Panisse Thirty-Fifth Birthday, 2006, 16" × 24"

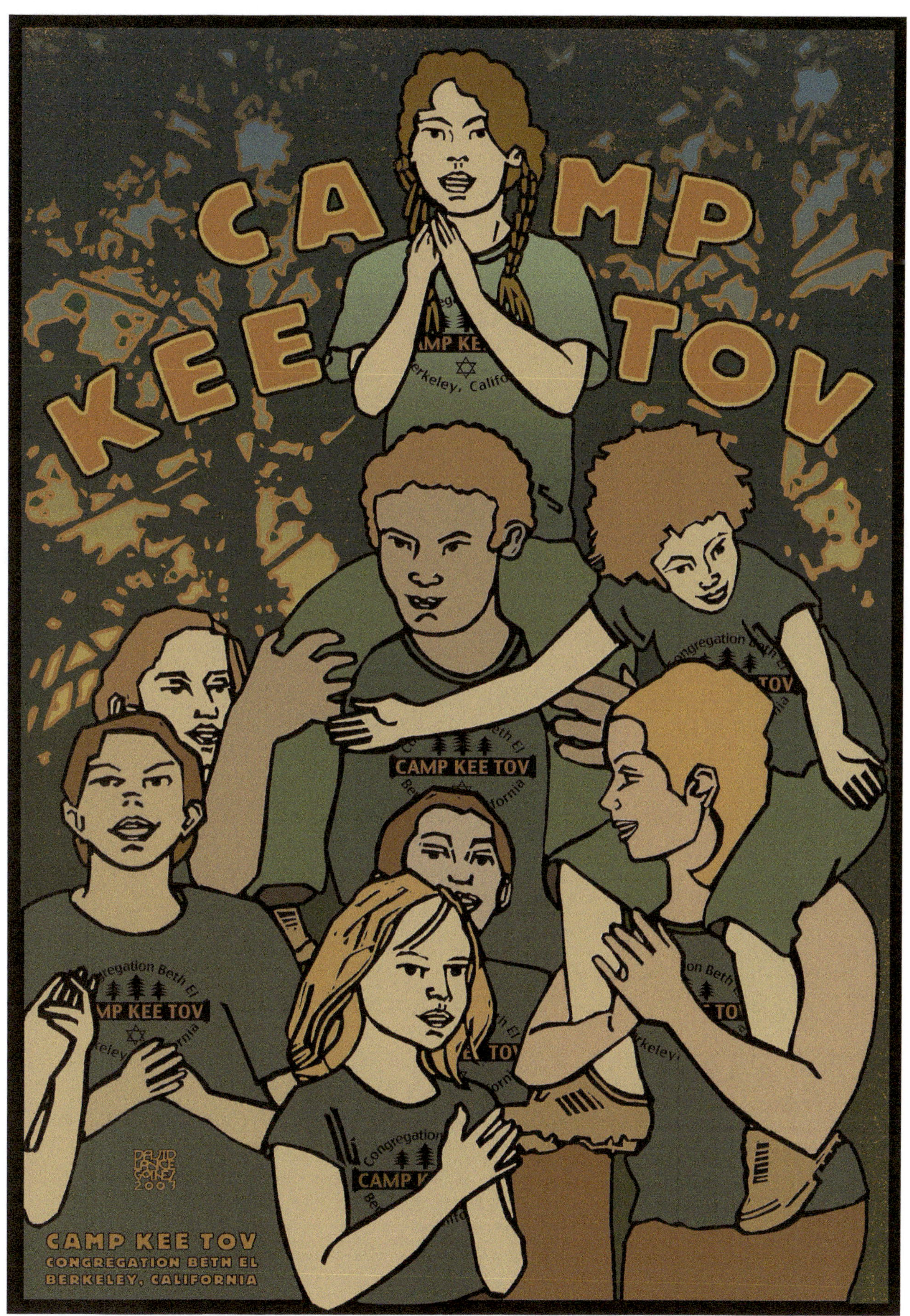

146. Camp Kee Tov, 2007, 16¼" × 24"

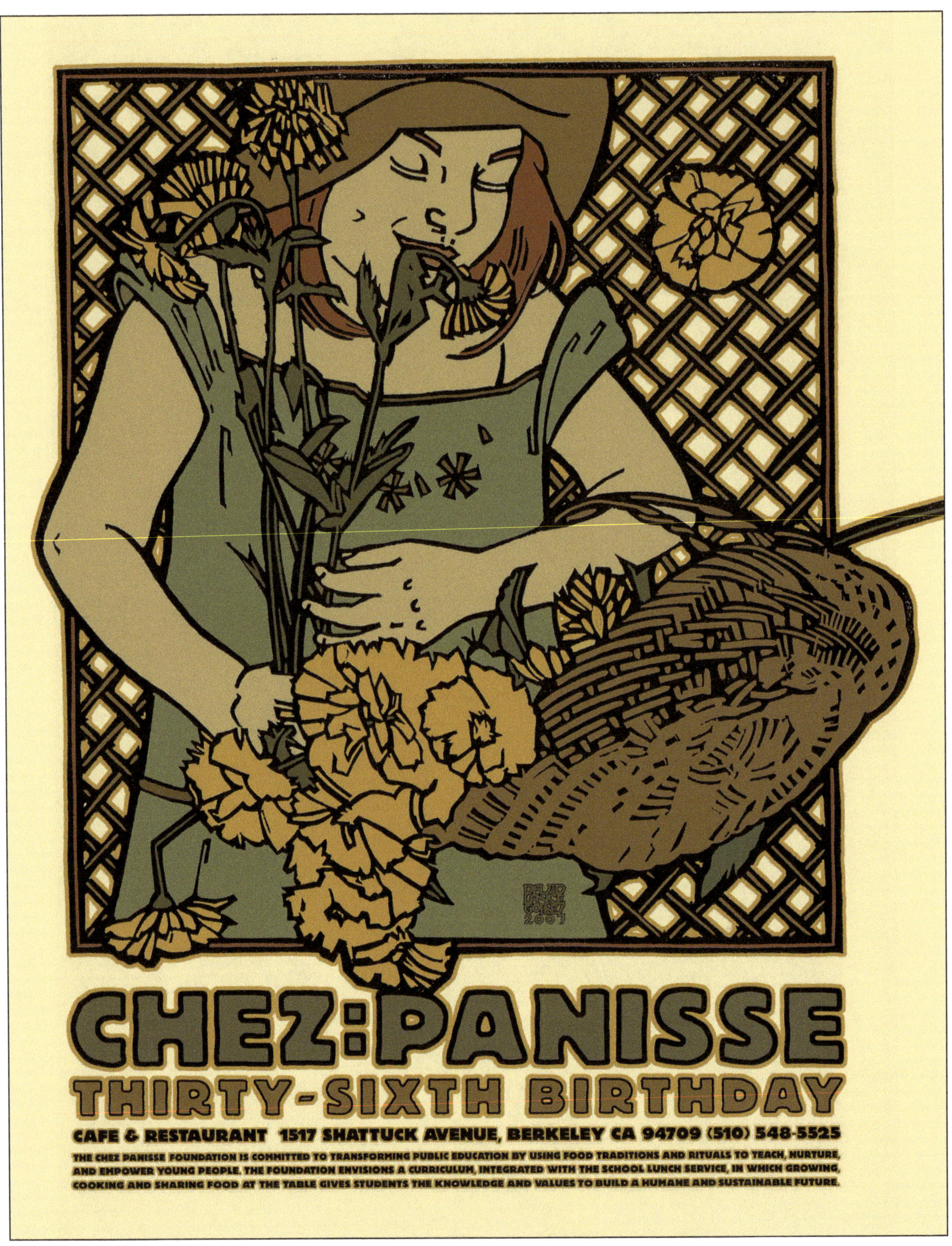

147. Chez Panisse Thirty-Sixth Birthday, 2007, 17½" × 24"

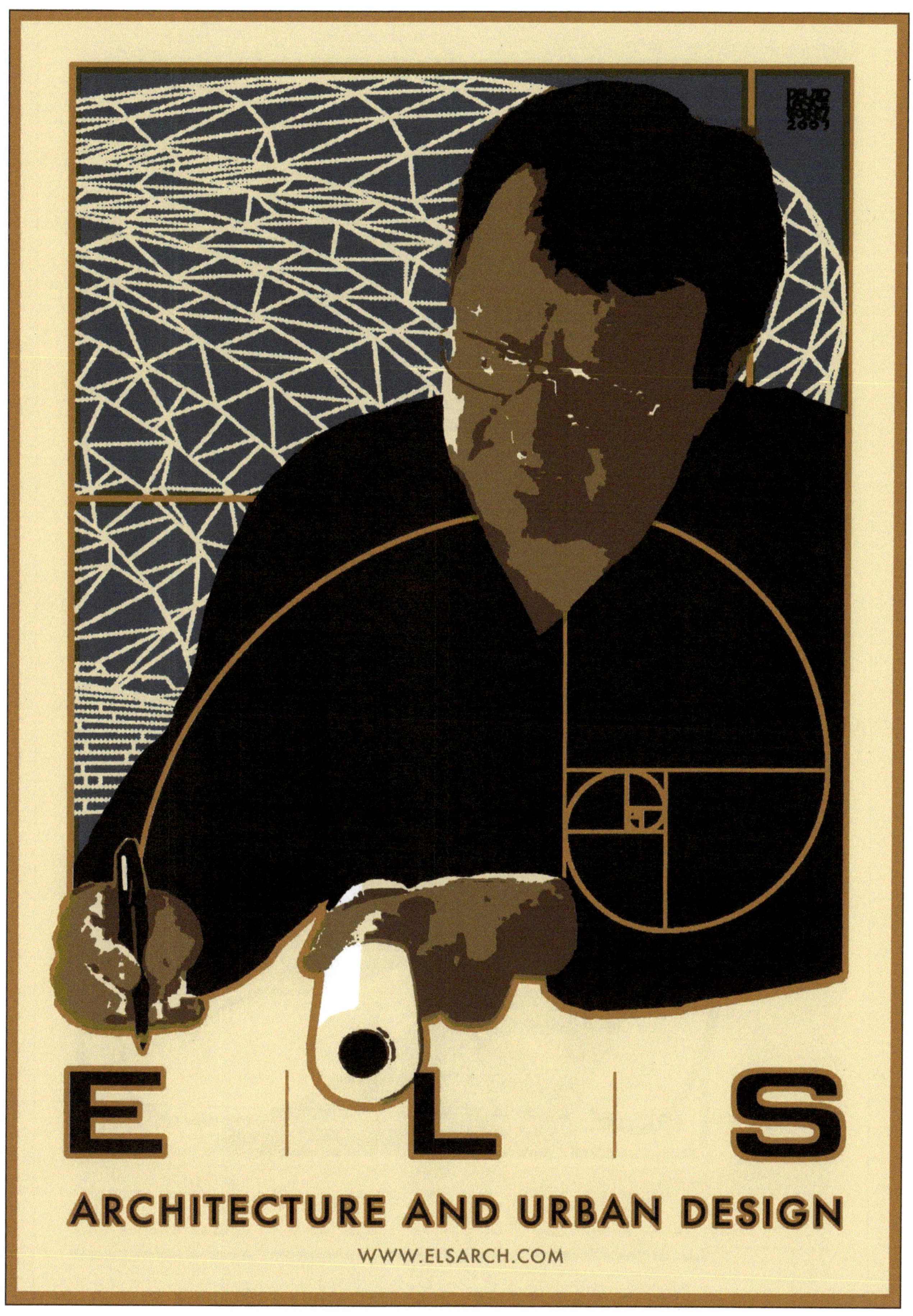

148. ELS Architecture & Urban Design, 2007, 16⅝" × 24"

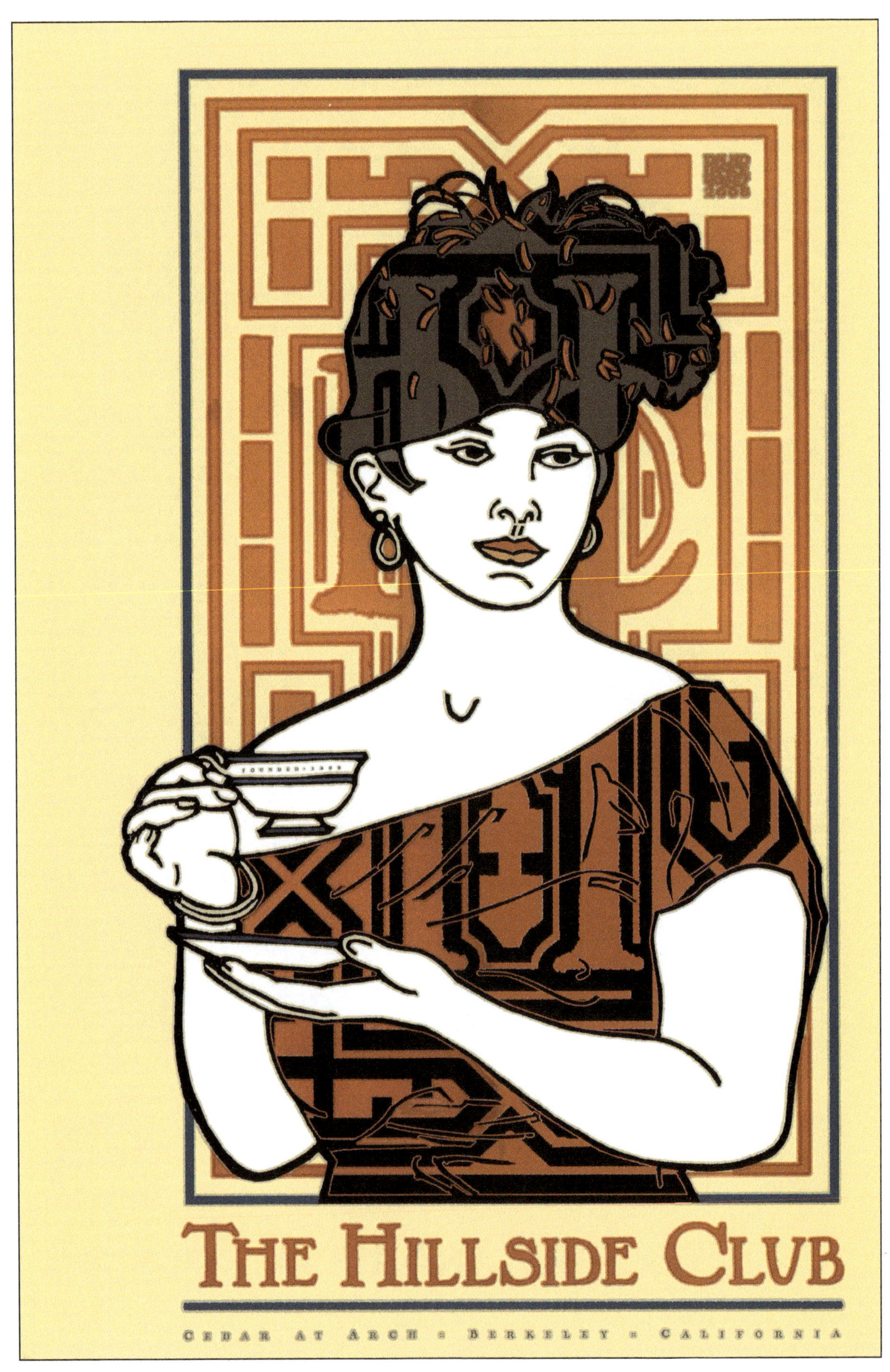

149. Hillside Club, 2008, 16⅝" × 24"

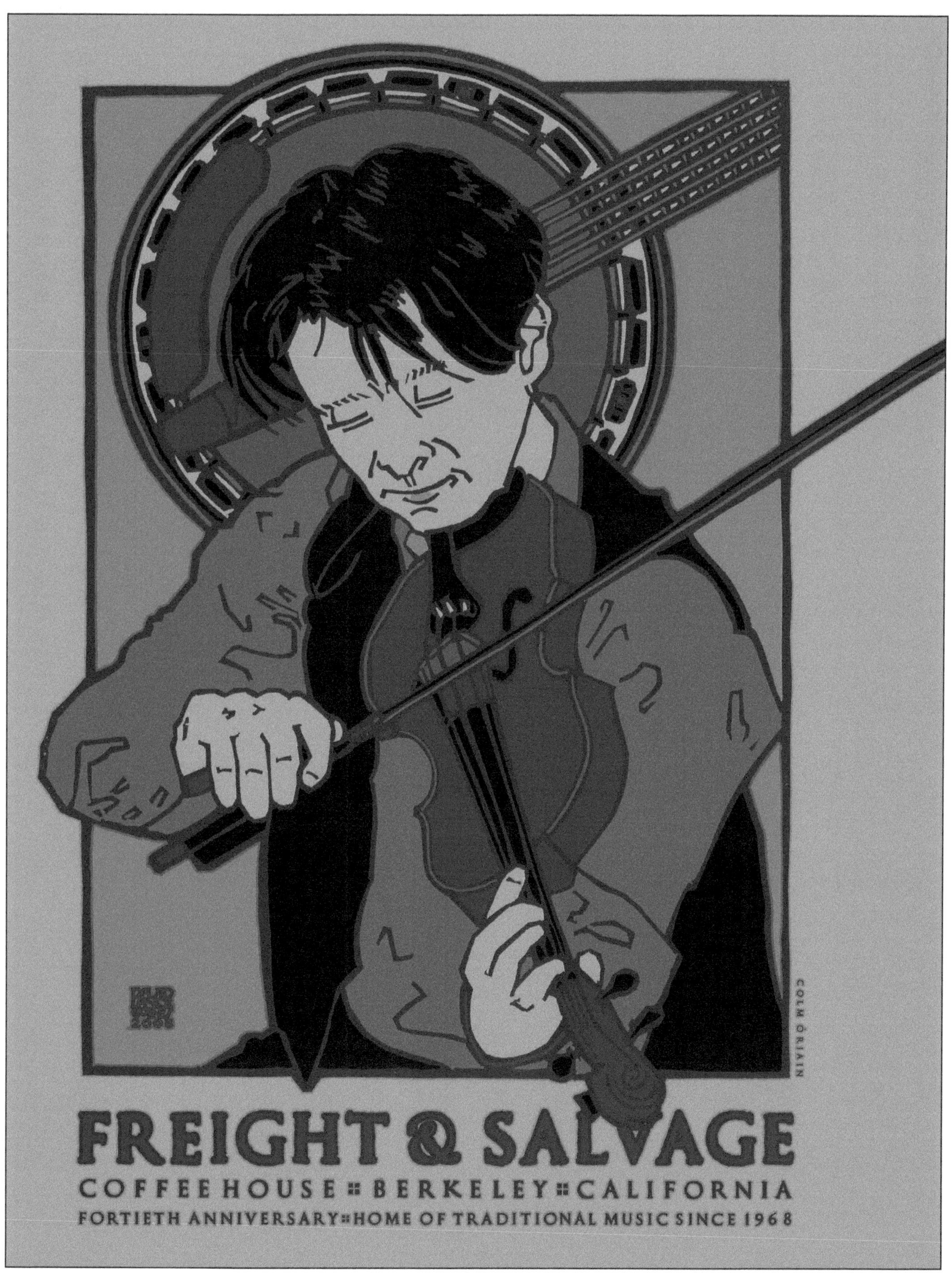

150. Freight & Salvage, 2008, 17⅝" × 24"

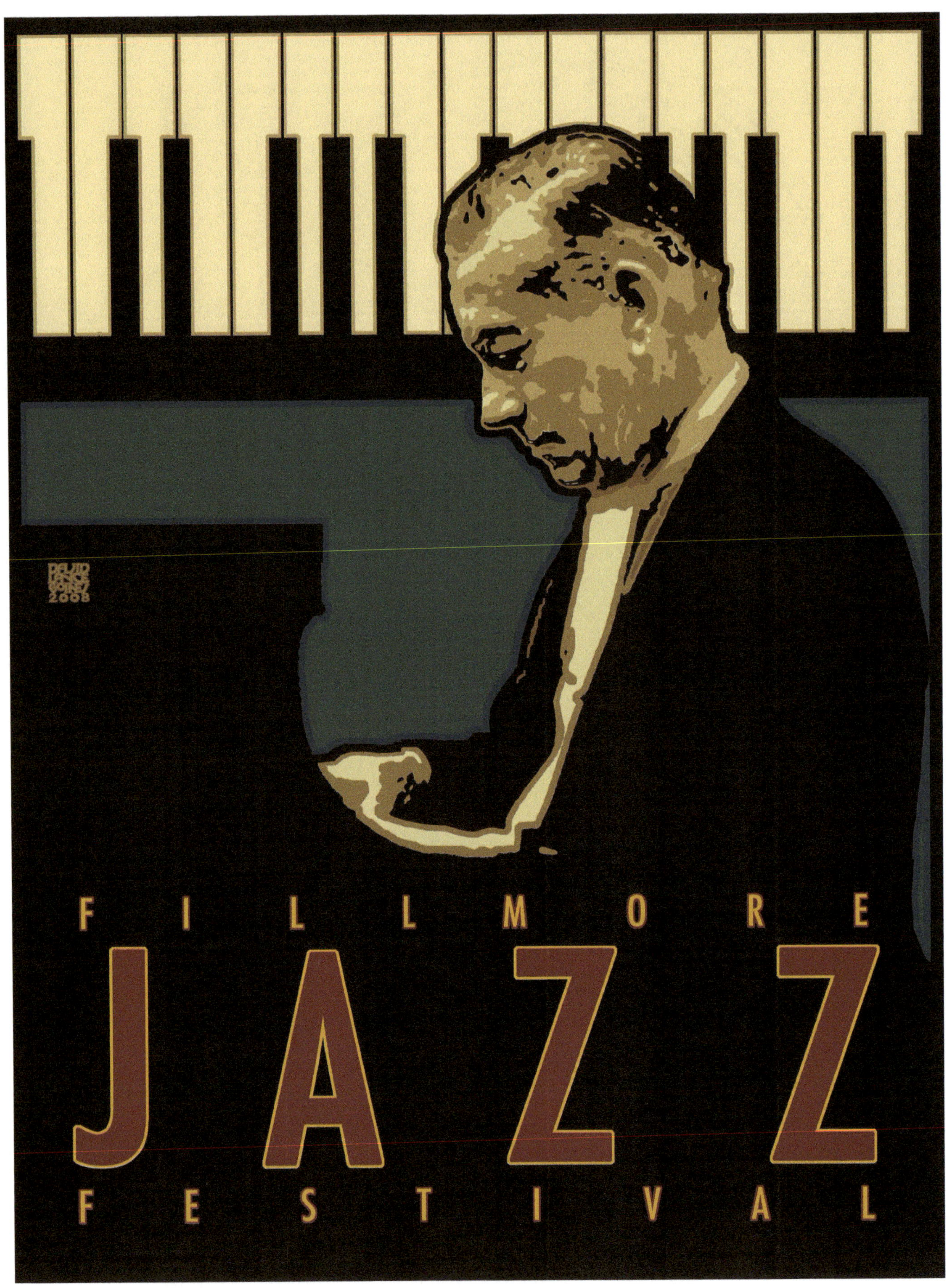

151. Fillmore Jazz Festival, 2008, 17⅝" × 24"

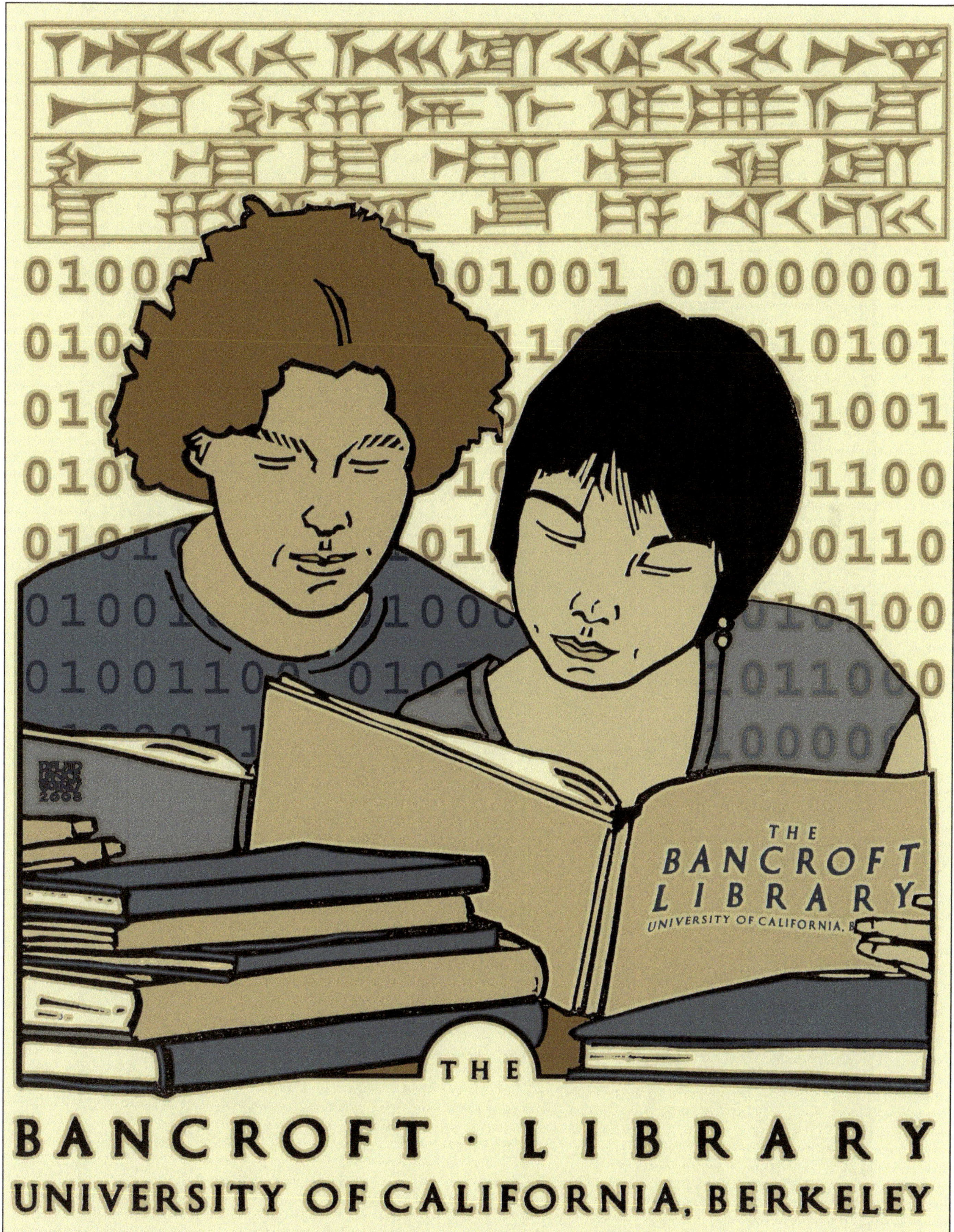

152. Bancroft Library, 2008, 17⅝" × 24"

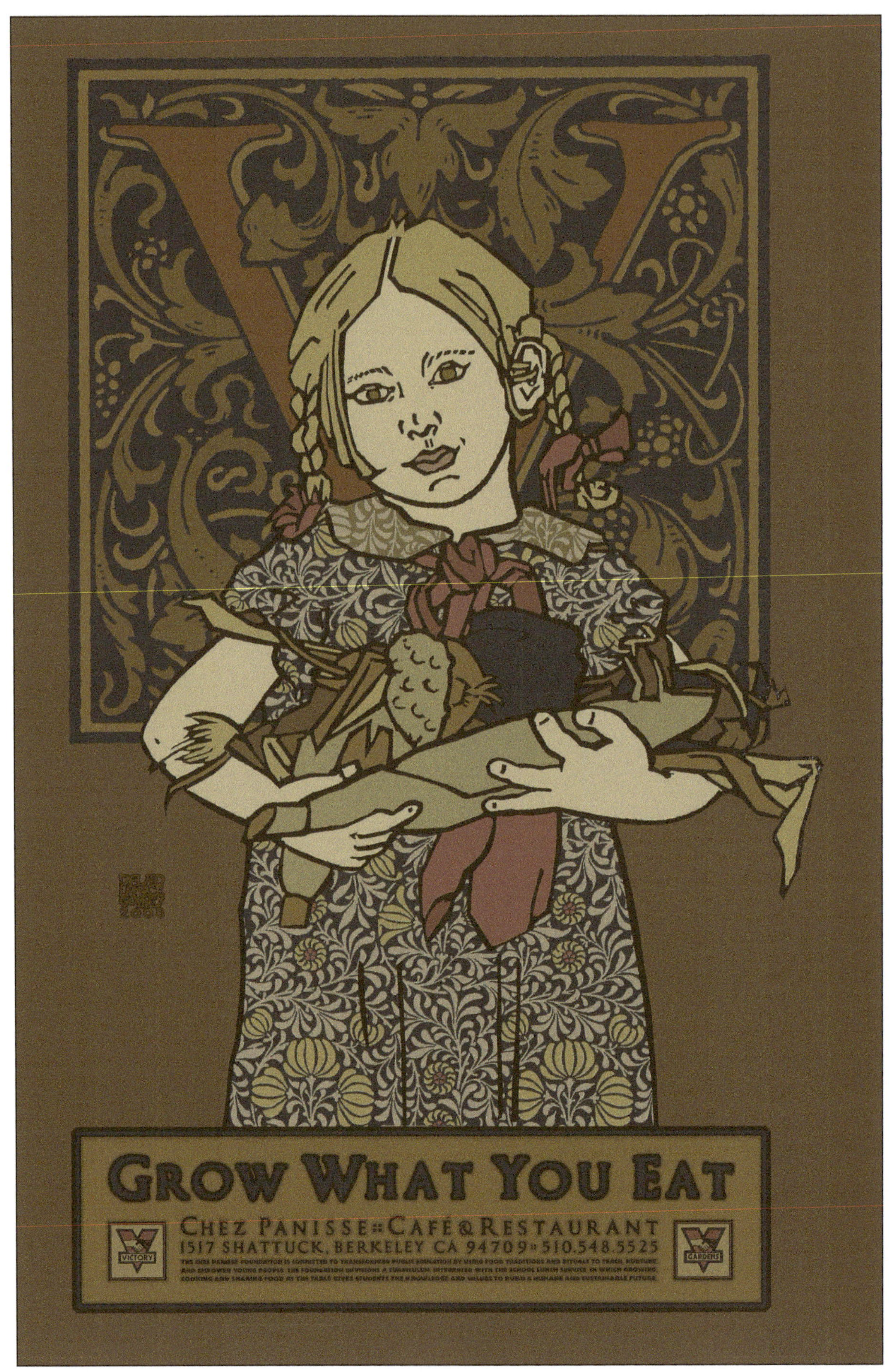

153. Grow What You Eat (Chez Panisse Thirty-Seventh Anniversary), 2008, 15½" × 24"

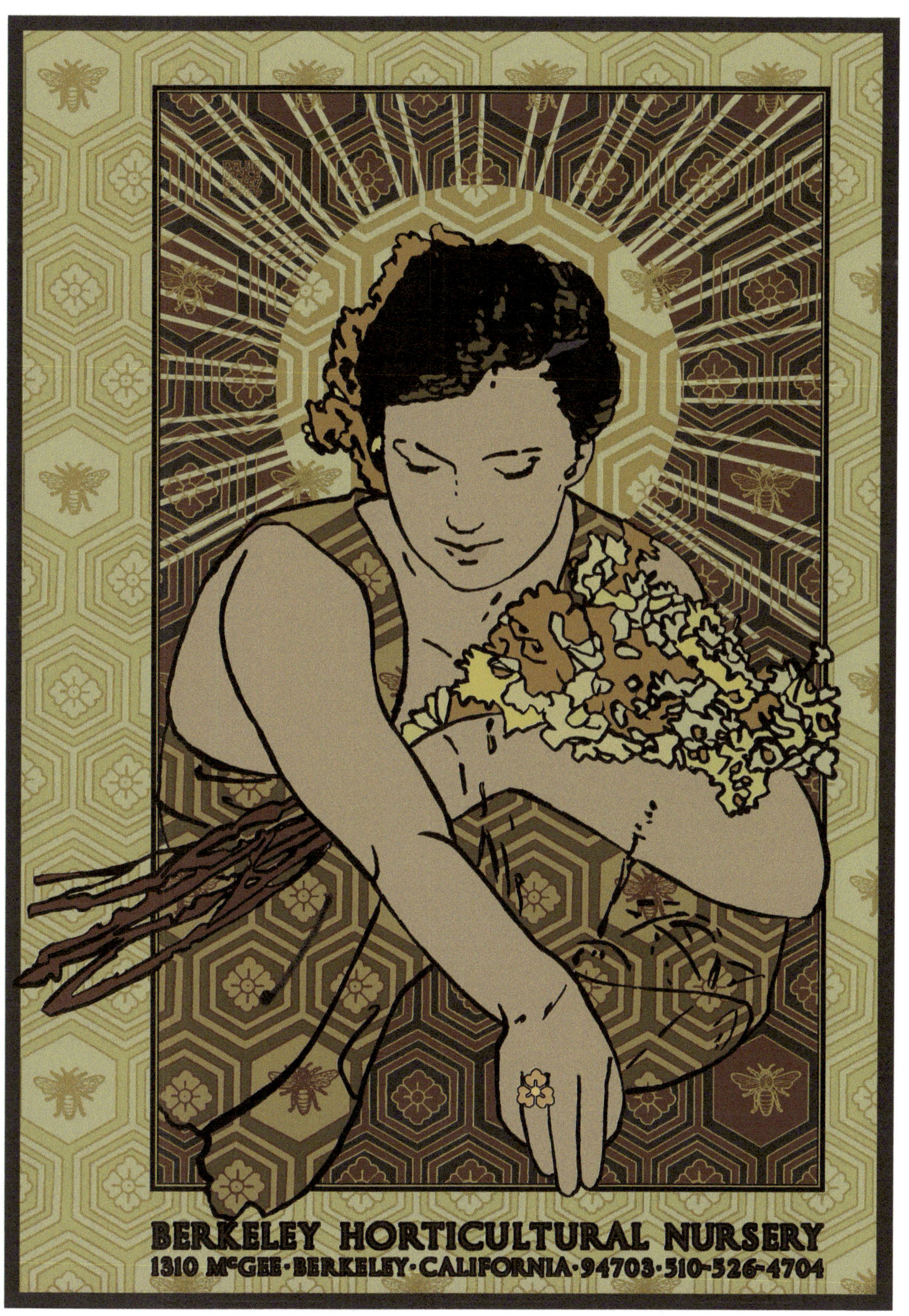

154. Berkeley Horticultural Nursery, 2009, 16¼" × 24"

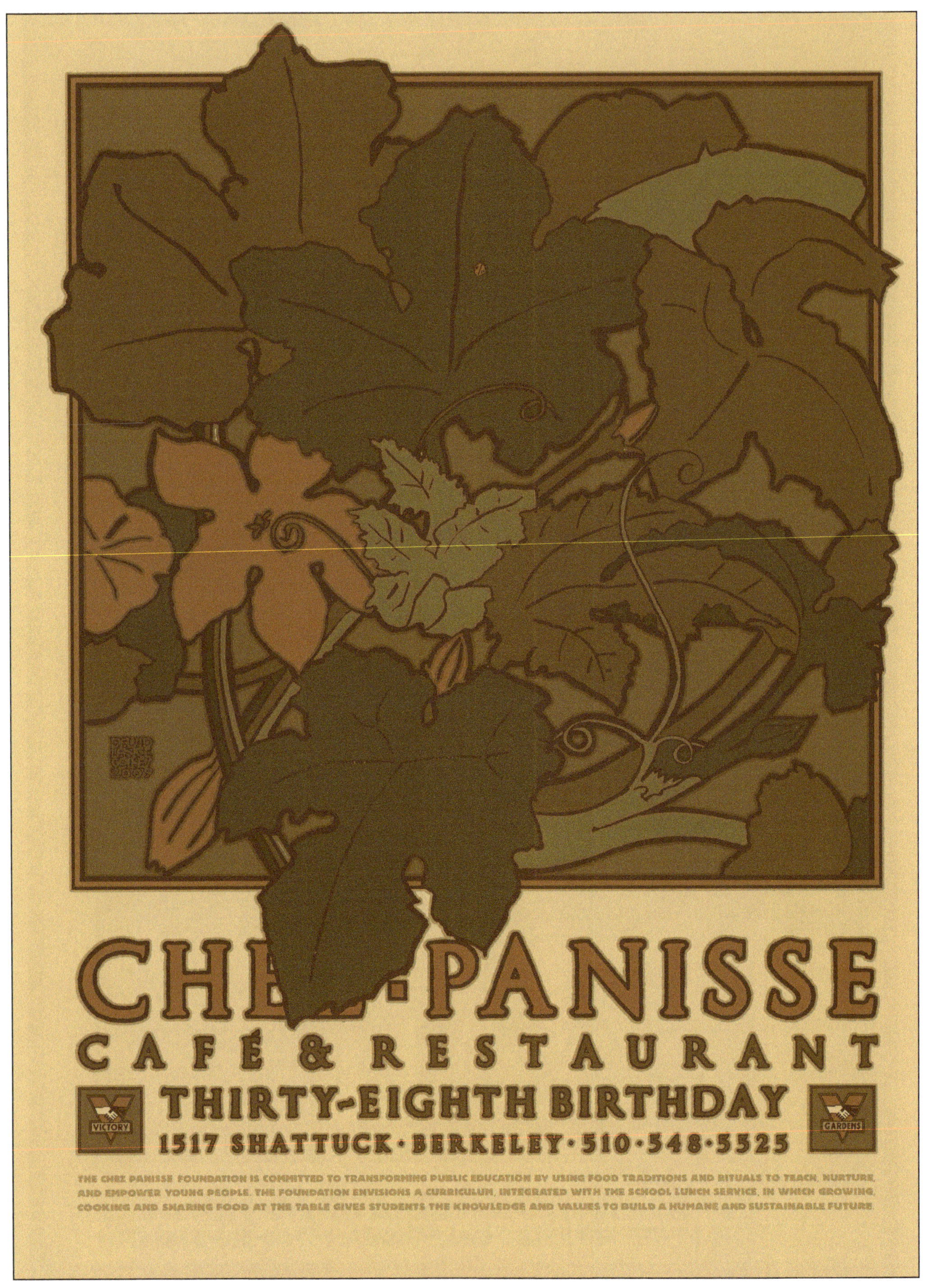

155. Chez Panisse Thirty-Eighth Anniversary, 2009, 17⅝" × 24"